Cognitive Rehabilitation of Memory
A Practical Guide

Minnie Harrell, MS, LPC
Psychotherapist
Supervisor of Cognitive Rehabilitation
Center for Psychological and Rehabilitation Services
Decatur, Georgia

Frederick Parenté, PhD
Professor of Psychology
Towson State University
Towson, Maryland

Eileen G. Bellingrath, MS
Cognitive Rehabilitation Therapist
Center for Psychological and Rehabilitation Services
Decatur, Georgia

Katherine A. Lisicia, MEd
Cognitive Rehabilitation Therapist
Speech/Language Pathologist
Center for Psychological and Rehabilitation Services
Decatur, Georgia

AN ASPEN PUBLICATION®
Aspen Publishers, Inc.
Gaithersburg, Maryland
1992

Library of Congress Cataloging-in-Publication Data

Cognitive rehabilitation of memory : a practical guide / Minnie Harrell . . . [et al.].
p. cm.
Includes bibliographical references and index.
ISBN 0-8352-0285-9
1. Memory disorders—Patients—Rehabilitation.   2. Brain damage—
Patients—rehabilitation.   I. Harrell, Minnie.
[DNLM: 1. Brain Injuries—rehabilitation.   2. Memory Disorders—
rehabilitation.   WM 173.7 C676]
RC394.M45C64   1992
616.8′4—dc20
DNLM/DLC
for Library of Congress
91-31706
CIP

The authors have made every effort to ensure the accuracy of the information herein. However,
appropriate information sources should be consulted, especially for new or unfamiliar procedures.
It is the responsibility of every practitioner to evaluate the appropriateness of a particular opinion
in the context of actual clinical situations and with due consideration to new developments.
Authors, editors, and the publisher cannot be held responsible for any typographical or other errors
found in this book.

Editorial Services: Barbara Priest

Library of Congress Catalog Card Number: 91-31706
ISBN: 0-8342-0285-9

Printed in the United States of America

1 2 3 4 5

Table of Contents

Acknowledgments

This book could not have been written without the expertise of thousands of survivors of traumatic brain injury who have shared their experiences with us over the years. Through them, we have learned to be hypervigilant for missing pieces in the rehabilitation process. Through their feedback, we have altered our treatment, developed models, and focused on teaching skills (strategies) in the process of cognitive rehabilitation to empower survivors to return to meaningful and full lives after the rehabilitation process. We thank each of them for their willingness to share their healing process and to assist us in our continual evolution of the field of cognitive rehabilitation.

We wish to thank Christiane O'Hara, Ph.D. for her support in the preparation and review of this book. We appreciate all her time and energy, as well as her moral support. Sarah Bellingrath assisted in typing, photocopying, and much-needed clerical back-up as the book reached the final production stage. Her efforts and patience are greatly appreciated.

* * *

Special thanks to my coauthors, who put forth great efforts in reaching deadlines; this required writing through a wedding, honeymoon, and various trips out of town, not to mention the other sacrifices of precious time and energy required in the preparation of this book.

I also wish to thank Vickie Byrd, who provided sisterly understanding, encouragement, and faith in my ability to write this second book. Thanks also to Michael Frank, who provided a much-needed distraction in the Caribbean when I needed it the most. And, thanks to Alberto and Patty Harrell who give me much joy and laughter.

I offer a special tribute to Marcus, who gave so unselfishly for 19 years. He is very much loved and missed; this book is but a small tribute to his meaning in my life. I dedicate my work on this book in eternal memory of his love.

M.H.

* * *

My gratitude and appreciation to my co-authors, especially Minnie Harrell; I have learned much from all of you.

Also thanks to Bob, Sarah, and Robert Bellingrath; who have contributed time, love, and moral support during the long hours devoted to completion of this undertaking. I could not have done it without them; they have been my mainstay throughout this undertaking.

Finally, my thanks and appreciation to Winifred T. Geary, my mother, who made many of the dreams and aspirations of my life possible with her unfailing support and love.

E.B.

* * *

I would like to give special thanks to Robert Jones, who provided love, encouragement, patience, and understanding throughout this challenge. I also thank him for the time he spent in researching catalogs as well as proofreading the text.

In addition, I thank my parents, Kay and Dick Lisicia, my grandmother "Anna," and the rest of my family (Joey, Mark, Karen, and Mary), who provided moral support when I needed it most.

Thanks to Minnie Harrell, who not only provided me with increased knowledge in the assessment and treatment areas of memory but also provided me with assistance in my contribution to the book as well as in using the word processing program.

A final word of appreciation to Mel White-Hicks, M.Ed., CCC-SLP for her review and feedback.

K.L.

Part I
Introduction

1
Overview of the Book

Memory is one of the most frequently reported cognitive problem areas experienced by much of the general population; this situation is paralleled in the field of cognitive rehabilitation with persons who have experienced neurological trauma. The ability to remember is crucial to a person's sense of self, and its loss is devastating. Memory is the fabric of our lives; it is the ability to recall old information, learn new information, and integrate the two. Without the ability to remember information, we experience a loss of control and empowerment.

Because memory is such a critical area, much treatment time is spent on it in rehabilitation settings. In discussions and training sessions with other clinicians, we are constantly asked for information and skills on the "how-to's" of rehabilitating memory. Clinicians in busy practices or rehabilitation settings do not generally have time to collect information from multiple sources and synthesize it into a usable tool.

At present, even if a clinician had time to peruse literature to search out techniques and skills, the endeavor would be a time consuming one. There is much literature available on memory, but that which exists on aspects helpful in hands-on clinical practice is less available (see Additional Readings at the end of the book for sample literature).

This book was written to provide the clinician with a practical manual for use in clinical practice. It does not provide in-depth research studies or extensive discussions on neuroanatomy and neurochemistry (see Additional Readings at the end of the text for information in these areas). Rather, we have compiled what we feel to be a generally comprehensive text that addresses both basic information needed by clinicians and hands-on skills they can immediately use in practice. Our intent is for it to be a *resource* that the clinician can rapidly access in any rehabilitation setting.

The book is divided into three parts. Part I contains this introductory overview chapter (Chapter 1) and a chapter introducing various memory theories and types of memory (Chapter 2). This information is important to clinicians since effective treatment cannot be done without a model on which to base memory recovery and an understanding of the various types of memory. With this basic understanding, clinicians can then begin identifying where in the process of memory the person is experiencing difficulty.

Part II of the book contains information on assessment (Chapter 3) as well as goal setting and treatment planning (Chapter 4). In Chapter 3, a variety of assessment techniques are introduced (both formalized and informalized), as are discussions of subjective ratings, questionnaires, and so forth. Assessments provide baseline information (from where to start treatment) as well as information about the types of memory impairments and recommendations for both present and future treatment interventions.

Chapter 4 introduces the concept of goal setting and treatment planning. These are crucial steps in designing treatment tasks to focus on memory (or any cognitive area). Therapists must set goals with clients (both short- and long-term goals) and develop treatment plans that focus on the needs of the client versus the needs of the therapist.

Part III is the primary clinical portion of the text and provides practical clinical applications. Chapter 5 introduces our philosophy of retraining memory functions (or any cognitive function). The concept of empowerment is introduced, which we feel is a critical component in rehabilitation. Other issues are discussed as well, including how to determine client readiness for treatment and basic training requirements of persons providing cognitive rehabilitation services.

Chapter 5 also presents a treatment model we have developed for use with clients. We feel this model incorporates all the elements needed to structure successful rehabilitation. This Eight-Step Model is discussed throughout the book, and various examples of its application in clinical settings are given as well. The appendix in this chapter provides several experimental models that can be reframed as treatment models that clinicians can adapt for use in their practices.

Chapter 6 introduces direct retraining tasks, including pen-and-paper, three-dimensional, and computerized, all of which are explained by sample task continuums using the Eight-Step Model discussed in Chapter 5. At the end of this chapter are appendixes that give various sample tasks, sample materials, a listing of various computerized programs on memory, and listings of materials and manufacturers from whom they can be obtained.

The book does not attempt to "prove" the effectiveness of rehabilitation or to argue the validity of computerized or other types of treatment interventions. Our treatment model encompasses providing clients and clinicians with a "menu" of skills and aids from which they may pick and choose as the situation demands. To this end, the text includes direct retraining of memory deficits using computerized, pen-and-paper, and three-dimensional tasks.

Chapter 7 provides a menu of compensatory strategies from which the client and therapist can pick and choose the ones most appropriate to their particular settings. These strategies are discussed in detail and are mentioned throughout the rest of the text. Strategies are the primary focus of our treatment model as acquisition of skills is the primary reason for doing rehabilitation in the first place.

Chapter 8 focuses on compensatory aids that can be used with clients. These include prosthetic devices (nonelectronic aids that assist in remembering) and orthotic devices (which make decisions for the client). Photographs are included in this chapter, along with descriptions of the devices. At the end of the chapter is an appendix that lists manufacturers' information.

Finally, at the end of the text we have included a list of additional readings that will assist therapists and clients who wish to have more information about the issues discussed throughout the text.

TARGETED AUDIENCE

This book is particularly targeted toward rehabilitation providers who are involved in the direct rehabilitation of memory functions. Such clinicians typically come from a variety of disciplines, such as neuropsychology, psychology, speech and language, occupational and physical therapy, education, recreational therapy, and social work. This audience includes clinicians involved in both inpatient and outpatient facilities (acute care, transitional living, day programs, out-patient, home health, and long-term care facilities such as nursing homes). Any clinician who provides cognitive rehabilitation services can use the information and skills contained in this text.

This text particularly addresses information and skills for use with persons who have sustained some type of neurological insult. This includes persons with closed or open head injuries, cerebrovascular accidents, aneurysms, cancer, tumors, and so forth. Tasks are generally designed for adults, but therapists who work with adolescents and children may be able to adapt some of the materials and strategies for use with these age groups as well.

The material can be used with persons who have sustained various levels of impairment as a result of a traumatic brain injury (TBI). That is, persons with mild, moderate, severe, or profound impairments can benefit from application of some of the techniques and strategies discussed in this text. Therapists are encouraged to be creative in modifying and applying these to their particular client population and in independently developing materials and strategies appropriate to their setting.

Clients, depending upon their cognitive strengths and limitations, may also be able to use this text to learn information about the process of memory rehabilitation as well as specific skills and aids. Family members can also benefit from the text, particularly in understanding the process of memory rehabilitation. Additionally, if the client and family are involved in home health or long-term care, the book can serve as a resource for at-home rehabilitation practice.

Other persons associated with TBI survivors may find parts of the text valuable as well. For example, in working with a college-level student returning to an academic setting, tutors, teachers, or special services department personnel may find the information and skills presented in this text helpful in understanding some of the limitations the client may have as well as how to assist the client in achieving success. This setting is particularly important since memory is a critical skill for success in academics. For a client returning to work, a job coach may find these materials valuable in transferring skills to the real-life situation of work.

In addition to rehabilitation facilities, others may find the information helpful in their provision of services. For example, teachers who work with non-brain injured students can use the resources, strategies, and aids in teaching students how to remember information in the classroom. The strategies discussed in Chapter 7 (mnemonics, organization, and note taking) are particularly valuable for students. Persons working in geriatric centers often encounter clients who have various degrees of memory loss which is not necessarily related to brain trauma. Persons in these facilities can extrapolate materials, tasks, strategies, and aids to assist these persons in maintaining (or regaining) quality of life. Finally, physicians may wish to use this text as a desk reference for use with clients who present with symptoms of memory loss not necessarily associated with brain trauma. Such clients might include persons who are depressed or those who historically have not learned strategies to assist in memory. The text, in these cases, can be used to assess and recommend treatment interventions.

A WORD ABOUT LANGUAGE

We believe in the dignity and empowerment of individuals. A person who has sustained a neurological insult is a person *with* an injury; the injury does not define the person. Therefore, we avoid terms such as *head injured, brain damaged,* or *brain injured.* Labels such as these are almost always disempowering and serve to group people into unequal categories (e.g., the "brain injured" and the "normals"). Instead, we choose terms such as *head injury survivor* or *person who has sustained a brain injury.*

Likewise, we depart from the traditional medical model that labels survivors as patients. We prefer the more empowering term *client. Client* denotes the person's choice and equality in paying for a service; *patient* denotes an inequality in the relationship (physician-patient), where the individual is "sick." In acute care settings, it may be appropriate to label a survivor as a patient, particularly since that person may really be sick. Calling the person who returns to work while continuing in treatment outside a hospital setting a patient, however, is disrespectful, particularly since the person is trying desperately to normalize life after injury.

Much of this discussion emerged from *listening* to survivors and appreciating their continued difficulty with labels. Our goal is always to reempower persons after trauma, not to disempower them with language.

2
Overview of Memory

To retrain memory, it is first necessary to understand the mechanisms that underlie this most complex of intellectual functions. The purpose of this chapter is to illustrate how memory works and to provide the therapist with a model to determine how to begin treatment. Several analogies are presented to illustrate the mechanisms of memory. A widely accepted model of memory is presented that will help the therapist and client in isolating and understanding memory deficits. Various types of memory are discussed, different memory processes described, and a discussion of forgetting and amnesia is provided.

ANALOGIES OF MEMORY

It is often difficult for persons to understand how memory works or how some types of memories are intact while others are impaired. Clients frequently ask questions such as: "Why is it that I can't remember what I ate for breakfast but I can remember my first grade school teacher?" It is important to assist clients in understanding memory, and to explain the information in a format the client can understand. Therapists can use drawings, figures, or written text and can teach the information to the client. The client can take notes on the material or use an audiotape recorder to listen to the information later (repetition). This teaching of general information can become a therapeutic task that has relevance to the client.

One particularly helpful way to think about memory is to compare the process to common experiences to which anyone can relate or by likening the process to something more concrete and "real" for clients. This can easily be done by using analogies, and several are presented in this chapter. It should be noted that not every client will need to know all the following analogies. Therapists can choose ones that fit their particular beliefs and assist clients in understanding. Later in this chapter, we present one of the most widely accepted models, which therapists may choose to use with their clients.

7

The Mountain Rain Analogy

Kolb and Whishaw[1] have described a useful memory concept that illustrates the dynamics or fluid nature of how information is stored in memory. The process of remembering is likened to the gradual erosion of a mountain by rain. Sensory information (that is, information confronting the client's senses) is similar to the rain that falls on the mountain and the other natural processes such as wind that gradually efface its terrain. As the rain falls on the mountain, it creates trails and furrows in the soil. These are analogous to memories that are formed in the brain from sensations over time and with experiences.

Future rains cut deeper trails, just as perceptions and sensations that we experience on a regular basis are permanently stored in memory. The effect of the rains is unpredictable, however. They may only slightly alter the existing trails. They may reinforce only a certain part of the trail or cut an entirely new path down the side of the mountain. By analogy, memories may be fully reinforced, partially reinforced, or completely changed with new experience. Moreover, the actions of wind and other natural causes can enhance or diminish the trail. Clearly, ancillary information and experience can alter our memories. Finally, if it does not rain for a time, the trails eventually succumb to the physical action of wind and become less distinct. Analogously, if we do not have the same experience repeatedly, that memory may diminish and eventually be replaced by others.

The Conveyor Belt Analogy

Murdock[2] describes memory as a conveyor belt. A person overlooks the conveyor and has only a limited time to process any episode of life as it passes by. Experience is fresh in our minds while it is directly in front of us but gradually begins to fade from memory as it travels down the conveyor belt and other information that is now passing before us begins to compete with it. Eventually it is lost from view, and we have a difficult time recalling it.

This model illustrates the point that memory is a dynamic process and that there are no distinct stages to remembering. It also points out the role of interference in memory. We lose access to information as it travels down the conveyor belt. Our attention is distracted by those items that are directly in front of us.

The Computer Analogy

This popular memory analogy assumes that memory functions are similar to the workings of a computer. There is a sensory stage that involves input from any of several sources. For example, computers accept information from visual scanning devices, keyboards, light pens, and so forth; humans can process from five senses. Inside the computer there is an information buffer called random access memory (RAM), which holds the input until it is processed. This is analogous to an individual's working memory (to be discussed later in this chapter). Information is maintained and altered in RAM and then is stored on a hard disk (analogous to long-term memory) until it is needed again. The electricity that surges through the machine is analogous to the rehearsal process of memory. The software that transforms the information in different ways is analogous to the encoding process of memory. The information is maintained so long as the electricity is on. Once the electricity is turned off, the information in RAM is lost, although files on the hard disk are maintained. Analogously, if information is not rehearsed, it is lost from working memory, although the information stored in long-term memory is still there when it is needed. Without the software, useful transformations of the information will never take place.

The computer analogy is an attractive one in that it describes several types of information processing that are intuitively similar to the way humans process information. It also gives scientists a convenient model of memory because the computer is familiar to many people. The computer analogy implies that information is processed in discrete places within a mental machine. This is precisely the impression the previous analogies discussed in this chapter tried to dispel, however.

There are many dissimilarities between human memory and computer processing. For example, computers can do many storage and retrieval processes much faster than humans. Also, there are many memory processes that are unique to humans, such as the tendency for humans to distort or embellish their memories. It is also unlikely that humans store information in binary form, and humans can store considerably more information than is possible in the current generation of computers.

The Desk Top Analogy

Memory can also be viewed as an office or work space that contains a desk, file cabinets, and various machines such as telephones, fax, and copiers.[3] Information enters the system through the telephone, conversations with others, visitors, and mail. Only a small fragment of information is processed: Some is filed, action is delayed on some, people are put on hold, and so forth. The rest makes it to the top of the desk, where it is processed for further action. This is analogous to the working memory system. The desk top is the location where the work takes place. Once the work is processed, the result is stored in a file cabinet. The work is analogous to the concept of encoding, which will be discussed in detail later. Putting the information in the file cabinet is analogous to storing it in long-term memory. Simply keeping the more important information on the desk top is analogous to the process of rehearsal.

Once information is stored, it can be retrieved from the file cabinet later for update and review. Analogously, after a person mentally processes something, it is stored in the mental file cabinet. The analogy describes a dynamic system where information enters the desk top from outside sources or the long-term memory and then is processed and completed, or it is stored away in the long-term memory for later retrieval and further processing.

This analogy illustrates that, if any office system is limited, then processing in the remaining systems is also limited. For example, if the phone line is disconnected, then the person has limited access to the outside world. Analogously, if any of an individual's sensory systems is diminished, then processing capacity is reduced. It also predicts that, if information is not maintained on the desk top, it will eventually be lost or confused with other papers and materials resident there. If information is not in memory, its distinctive character is lost, and it eventually is blurred with the other sensations of the day. If the name of a file is forgotten, then it cannot be retrieved from the cabinet. If the cue for recall is forgotten, then the memory cannot be retrieved.

The General Information Processing Model

This model uses many of the same analogies discussed previously to describe the workings of human memory. It is most similar to the computer and desk top analogies, although the elements of the other systems are also apparent in its logic. It was originally developed by Atkinson and Shiffren[4] in the mid-1960s and is still cited as perhaps the best description of memory functions. Parenté and Anderson-Parenté[5] have revamped this model and present their modifications as a useful schema for describing memory dysfunction after head injury (Figures 2-1 and 2-2).

These systems involve three types of memory. This is not to say that there are three distinct types of memories resident in the brain, only that there is evidence for at least three types of memory. The first is the sensory information store, the second is working memory, and the third is the long-term memory.

Sensory Memory

Sensory memory is the first stage of information processing. It is of brief duration but is a high-capacity information storage system that functions to retain information for selection and processing. Each of the senses has a sensory store, but only the visual system has been well researched.[6] Information in this system lasts for about a third of a second. Visual images are processed as literal pictures that are scanned in the visual memory to extract crucial features. For example, an individual can seldom report a complete description of a person met on a busy street. What initially seems to be a complete image immediately begins to fade from memory,

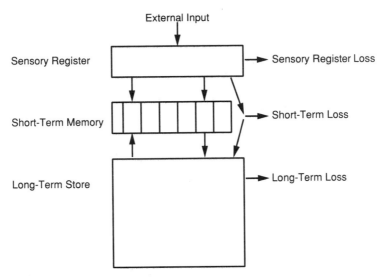

Figure 2-1 Atkinson and Shiffren model of memory. Information enters the sensory buffer and is lost if not scanned. It then enters the limited-capacity short-term buffer and is lost if not scanned. What is rehearsed and encoded enters the long-term memory, where it decays or is lost by interference from other memories.

and only certain aspects of the person are recalled. The image is mentally scanned, and only those characteristics that stand out or are important for some reason are retained. This same process occurs in audition, gustation, the tactile sense, and olfaction. The complete sensation may last longer in some senses, but the process is the same.

This example illustrates that an individual's initial perceptions are complete and isomorphic. The percept is then scanned to make the crucial features available for further processing in the working memory.

Working Memory

Working memory is the crossroads of the system. It is not a place in memory; rather, the concept refers more to the time that the information is processed relative to the time of initial perception. For example, if a visual image is retained longer than half a second, it has probably been scanned in sensory memory, and a portion of it is maintained in working memory. This description emphasizes the time frame of processing and the changes that probably occur with the passage of short intervals of time.

There are several processes that occur in working memory. The two that have been most thoroughly investigated are the rehearsal and encoding processes. To maintain information in working memory, it is necessary to rehearse it; if the

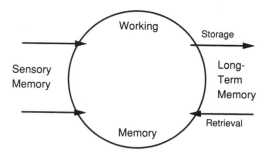

Figure 2-2 Information processing model of memory. Information enters the sensory memory and is scanned, and then portions of it enter the working memory, where they are rehearsed and encoded. The encoded information is stored in long-term memory, where it is retrieved, updated, and then restored in the long-term memory.

information is not rehearsed, it is lost. As with the computer analogy discussed earlier, when the electricity is turned off, all information in RAM is lost. Rehearsal is, analogously, the electricity of memory. It functions simply to keep the information resident in working memory. Encoding is similar to the software discussed in the computer analogy. These are the methods that are used to make the information more memorable. In this process, the individual may develop pictures, form mnemonics, or try to remember by verbally labeling new information. Regardless of the strategy, each is a method of encoding, or the software of the mind.

Working memory has also been called short-term memory. Although there is still considerable use of this phrase, it has been largely abandoned by some memory researchers in favor of the working memory concept. The reason is that short-term memory implies a place where information is held for processing in a system with limited capacity. The working memory concept emphasizes the dynamic quality of memory at this temporal stage of processing. It also illustrates that information is processed from two directions, the sensory system and the long-term store.

Working memory efficiency is usually impaired after injury to the brain. Rehearsal is also adversely affected. Without rehearsal, information cannot be maintained for encoding. The client may not be able to generate cues that are effective for retrieval. In general, the therapist must assess each of these processes and plan therapy with the client accordingly.

Long-term Memory

Long-term memory is analogous to the file cabinet in an office, the hard disk on a personal computer, or the deepest riverlet in the mountain after a torrential rain. It is the place where information is stored, largely in inactive form, and remains available for retrieval on demand. The capacity of long-term memory has never been determined. It is probably boundless; certainly it is larger than any existing computer system's mass storage device. The function of long-term memory is to store information for later retrieval.

TYPES OF MEMORY

Most clients think of memory as the ability to recall information independently. Actually, there are a variety of different types of memory, and some but not others may be affected after head injury.

Recognition and Identification

Recognition is the ability to choose a familiar item, event, or person from among similar-looking things. For example, imagine a man standing in a busy airport waiting for a friend to arrive. He searches the passengers as they leave the plane. Occasionally he thinks he sees his friend, only to realize that the person only physically resembles the friend. Eventually he sees the person and greets him by his correct name. Recognition memory is the search process: scanning the available selection of passengers, eliminating the distractions, and eventually deciding that a certain person is the one who was sought. Identification is similar to recognition memory but requires the labeling of the familiar thing with a name. Recognition memory is relatively unaffected by head injury. Identification memory may be seriously impaired. For example, few clients report difficulty determining whether a person is familiar, but it may be difficult to recall his or her correct name.

Recall

As previously stated, recall is often what is thought of when the word *memory* is used. It involves generating the memory with an appropriate internal cue. It is a far more complex memory process than recognition, and it is usually deficient after a head injury. Recall involves several memory processes, and if any one is not functioning normally, recall may be seriously impaired. For example, recall involves generating the appropriate internal cue for retrieving the information. Recall involves a search of memory, whereas recognition simply requires that the person make a yes or no decision concerning whether the information has been seen or heard before. Recall is also enhanced by the organization of information and its relation to other well-learned information.

Recall may be seriously impaired after a head injury. The impairment is selective, however. Recall may be fine for the events or information of the distant past but may be seriously impaired for such data in the present. Recall is similar to writing an essay question on a test: The client must pull the information independently from memory. Recognition, on the other hand, is similar to answering multiple-choice questions on the test: If the client is given choices, the correct answer is cued and pulled from long-term memory.

Semantic Memory

This memory retains knowledge, skill, and understanding. For example, semantic memories include the knowledge that a dog is an animal or that the use of *ain't* is poor grammar. This is the type of memory that is tapped when a person recalls the alphabet, names of presidents, dates in history, language use, and so forth. Semantic memory also contains the wisdom that is abstracted from a lifetime of episodic experiences. Semantic memory appears to be relatively unaffected after a head injury.

Episodic Memory

Episodic memories are recollections of the novel episodes of life that we unpredictably encounter every day. This type of memory tends to be more personal in that the events are ones that affect the individual directly. Such events include one's personal history of memories (first day of school, weddings, birthdays, vacations, and so forth). TBI survivors usually indicate that their short-term memory is not functioning normally after a head injury when short-term memory may actually be functioning quite well. The deficit may involve the inability to transfer this episodic information to the long-term memory. The real problem is an inability to store and retrieve episodic information.

Episodic memory probably precedes semantic memory. The latter includes abstract knowledge that results from interaction with the world. It is therefore likely that the episodes of life are retained and that certain consistencies are simply extracted. This type of information can exist separately as semantic memories. Although the term *semantic* implies that this is a verbal process, it is quite possible that the same type of abstraction goes on at a nonverbal level; episodic memory can also be visual, or it can involve some other sensory modality.

Procedural Memory

Procedural memory (also called motor memory)[7] is the ability to recall a skill. Procedural memory is the ability to remember sequences of actions (typically motor movements) and to improve the execution of that sequence with practice. For example, playing a musical instrument involves procedural learning. Although procedural memory involves other types of senses (e.g., visual and auditory), it can exist independently. For example, blind individuals who are unable to read music or to see their finger placement on a keyboard can still learn to play the piano. Moreover, persons with head injury can frequently improve their performance on procedural tasks but cannot recall having done the task before.

Declarative Memory

This is the ability to remember facts, to describe procedures, and to recall types of categories of information. Declarative memory therefore encompasses a variety of different memories such as identification, recall, the ability to elaborate on a topic, and the ability to describe a sequence or procedure. Declarative memory functions are usually impaired after head injury and may also be quite difficult to improve.

INPUT/OUTPUT CHANNELS

Input/output channels refer to the manner in which information is processed. Input refers to the way information enters the brain; output refers to the way information leaves memory and is expressed. Several input channels are discussed below: visual-verbal, visual-figural, auditory-verbal, and auditory-nonverbal. These are discussed because they are the most commonly measured channels, although output can be through any sensory modality or a combination of several.

Visual-Verbal

Visual-verbal information consists of verbal content (e.g., words and sentences) that is presented visually. Deficits in this area limit the ability to recall what is read in textbooks or novels and to read directions, instructions, and so forth. This input channel is particularly important for persons involved in activities requiring much reading (e.g., school or work).

Visual-Figural

This involves memory for nonverbal information: pictures, charts, diagrams, maps, schematics, and so forth (the presentation is of course visual). Damage to the right hemisphere, especially the occipital area of the brain, usually produces difficulties with visual-figural memory. The person may be unable to learn new skills that require recall of pictures, charts, or routes. He or she may not be able to learn place relationships, navigate an office building or shopping mall, or understand figural directions. It may be difficult to learn new skills such as high-level math, which requires visualizing three-dimensional structures. Certain types of therapy such as imagery training may also be ineffective.

Auditory-Verbal

Auditory-verbal information consists of verbal content such as words, numbers, or sentences that is presented orally. This includes information heard in lectures, in daily conversations, on television, and so forth. This is an extremely crucial area, and one that is often impaired after brain trauma.

Auditory-Nonverbal

This is information that consists of nonverbal content that the client hears. Such information includes tones, noises, and music (without words, such as symphonies).

TYPES OF MEMORY PROCESSES

For information to be encoded and stored into memory, there are several processes that must occur. Each of these is discussed in the sections that follow.

Scanning in Sensory Memory

Much of the information in sensory memory is lost in less than a second. Scanning is the procedure for selecting information that is further processed in working memory. The capacity of sensory iconic memory cannot be increased, but clients can learn to scan it more efficiently. Parenté and colleagues[8] have shown that TBI survivors can learn to scan the sensory memory more effectively and that this training can be transferred to another functional skill, such as reading.

Orientation, Attention, Concentration, and Vigilance

Orientation is the ability to orient oneself physically to a source of stimulation. This usually involves the physical process of turning the body or making some other gross motor movement. Attention is the ability to focus on a stimulus once oriented. Concentration is the ability to maintain attention over time (vigilance), such that the person can work with the information in memory (i.e., mentally process and organize it). These terms are frequently confused and are often difficult to separate or discern. These processes are the predecessors of memory. Information cannot be stored in memory unless the person can orient to the material, attend to it, and concentrate on it. A complete event will never be experienced if the person cannot remain vigilant.

Rehearsal in Working Memory

Rehearsal is the mechanism for keeping information resident in working memory. Without rehearsal, most information would be lost before it could be processed and stored in long-term memory. Rehearsal is the precursor to encoding. After a head injury, the client may lose the ability to rehearse automatically and may need to relearn this strategy. In many cases, simply teaching rehearsal skills is sufficient to improve memory.

Encoding

This is the process of transforming information for storage into long-term memory. Without encoding, the client is unable to form the access codes necessary to retrieve the information from long-term memory. It is literally impossible to recall anything unless it is organized in some way. Head injury disrupts the person's ability to form organizational schemes automatically. Moreover, the client may not have organized effectively before the injury. Therapy therefore should stress teaching categorization, imaging, mnemonics, and other strategies that improve the person's ability to encode. The general process involves showing the client that, to remember well, it is necessary to organize the new information, that is, to relate it to something he or she already knows.

Cuing

This is the process of forming access keys to the information in long-term memory. Without cues, memories are available but not accessible. The analogy to the computer model mentioned earlier is obvious. Without knowing the file name, it is impossible to find the file on the hard disk. The information is therefore available but not accessible. TBI survivors may also lose the ability to generate cues spontaneously. When working with TBI survivors, the therapist quickly realizes that memory improves immediately with appropriate cuing. The information is therefore resident in memory, but it may be inaccessible unless the therapist and client can find the appropriate access code. Therefore, the methods for training encoding (see Chapters 6 and 7) ensure that the client's spontaneously generated cues are effective. Likewise, prosthetic devices (see Chapter 8) are simple ways to improve the client's ability to cue recall externally (and to compensate).

Storage and Retrieval

These two processes refer to the entry and removal of information from long-term memory. In storage, information enters the long-term memory from the working memory; retrieval is the process of removing information from long-term memory. The ability to store and retrieve is usually diminished after a head injury. Since encoding strategies facilitate storage and retrieval, memory therapy focuses on teaching many different techniques until the client finds one that is effective.

Organization

The organization of memory involves finding structure in what we experience. Organization is a strategy that most persons perform in an automatic way before injury and is often a strategy that is taught after injury to assist in memory (see Chapter 7). Organization can be subjective, categorical, imaginal, spatial, or procedural.

Subjective organization implies a unique memory structuring that will differ from person to person; that is, the person's individual experiences will affect how he or she will view and impose structure on the world and learn new information. To the child, the words *silver, brass,* and *steel* may imply colored metals. A metallurgist may immediately group the metals by their density, whereas a jeweler may group them by their value.

Developing categorical organization involves giving the person a specific grouping or structure to facilitate recall. Categorical organization can be hierarchical, semantic, or conceptual. For example, businesses frequently group people by an organizational chart. The military is grouped by rank. The phone book is grouped alphabetically, and words in the English language can be grouped into synonyms. Ideas are grouped into theories. These are not subjectively derived systems.

Imaginal, spatial, and symbolic organizations are pictures, maps, or other nonverbal means of organizing otherwise unrelated facts. Computer systems use icons for organizing commands. Most persons have grossly organized the states in the United States according to the map. Advertisers constantly try to conjure certain images or looks in the minds of their customers to sell their products. Other symbols include flags, crosses, and so forth.

Serial and procedural organizations are ways of structuring a series of steps that must be taken in a certain order. Operating a microwave oven involves pressing buttons in a certain order. Playing a musical instrument entails playing notes in a specific sequence. We therefore organize much of our everyday experience as a series of specific actions that follow one another in a structured sequence.

Clients frequently try to remember facts, faces, objectives, and events in vacuo. Retraining memory can therefore be viewed as a process of teaching the person how to organize information and how to use the organization to facilitate memory. It is necessary to impress on the client that organization, in any form, facilitates recall.

THEORIES OF FORGETTING AND AMNESIA

It is convenient to think of forgetting as the opposite of remembering; however, this comparison is probably too simplistic. Although forgetting and remembering share many common processes, the two are not simply flip sides of the same coin. There are many and varied theories of forgetting; for convenience and ease in understanding, we divide these into classical theories of forgetting and theories of amnesia. The former type of theory was developed to explain why most people forget; the latter type is an explanation of forgetting that results from injury to the brain. Most theories of amnesia borrow heavily from the classical models discussed in the next section.

Classical Theories of Forgetting

Classical models of forgetting can be grouped into three broad categories.[9] The first assumes that forgetting results from decay of information over time. Literally, if information is not used, it is forgotten. Memories are similar to sand castles. Unless the castle is continually reinforced, it will eventually be eroded by the waves and swept away. It is therefore necessary to keep information active through rehearsal, or it will, like the sand castle, be effaced by time and experience to the point where the person can no longer recall it. There is no assumption concerning which types of experiences erode in memory faster than others. The theory simply assumes that memory will decay if it is not rehearsed.

Hebb[10] was the first to propose a physiological mechanism of memory. His theory, which is still generally accepted today, is that rehearsing any experience causes a structural change in the brain. Rehearsal and encoding cause cells to fire and to stimulate other cells. This process goes on even after the initial physical stimulation has ended. Eventually the stimulated cells connect into a circuit, which forms a memory. The process of forming the circuit is called consolidation. If anything happens to disrupt the consolidation process, then memory for the event will be incomplete.

Hebb's theory explains the typically poor memory for events that precede a traumatic experience. For example, clients treated with electroconvulsive shock therapy usually cannot recall events that occurred immediately before the treatment because the shock disrupted consolidation. It is therefore reasonable to suggest that one reason TBI survivors cannot recall their accidents is that the trauma disrupted consolidation of the event.

The third model, interference theory, assumes that new experiences interfere with memory for old ones. Alternatively, old experiences can interfere with memory for new ones. One type of interference is called retroactive. Another type is called proactive. Retroactive interference occurs when new information interferes with the ability to retrieve old information. For example, if a TBI survivor is tested on different text passages for several days, he or she may experience interference when trying to recall yesterday's passage after reading today's. Proactive inhibition occurs when old information affects the ability to remember new information. As the person reads more and more passages, it becomes progressively more difficult to recall the most recent ones because of interference from preceding paragraphs. Proactive inhibition therefore accounts in part for the fatigue and progressive inefficiency that clients experience when performing similar tasks.

These models differ in several ways. Decay theories assert that memory and retention are determined by whether information is used. For example, an event should be recalled equally well regardless of whether it is experienced in the evening before going to sleep or in the morning before an entire day of activity. Interference theory asserts that what is done during the interval of time after learning something and before recalling it determines the ability to remember it. It also emphasizes the effect of cumulative experiences on memory. Consolidation theory stresses the physiological aspects of memory. It illustrates the importance of events that immediately follow the episode the person is trying to remember. If the consolidation is disrupted, memory will be affected.

Theories of Amnesia

Whereas the term *forgetting* describes a normal condition of mind, amnesia is a pathology that usually accompanies injury to the brain. It is important to distinguish three types of amnesia.[11] The first type is global amnesia. The TBI survivor is unable to recall personal life history, to recognize familiar people, or to recall newly learned information. Global amnesia is commonly portrayed on television when a person totally forgets his or her past. Global amnesia is actually quite rare and resistant to therapy.

A second type of memory loss is primary amnesia. The person is unable to recall novel information, although most old memories seem to be intact. The person's intellectual functions may not be obviously impaired. This type of memory loss usually results from head injury or stroke.

A third type of memory loss is secondary amnesia. Secondary amnestic effects result from the primary disorder. For example, language may be impaired, which results in an inability to understand instructions, not necessarily the inability to remember them. Visual deficits may make it difficult to perceive information correctly. Recall may therefore be complete but incorrect because of the original misperception. Hearing loss may limit the person's ability to process the nonverbal aspects of speech, voice, and tonal inflections that convey meaning. Memory may therefore seem impaired because the person cannot perceive the meaning of the conversation correctly.

The theories outlined below were developed with clients with secondary amnesia. Since, most theories are based on studies of clients in this population, it is difficult to develop an adequate theory of primary amnesia.[12] None of the theories has been clearly validated, and it is likely that each of these theories describes a portion of the amnestic syndrome. The reader should note the similarities between the types of amnesia and the theories of forgetting discussed above.

Storage Theories of Amnesia

Storage occurs as information moves from working memory to long-term memory. If the process is interrupted or partially diminished, then information would never be available for recall. Wilson[13] has identified two models of this process. One model assumes that the information decays rapidly in working memory and is therefore unavailable for retrieval. The second type of storage model assumes that the person never consolidates the information in long-term memory. Either of these explanations assumes that the information is not available for recall. This is a fundamentally different assumption from the one that underlies the retrieval deficit theory discussed next.

Retrieval Theories of Amnesia

Retrieval occurs as information moves from long-term to working memory. Retrieval theories therefore describe the amnestic syndrome as a break in the process (literally, the inability to get information out of memory). Cuing facilitates recall after head injury. If the information was never stored, then cuing would have no effect on recall. Recognition memory is relatively unaffected after head injury. Again, there must have been some storage of the information if recognition has been spared. Although neither of these facts alone provides clear proof of the retrieval theory of amnesia, together they indicate that some portion of the problem may be due to the inability to gain access to information rather than the inability to store it.

There are generally two types of retrieval theories of amnesia.[14] The first type assumes that a TBI survivor cannot generate the cues that are necessary for retrieval.

The second model asserts that the inability to recall new information is the result of different types of interference. For example, the person may have difficulty distinguishing the context in which the information occurred, determining when the event occurred, or forming associations with familiar information or knowledge.

Processing Theories of Amnesia

This type of theory assumes that the TBI survivor loses the ability to rehearse and encode information automatically. The automaticity of processing is the key characteristic that distinguishes this class of theory from all others. Specifically, the notion is that the TBI survivor loses the ability to rehearse and transform information unconsciously into easily retrievable units. He or she may be easily distracted, unable to attend, or otherwise unable to allocate cognitive effort. The client must relearn to rehearse consciously to maintain information in working memory. He or she must also learn new ways to encode the information to retrieve it from long-term memory. Although the therapist may find that training rehearsal and encoding techniques clearly improve the client's memory, the challenge is to assist the client in using these techniques spontaneously.

IMPLICATIONS FOR TREATMENT

Several practical suggestions for working with TBI survivors are apparent in this survey of memory. Amnesia can result from a failure of rehearsal, encoding, storage, retrieval, or attention. It is therefore necessary to assess the memory deficit before an effective treatment program can begin. In some cases, all these processes will have been diminished. In others, only one may be defective. Assessing the client allows the therapist to allocate therapy time efficiently.

Retraining memory will involve teaching the client compensatory strategies that may require conscious effort. Many clients may be unwilling to make the effort at first, and the therapist may need to demonstrate that memory will improve markedly only when the person uses the strategy. For example, simply showing the person that rehearsing most things two or three times may result in a 100% improvement in memory can provide the type of immediate reinforcement that is necessary to get the person to continue to rehearse spontaneously.

The client's ability to consolidate and to store information will be partially determined by attentional factors. If the therapist suspects an attention deficit, then it will be necessary to work with this problem before beginning memory training. Sohlberg and Mateer[15] provide a highly structured training program specifically designed for retraining attention. Playing computer games can also improve attention and concentration.

In our experience, much of the amnestic syndrome can be overcome with compensatory strategies such as mnemonics and imagery or obviated by training the

TBI survivor to use prosthetic devices (see Chapters 7 and 8). The compensatory strategies improve the storage and retrieval of information, whereas the prosthetic devices facilitate the cuing process. Simply showing the person how to form mnemonics or how to use a device, however, is not sufficient to ensure that he or she will use the strategy. The therapist may have to create mnemonics with the client to be memorized. The client may or may not be able to create his or her own. The therapist may spend hours showing the client how to use a calendar or notebook before the person can use it unassisted.

Therapists and family members may find it necessary to phrase questions so that the TBI survivor is cued to recall the answer. For example, for some clients a question such as "What did you have for lunch yesterday?" may not elicit a response. However, asking the person "What did you eat for lunch when you went to Harvey's restaurant yesterday?" provides specific information about the context of the event. It is therefore more likely to get a correct response. This provision of external cues is especially important in the early stages of recovery as internal cuing mechanisms are often impaired.

Different types of memory may be completely spared or generally uncorrelated with other memories that are more obviously affected by the injury. For example, even though the TBI survivor may not recall participating in a training program, performance may improve from session to session. It may therefore be possible for that person to learn an employable skill even though deficiencies in declarative memory would seem to contraindicate employment.

NOTES

1. B. Kolb and I.Q. Whishaw, *Fundamentals of Human Neuropsychology* (New York: Freeman, 1990), 526.

2. B.B. Murdock, "Short-term Memory," in *The Psychology of Learning and Motivation: Advances in Research and Theory,* ed. G.H. Bower (New York: Academic Press, 1972), 5.

3. H.C. Ellis, J.P. Groggin, and R. Parenté, "Human Memory and Learning: The Processing of Information," in *Foundations of Contemporary Psychology,* ed. Merle Meyer (New York: Oxford University Press, 1979), 327–358.

4. R.C. Atkinson and R.M. Shiffren, "Human Memory: A Proposed System and its Control Processes," in *The Psychology of Learning and Motivation,* eds. K.W. Spence and J.T. Spence (New York: Academic Press, 1968), 2.

5. R. Parenté and J.K. Anderson-Parenté, "Retraining Memory: Theory and Application," *Journal of Head Trauma Rehabilitation* 4 (1989): 55–65.

6. A.O. Dick, "Iconic Memory and its Relation to Perceptual Processing and Other Memory Mechanisms," *Perceptions and Psychophysics* 16 (1974): 576–596.

7. Ellis, Groggin, and Parenté, "Human Memory and Learning," 335.

8. R. Parenté, J.K. Anderson-Parenté, and B. Shaw, "Retraining the Mind's Eye," *Journal of Head Trauma Rehabilitation* 4 (1989): 53–62.

9. R. Parenté and J.K. Anderson-Parenté, *Retraining Memory: Techniques and Applications* (Houston: CSY Publishers, 1991), 35–45.

10. D.O. Hebb, *The Organization of Behavior* (New York: John Wiley & Sons, 1949), 500–520.

11. B. Wilson, *Rehabilitation of Memory* (New York: Guilford Press, 1987), 47.

12. Ibid., 48–56.

13. Ibid., 47–51.

14. P.R. Meudell and A.R. Mayes, "Normal and Abnormal Forgetting," in *Normality and Pathology of Cognitive Functions,* ed. A.W. Ellis (London: Academic Press, 1982), 51–63.

15. M.M. Sohlberg and C.A. Mateer, "Effectiveness of an Attention Training Program," *Journal of Clinical and Experimental Neuropsychology* 9 (1987): 117–130.

Part II
Assessment and Treatment Planning

3
Memory Assessment

Any memory system may be dysfunctional after injury to the brain. There is little consistency in the clinical picture, however, and the therapist must be prepared to evaluate a variety of different types of memory to determine which are the best candidates for rehabilitation. This chapter discusses basics of assessment (training of the assessor, selection of tests, the client's level of functioning, and missing links in assessment), the reasons for evaluating memory, and the types of assessments available to clinicians. In addition, it focuses on how the therapist can use information gained in the assessment to plan the most effective treatment regimen.

ASSESSMENT BASICS

Before beginning an assessment of memory, there are several basics to be considered. These are discussed in the sections that follow.

Training of the Assessor

The issue of who can assess memory and other cognitive areas is controversial. Many clinicians feel that it is not necessary to be a licensed or certified clinician to evaluate memory effectively. What is necessary is training and experience. Indeed, many hospitals and rehabilitation facilities use unlicensed technicians to do testing. With adequate training and supervision, these individuals can eventually become highly skilled and proficient administrators and, often, interpreters of memory assessment instruments. Conversely, some clinicians believe that persons who provide assessments should meet minimum requirements, such as those outlined by the American Psychological Association (APA).[1] The APA has developed recommendations which include a minimum of a Bachelor's degree, preferably in Psychology, along with training in administration, scoring, ethics, and situations that may arise within the context of testing.

Regardless of beliefs about guidelines for training, it is necessary for the assessor to practice administering tests until his or her results are similar to those obtained by practiced clinicians. The clinicians who perform evaluations are usually neuropsychologists, speech and language therapists, or psychometrists. In most cases, the decision to entrust an individual with administering various tests is made by the supervising clinician after a period of training. Training to administer a specific battery of tests is also part of the internship experience for some degree programs and typically includes administration, scoring, interpretation, and preparation of reports. The actual time to train an assessor will vary with the person's educational level and previous experience and skills. In some cases, the test manuals prescribe limits for the number of administrations necessary to achieve consistent and accurate results. In others, the test developers assume that persons administering tests will have adequate training to do so.

Testing is a specific and often taxing process for both the client and the therapist. Persons who test must do so only if they have the requisite skills. Therapists must honestly evaluate their expertise and not test clients if they are unqualified to do so. If a test is given, scored, or interpreted inaccurately, it is not helpful to clients; in fact, it may be harmful in that clients may feel frustrated, results may be inaccurate, and this information can distort treatment planning.

For therapists working with clients on the rehabilitation of memory, access to test data is important; the therapist who is unqualified to administer such testing will need access to someone who is.

Selection of Tests

This section discusses selection of tests specific to memory areas. It should be noted, however, that clients are typically evaluated in multiple cognitive areas; individual areas of memory are not assessed in isolation. Clinicians must have access to other test data to obtain a holistic assessment of strengths and limitations.

Before administering tests, the assessor must decide which types of assessments and which particular tests to use. This is based on the specific questions to be addressed in the evaluation. Typically, evaluations are performed to determine the client's pattern of strengths and limitations and to make recommendations for treatment or other interventions. Testing is done to assist in measuring progress and in planning for discharge from a particular facility or to document injury (typically at the request of an insurer or an attorney). Testing is also conducted for a variety of other reasons such as to determine competency or to provide data for use in litigation.

A primary consideration when selecting tests for use is the client's level of cognitive, emotional, and physical functioning. Clients must be able to sustain concentration and energy levels for some amount of time to participate in testing. Creative testing procedures are often necessary. For example, the client may be severely agitated or visually limited. Spasticity or shortened attention span may also require creative efforts by the therapist in collecting test data. Or, testing may be deferred until the client is more able to give or receive maximum effort and benefit.

In some cases, a self-report or rating instrument may be the only feasible evaluation. It is impossible to determine exactly which tests will apply without first interviewing the client. The examiner must therefore have a variety of tests available and must also be prepared to use different ones to conform to the individual needs of the client.

Another consideration is the issue of whether to administer a standard battery of tests or to choose tests individually. The clinician will need to decide this issue based on the reason for referral, the cognitive level of the client, funding and time re-straints, and the range of skills measured by particular tests.

Missing Links in Assessment

Rehabilitation is a learning process for both the client and the therapist. The client works on improving memory by learning ways to remember (skills). The goal is to acquaint the client with a variety of memory strategies and to ensure transfer and generalization of one or more of those strategies into novel situations. One missing link in traditional memory assessment is the lack of measurement for how well the person acquires new skills or the ability to generalize strategies to real-world settings. Although most tests provide only a one-shot assessment of the client's memory performance in a static clinical setting, there are few exceptions that allow the clinician to measure the client's performance with practice and learning potential (e.g., the Visual and Verbal Paired Associates sections of the Wechsler Memory Test,[2] the Rey-Auditory Verbal Learning Test,[3] etc.). Often, however, the clinician is left with the knowledge that some aspect of memory is impaired, but there is little insight concerning where most profitably to invest the therapy effort.

Another limitation to conventional memory assessments is that there is little documentation of the relationship between the scores on performance-based tests and everyday life functioning.[4,5] Therefore, many standardized tests provide little more than benchmark evaluations of memory that simply document how much recovery has taken place. A third problem with traditional memory assessments is that most of them do not measure change in performance with practice. The client may require time to warm up, focus attention, understand instructions, or otherwise orient to the task at hand. Clients with attentional deficits often fail to understand instructions and will perform considerably better on repeated testings after the task demands are clear. This rate of improvement with repeated testing is usually ignored in a conventional neuropsychological or speech-language evaluation.[6] This will limit the therapist's ability to evaluate the client's learning potential. This is an important point that requires elaboration.

A client may begin testing at a low level of performance but may also improve markedly after practicing. Another may begin with an average level of performance but may not improve at all. This rate of improvement, or learning potential, is a better predictor of success in therapy than the traditional performance score on static, one-shot testing.[7] Indeed, the term *learning* is defined as improvement of performance with practice.[8] Although many psychological and speech-language assessments discuss the client's potential (capacity) for learning, rate of improvement (i.e., learning potential) is generally not scaled and norms for learning scores are not typically published.

A final problem with conventional assessments is that the tests are usually timed. Most clients have a difficult time performing at peak efficiency within the time frame of the test, and scores may therefore reflect slow performance rather than impaired intellectual functioning. When therapists test limits with clients by allowing them to complete tasks after time limits have expired, clients may be able to perform the task accurately. This is valuable information for the therapist in that therapy tasks can focus first on accuracy and later on speed.

RATIONALE FOR ASSESSMENT

The reasons for assessment are tied to the overall philosophy of retraining memory discussed in Chapter 5. As previously stated in this chapter, there are many reasons to perform assessments. Each of these reasons are discussed in the sections that follow. This includes obtaining a baseline measure of strengths and limitations, determining when to begin treatment, determining long-term treatment needs, treatment planning and goalsetting, and providing an ongoing measure of progress.

Baseline Data To Determine Strengths and Limitations

A complete memory assessment will necessarily include an evaluation of several different functions. Many of the standardized batteries for assessing memory will facilitate this type of global assessment. At a minimum, the assessment should determine which of several different memories are functioning normally and which are not (for example, visual and verbal memory). It is also necessary to assess the mental control capacity of memory. This is the ability to perform mental work, to attend and concentrate, and to encode or transform information for effective storage. The assessment should determine whether or not the client is storing information in long-term memory and whether the information can be retrieved. Testing each of these functions is a complex and often time-consuming process. The assessment usually begins with standardized tests of memory, but much of what the therapist learns about the client can only come from long-term interaction, observation, and treatment.

The assessment of memory, when occurring in the beginning of treatment, serves as a baseline measure against which all future treatment and change can be compared. It is these initial data that give the client and the therapist information and structure within which to work and a basis for treatment. The client must know where he or she is starting before goals can be set and progress measured. Baseline measures in treatment are discussed further in Chapter 6.

When To Begin Treatment

Another reason for assessment is to assist the client, therapist, and treatment team in deciding when to begin treatment. There are generally two schools of thought on the issue of when to begin treatment.[9] One assumes that treatment should begin as soon as possible. This is because the person has a limited time frame for maximum recovery (somewhere between 6 months and 2 years), and it is necessary to maximize recovery during this period (it should be noted, however, that we have seen improvement in brain injury survivors years after injury). Another school of thought assumes that the client will benefit from treatment only after the initial period of disorientation has subsided. It may take the client 6 months to 1 year (or longer) before treatment is feasible.

According to these two positions, different types of treatment are feasible at any stage of recovery. It is, however, necessary to identify the client's functional capacities and to assess which types of memory show the greatest potential for improvement with practice (learning potential). By using appropriate assessment techniques and baseline measures, the therapist can avoid treatments where there is limited learning potential. The therapist can begin working with those areas where the client is capable of improving with practice as soon as possible. The memory assessment must identify these skills and make suggestions for which areas of memory are trainable and which are not.

Treatment Planning and Goal Setting

Assessments are crucial in helping the client and therapist plan treatment interventions and set goals. The therapist must determine what memory skills are strongest and most likely to respond to treatment. With this type of assessment, the therapist is more likely to use valuable time effectively, and frustration for the client is minimized. The therapist must assess the interests of the client. Schultz[10] has developed a client information and interest form specifically for this purpose. This interview instrument helps the therapist determine the client's interests and plan treatment that will engage the client and foster vigilance.

The therapist and client must discuss realistic treatment goals. This process can be facilitated by effective use of assessment techniques to provide information to the client and therapist about the client's level of functioning.

Goals must be specific and behavioral. For example, the client's goal may be to remember a sequence of seven numbers (so that telephone numbers can be remembered). This goal is quantifiable and concrete. Goals such as "become more aware of memory impairment" or "make substantial improvement in everyday memory functions" are functionally useless to clients and therapists. Goal setting and treatment planning are discussed later in this chapter and further in Chapters 4 and 5.

Periodic Evaluations To Assess Progress

Memory functioning can change rapidly in the early stages of recovery from brain trauma. It may also change as medications are altered and with motivation, and it may also plateau and then accelerate unpredictably. Memory may change in the middle of therapy simply because the client and therapist stumble across a treatment that is effective with that particular client. For all these reasons, it is necessary to evaluate the client on a regular basis. As with initial memory assessments, periodic testing options include a standardized memory scale and an assessment of the client's rate of learning on various tests to determine which treatments have the greatest potential to affect learning.

As the client improves, it may be necessary to use different memory assessments or to use alternative forms of the same one. This is because the client may begin to remember specific test items or procedures with repeated testings. Performance may therefore appear to improve, but the change may be an artifact of repeated long-term testing. Even so, this type of improvement also indicates that the client can store and retrieve information about the test, and in that sense it indicates improved memory. Nevertheless, the therapist is wise to vary the schedule and selection of different memory assessments to limit practice effects on any one.

Reevaluation To Determine Long-Term Treatment Needs

At the end of treatment, reevaluations are performed to assist in determining which areas need more work, which memory skills have been strengthened, and a time frame for any additional treatment. Throughout the course of therapy, the client may demonstrate frustration and intolerance for certain treatments. This may be due to lack of interest, although it is more often the result of the therapist's error in assessment or inappropriate goal setting with the client. Reevaluation documents improvement and establishes the need for further specific treatment that may only become apparent as the abilities and skills of the client change with time.

Certain areas of memory may not show improvement with therapy or may improve much slower than others. This is usually the case with everyday memory for conversations and detail. The therapist can document which memory skills will require extended treatment and make suggestions for continued therapy in the long term, often long after a particular therapist discontinues work with the client.

Reevaluation at the end of treatment provides a measure of progress and is often used to recommend whether a client can return to work, school, or other pursuits. For instance, the test data, in combination with progress in treatment, can assist clients in choosing coursework in college and in structuring the experience for success. The student may need additional time on exams or may need to take exams in a separate area to minimize distractions. Test data can also be used to recommend placement in a particular job, when requirements are compared against performance.

In addition to reevaluation at the end of treatment, it is valuable to assess clients at intervals thereafter (e.g., one, two, or three years) to assess any changes and to make ongoing recommendations. This is particularly important for those clients who continue to be seen in treatment on a long-term, follow-along basis.

TYPES OF ASSESSMENTS

Several types of assessments are discussed in this section, including objective and subjective measures. We have also included a sampling of memory assessments available for clinical use.

Objective, Standardized Memory Evaluations

There is no such thing as a truly objective evaluation. This is because the client's abilities change with time, motivation fluctuates, different test administrators vary instructions or scoring, and a host of other factors determine performance on any single administration of a memory test. There are, however, standardized tests (tests that are normed on sample populations) that limit the effect such factors have on the measurement of a client's performance. Even here, the interpretations vary with the perceptions of the evaluator. Many tests require subjective judgment of things such as correctness of shapes that the client reproduces from memory or descriptions of story content. This is one reason why repeated testing over time is crucial for objectively assessing how much memory has recovered. Ideally, several different evaluators can independently administer and interpret the same sort of assessment. Agreement among these evaluators is necessary to determine the overall effect of the treatment. It may therefore take years before a stable assessment of the client's memory functioning can be gleaned from a number of independent evaluators. This does not mean that the results of a single evaluation are meaningless. It is to say that a single test result is best interpreted as it contributes to an overall trend that emerges after months of therapy.

There are a number of standardized memory test batteries available that evaluate a variety of different memory skills. Some of the more commonly used instruments are described in the sections below, together with others that are less well known but particularly well developed. This discussion is certainly not exhaustive but is representative of available tests. See Appendix 3-A for listings of tests and vendor information.

Wechsler Memory Scale

The Wechsler Memory Scale[11] is, perhaps, the most widely used instrument for clinical memory assessment. It was originally developed during World War II for assessing memory dysfunction with returning troops. The instrument was normed on 100 subjects. An alternative form of this version of the test is also available.[12] The original test was quick to administer and generally reliable and valid. Indeed, for many clinicians, the original Wechsler Memory Scale is still the preferred assessment instrument. An excellent review of the development of this test is provided in the manual for the revised version.

The Wechsler Memory Scale–Revised[13] is a comprehensive memory assessment with extensive norms and validation. The test measures orientation in time and place, short-term verbal memory, short-term visual memory, general memory functioning, attention and concentration, and delayed memory. Its standard scores are comparable to those of the Wechsler Adult Intelligence Scale (WAIS), so that direct comparisons of memory and intelligence are possible. It takes approximately 1½ hours to administer. Its standard sample is the normal population of the United States, based on 1990 census data. Persons are between the ages of 16 years, zero months and 74 years, 11 months. It reflects appropriate age, sex, race, education, IQ, and geographical stratifications.

Rivermead Behavioural Memory Assessment

Wilson[14] developed the Rivermead instrument to assess changes in everyday memory. The subtests are unlike most others because they do not measure memory for unfamiliar materials, nor do they measure memory in a quasi-laboratory fashion. The items assess the client's ability to remember a functional memory activity or to perform a functional skill that requires memory. For example, the client is asked to recall a name and face association after a delay. The examiner hides an object such as a comb or pencil at various locations in the room, and the client must recall the object and its placement after a delay. The client must recall the purpose of an alarm (a signal for an appointment) when the alarm goes off. The test also evaluates ability to recall prose passages, short routes, and simple errands. It evaluates the client's fund of personal and current information, ability to recognize faces, and ability to learn a new skill such as putting a given message into the memory of a calculator. Conventional memory tests for paired associations are used to supplement the battery.

Items on the Rivermead have been shown to discriminate successfully a memory-impaired from a non–memory-impaired sample. It was also demonstrated that the test could discriminate two groups of clients who were previously identified by occupational therapists as having everyday memory problems. The test correlates moderately with a variety of standardized memory tests but does not correlate strongly with tests of intelligence. Different administrators provide reliable and comparable scores; the alternative forms also correlate strongly. In general, the test is a viable alternative or supplement to the Wechsler battery or other standardized procedures in common use.

Ross Information Processing Assessment (RIPA)

The RIPA was originally developed at the University of California, Davis Medical Center.[15] The test is for adolescents and adults and is designed to assess cognitive linguistic deficits after brain injury. Specific cognitive functions measured include immediate memory, delayed memory, temporal orientation (recent memory), temporal orientation (remote memory), spatial orientation, recall of general information, problem solving and abstract reasoning, organization, and auditory processing and retention. Therefore, although the scale measures memory and retention, it does so by examining overall information processing skills. The RIPA takes between 30 and 45 minutes to administer. It is well normed with percentile ranks for each of the subscales mentioned above. The manual also cites moderate to high levels of content and concurrent validity and reliability.

The Randt Memory Test

The Randt Memory Test[16] was designed to provide an overall evaluation of memory. The test is a series of sections that are administered in a special order. The first, a general information section, requires the client to provide personal information and common knowledge. The second section requires the client to recall a list of five words presented in as many as three trials. Each trial is separated by an interval of 10 seconds during which the client engages in a rehearsal prevention task. He or she is then asked to recall the five words. Then, the client is told the words that were left out as well as any intrusions. The client again recalls as many of the words as he or she can. Section 3 is a digit span task, similar to the Wechsler Memory Scale. The fourth section is similar to the second except that word pairs are used rather than a simple list of words. Section 5 involves the immediate recall of a story and additional recall after two delay intervals to assess remote memory for the same passage. The sixth section involves recognition of pictures of seven common objects. The client selects the pictures from a batch which contains the original items plus additional distractor items. This task measures both immediate and delayed recognition. The seventh section measures the client's ability to recall the various names of the different sections of the test.

One interesting procedural feature of the Randt Memory Test is that the examiner continually returns to previously administered sections to evaluate the client's delayed recall or recognition for those materials. The Randt Memory Test is also unique because it tests delayed memory for the word list, paired associates recall, story recall, and picture recognition sections after a 24-hour interval.

The Randt Memory Test is scaled for ages 20 through 89. It measures acquisition of novel information, immediate memory, and delayed recall in both visual and verbal domains. It also provides a single global index of memory functioning. However, normative data and research are limited.

The California Verbal Learning Test

The California Verbal Learning Test[17] was designed to assess verbal learning in neurologically impaired and elderly populations. It measures different strategies of encoding as well as rate of learning, how information is processed, and different types of errors. Immediate and delayed memory are also examined. The test involves learning a list of 16 words that are divided into four semantic categories. The client receives five study and test trials to learn the words. The client then learns a second list of 16 words which is presented for only one trial. Finally, the examiner waits 20 minutes before testing the client's memory for the first list. The delayed memory test examines free recall, recall of the list after presenting the semantic category labels, and recognition of the list words.

The California Verbal Learning Test is designed for clients ages 17 and older. Norms are provided for several ages although the actual norming population is rather small (273 adults between 17 and 80 years old). The test takes one hour to administer. Scoring procedures are complex and the user should consider purchasing available computer scoring materials.

Rey Auditory-Verbal Learning Test

The Rey Auditory-Verbal Learning Test is designed to measure memory for lists of words. It provides information about several different features of memory such as the rate of learning the list, long-term retention, and the effects of interference.

A list of 15 words is read and the client is asked to recall the list on five separate test administrations. The examiner records the words recalled during each trial. After the five trials, the examiner reads a second list of words and instructs the client to recall this list. The client is then asked to recall as many words from the first list as possible.

Norms for the test were originally published by Lezak.[18] The number of items recalled on each trial is scaled for several different occupations. The test also provides information about errors due to intrusions from the second list. Norms for recognition of the words are also available from the same source.

The Rey Auditory-Verbal Learning Test is frequently reported in the literature on head injury. It is simple to administer and takes less than one half-hour. The materials are inexpensive and the amount of information gleaned from the test is quite large. The norms are not well developed, however.

Rey-Osterreith Complex Figure Test

The Rey-Osterreith Complex Figure Test was designed to evaluate both visual memory and visual perception. Materials include only three sheets of white paper and several colored pencils. The procedure involves presenting a complex figure for the client to copy. The examiner places the figure in front of the client with instructions to reproduce or copy its shape. The examiner then watches as the client completes the copy portion of the task. Each time a new section is completed, the examiner gives the client a different colored pencil and records the order in which the colors are used. The examiner also records the time the client requires to complete the drawing. After completion, the figure and the client's reproduction are removed from view and the client is asked to draw the shape again, this time from memory. A third trial is given several minutes later to measure delayed recall. The examiner may record whether or not the client draws the shape in the original order by noting the order of colored pencils during the delay task. Scoring procedures are adapted from Lezak's work.[19] A total score for both the copy and recall score are compared to norms and converted to percentiles.

The major advantages of the Rey-Osterreith Complex Figure Test are that it is quick to administer and the scoring procedures are well defined. It also provides a screening tool for perceptual-motor dysfunction, along with a quantitative index of visual memory. Although it was never intended as a comprehensive visual memory test, it is well documented and is often reported in head injury literature.

The Benton Visual Retention Test

The Benton Visual Retention Test[20] is available in two versions. Each version consists of a group of 10 cards, each of which displays one or more figures. Most of the cards have two large figures and one small figure. The cards are exposed for 10 seconds and the client is asked to draw the shape from memory. Scoring involves both the number of correctly drawn shapes and the number of errors. The norms are based on both the client's age and IQ, a unique feature of the test.

The Benton Visual Retention Test takes approximately five to ten minutes to administer. It is normed for those aged eight to adulthood. The test has been well researched and is a reliable discriminator of brain damage, but it does not measure delayed retention and is not meant as a comprehensive memory test battery.

Other Memory Tests

The following tests are frequently cited in the literature on traumatic brain injury (TBI), although their use is restricted to specific applications. Therefore, the tests are not comprehensive batteries. Nevertheless, these instruments are frequently used for examining memory dysfunction after injury to the brain.

Webster Memory Scale. Webster, Parenté, and Bowersox[21] developed a multifunction memory scale specifically for clinical applications. Because of previous criticisms of the original Wechsler Memory Scale, the instrument was specifically designed to assess both verbal and nonverbal memory functions, working memory and long-term memory functions, both recall and recognition memory, and memory for information that was initially learned to a common performance criterion.

The test includes 10 different subscales that, more globally, examine ability to learn paired associations, immediate memory capacity and attention, working memory and concentration, delayed recall, and verbal-visual recognition memory. The factoral validity of the instrument is clearly documented, and the test also has moderate to high test-retest validity and interrater reliability. The test was also shown to discriminate survivors of brain trauma from a noninjured population.

The Webster Memory Scale was originally normed on 100 college students. It has not been widely used, largely because it is a relative newcomer on the clinical scene. Its main advantage is that it attempts to correct many of the flaws in the original Wechsler battery. It also allows the examiner to evaluate critical features of learning and memory such as visual versus verbal recall, recall versus recognition, and delayed recall. It was also specifically designed for clinical use. The major disadvantage is that it has not been widely adopted and the research base is therefore limited.

Memory Assessment Scale. Williams[22] has recently published a comprehensive assessment scale for evaluating adult memory functioning. The scales examine verbal span, visual span, list-learning skill, memory for text, name-face association, ability to reproduce shapes, and visual recognition memory. The test is exceptionally well normed and measures several different types of memory, including immediate and delayed recall and recognition of both verbal and visual information. The scaled scores are directly comparable to the Wechsler IQ norms. Reliability is moderate to high. Validity studies indicate that the scale can distinguish normal from neurologically impaired individuals. It can also discriminate various neurological disorders such as right versus left hemisphere lesions.

Objective, Nonstandardized Memory Evaluations

Nonstandardized memory evaluations are those that have not been formally normed but provide an objective measure. The tests are objective in that the examiner must specify a certain set of test procedures that can be duplicated. These assessments are easy to create and can provide useful information in a variety of situations. In some cases they may be the only feasible measure of memory (e.g., for clients with special needs or severe limitations). In other cases the measures can be used to supplement more norm-referenced data. These measures can also be used as baseline measures for therapy tasks.

Many measures of memory and learning do not require normative data. For example, informal tests of everyday memory functioning, such as asking the client to recall the breakfast menu that morning, can be quite useful for evaluating a client's functional skills at home.

When the purpose of the evaluation is to assess the viability of different treatments, then standardized measurement is often secondary. This type of evaluation involves therapy designs (see Chapter 5). No normative information is necessary because the client is evaluated relative to his or her baseline performance on some task. That is to say the client is tested to determine his or her unique baseline performance. The therapist then presents a training strategy and the client is retested on the same task to determine if the strategy has improved memory.

Nonstandardized objective measures provide the flexibility to expand the evaluation process. In the sections that follow, several non-standardized objective techniques are discussed including the Buschke Selective Reminding Procedure, training to criteria, delayed testing, and ecological validity issues.

Buschke Selective Reminding Procedure

Buschke and Fuld[23] developed an interesting procedure for assessing a variety of types of memory. This is not a specific test, but a *procedure* for evaluating different memory processes. The materials used are not standardized, and will vary depending on materials the therapist may have available. The technique is especially flexible and yields a great deal of information. The examiner begins by showing the client a list of items with instructions to remember them. After the client sees all the items, the examiner asks for recall of as many as possible. When the client can no longer recall any items, the examiner then reviews only those items that were not recalled. The client then tries to recall all the items again (i.e., the entire list). When the client can no longer recall any items, the examiner reminds the client of those that were missed, and the client tries to recall the entire list again. This procedure continues until the client can recall the entire list of items on two successive test trials with no errors.

Hannay and Levin[24] report a scoring procedure and normative data base for the Buschke procedure. The unique test procedure permits an examination of different components of a memory model that includes total recall, short-term registration, long-term registration, long-term storage, consistent long-term retrieval, and inconsistent long-term retrieval. The norms also include data for assessing other characteristics of memory such as cued recall, recognition memory, delayed recall, the number of intrusions at recall, and the number of reminders necessary to cue recall. Parenté and DiCesare[25] have shown how the Buschke procedure can be used to evaluate the results of memory strategy training.

The test does not cost anything because instructions are available in Buschke and Fuld's original publication in *Neurology,* and the examiner constructs the materials. The normative information is based on recall of word lists, and there are four alternative forms available. There are few data to validate its reliability or validity. Literally hundreds of uses for this test procedure have been cited. It is a flexible procedure for assessing improvement in memory with long-term follow-along.[26] Reisberg and colleagues[27] report that the Buschke procedure is capable also of distinguishing normal elderly subjects from those with early Alzheimer's disease. Jernigan[28] reports that the Buschke procedure correlates significantly with computerized tomography parameters.

The Buschke procedure is not a commercially available test. It is, strictly speaking, a selective reminding procedure that can be used with a variety of materials. Fuld[29] has developed an object memory scale based on the Buschke procedure. Conceivably the examiner could use any stimulus materials, such as categorized lists of words, name-face paired associations, or random shapes. It is therefore best discussed as a nonstandardized experimental tool, not a test. The examiner should not be dissuaded from using the Buschke procedure simply because there are no commonly accepted norms. The test can always be used to document change over time and can provide a clear picture of which types of memory are making the most rapid improvement with therapy.

Training to Criteria

One problem with traditional memory assessments that has been consistently cited in the literature is that most do not bring the client to a stable criterion before testing for delayed recall.[30] That is, if the client only remembers 20% of the information given on a task and then is not given the opportunity to practice to criterion, the delayed recall score will obviously be impaired. Therefore, performance after the delay may be due to the fact that the client never learned the material well to begin with. Parts of the Webster Memory Scale and the Wechsler Memory Scale–Revised eliminate this problem (see the discussion in this chapter).

Another objective way to assess performance is to determine the number of trials a client takes to reach a specific performance criterion during the initial learning phase of a task. It is a direct measure of learning potential. Unfortunately, many clients may not be able to learn the test materials within the stated time limits of the test. For example, on the Wechsler Memory Scale–Revised, some clients take more than six trials to learn the verbal-visual paired associations. Consequently, delayed recall for those materials may not result from poor memory; rather, it may be the result of inability to store the information during the initial study.

When using nonstandardized objective data, the examiner can administer test materials repeatedly to bring the client to a certain level of performance before administering tests of delayed recall. Repeated testing allows the therapist to observe how rapidly the client assimilates novel information, and it also ensures that tests of delayed memory are unbiased.

Delayed Testing

Delayed testing simply means testing the client's memory for information following a delay. The length of time from initial presentation of information to delayed testing can range from a few seconds to several minutes or hours. Testing for delayed memory is a very useful portion of the evaluation.

Delayed testing allows the examiner to determine the client's patterns of strengths and limitations and permits inferences concerning specific deficits, such as storage versus retrieval problems. Clients will usually have difficulty recalling without cues. If cuing helps recall, then the client is probably able to store information in memory. The problem is that he or she is unable to develop the cues that are necessary for retrieval. If cuing does not prompt the client's memory, then it is likely that the deficit involves an inability to store information. Several other methods should be used during the delayed testing to define the problem. For example, if the client can recognize novel information but not recall it, then retrieval failure is implicated. Clients who cannot recall or recognize effectively are probably not attending to the information or do not store it into long-term memory.

The delayed testing data also allow the therapist to determine which of several potential memory training techniques will best promote long-term retention. After measuring several baseline skills, the therapist can then suggest memory strategies and determine the effectiveness of each relative to the baseline measures. For example, after an initial baseline assessment, the therapist can train the client to use imagery and mnemonics. After a period of training, the therapist can reevaluate the client to determine whether the training facilitates memory relative to the baseline scores. The therapist should also evaluate whether or not the client is using the strategies spontaneously.

Another delayed testing measure is termed *savings*. This measure involves presenting the information again after the delay interval and asking the client to relearn it. If the client's performance exceeds his or her initial learning, then there must have been some storage. The problem is with retrieval of the information. If there is no savings, then storage is the problem. One typical pattern observed following brain injury involves poor delayed free recall with cuing usually improving memory markedly. The client's recognition memory may be unimpaired, and there are clear savings effects. This pattern implies loss of the ability to retrieve information and to generate appropriate internal cues.

Ecological Validity

Ecological validity refers to skills that can be transferred and generalized to real-life situations. These are perhaps the most important skills the client can acquire. In lieu of generalization, the client should show some evidence that the training transfers to a related task. For example, the client may learn a chunking technique (see Chapter 7) for remembering groups of numbers rather than individual digits. The client may then use this technique to remember phone numbers, demonstrating transfer of the skill. However, unless the client can use the chunking strategy to remember other types of numbers, there is limited generalization.

It may be impossible to measure generalization and transfer without observing the client or interviewing others outside the therapy session. Within the testing session, the opportunity for evaluating transfer and generalization can come from presenting new test materials and determining whether the client uses the learned strategy spontaneously.

Most standardized tests are not ecologically valid. That is, they do not measure functioning in the real world. Tests such as the Rivermead Behavioural Memory Scale previously discussed in this chapter are steps in the right direction, however. Perhaps the best way to test the client's ability to generalize is to build this type of nonstandardized test into the assessment procedure to supplement other standardized techniques.

Subjective Evaluation of Memory

Subjective measures are problems reported by clients or others (e.g., family members) or derived from clinical observation. Clients' self-reports concerning memory deficits after TBI are usually quite consistent. The common complaint is a "short-term memory loss," when actually what the client is describing may be failure of episodic memory (see Chapter 2) or difficulties with attention, concentration, or information processing. The deficit refers to the inability to store and/or retrieve novel information in long-term memory; that is, old memories are accessible, but the client cannot recall recent information. Although the explanations for this deficit vary, the phenomenon is quite consistently observed following head injury.

A clinical interview technique can be used to clarify what factors may contribute to the client's memory loss and in which specific situations difficulty with memory occurs. Another purpose of the interview is to discern the types of memory that may have been spared. Clients may sometimes make global statements such as "My memory is shot" or "I can't remember anything any longer." The examiner can assist in identifying problems more specifically than this by closed-ended questions rather than open-ended ones. For example, questions such as "Is it easier to remember pictures or words?" and "Can you remember what you hear better than what you see?" are specific, whereas a question such as "What problem do you have with memory?" is more vague and unstructured. The examiner may also wish to question the client's family members who see the client on a regular basis to gain additional information on specifics of memory loss. We have found it useful to use a simple questionnaire that can be filled out by the client and available family members. The questionnaire contains questions such as "Do you have difficulty remembering where you put items such as keys, purse, etc.?" and "Do you have difficulty remembering conversations you have with others?" The results of the client's and family's responses can be amalgamated to yield a picture of what types of memory are problematic.[31] Various other structured interview instruments are described below.

Memory Questionnaires

A number of questionnaires for measuring functional memory have been published. Crook[32] provides an excellent review of these scales. The focus of these instruments has been to identify frequency of forgetting, changes in memory over time, the seriousness of memory complaints, and the spontaneous use of strategies. Other questionnaires assess the client's overall judgment of memory, knowledge of memory, the demands on memory in daily life, memory for past events, cognitive effort when something is forgotten, and the relationship between personality and memory. Most of these scales, however, identify memory failures for non-injured populations or for persons who have been injured for extended lengths of time. Clients less reliably report deficits in the months immediately after the injury, which is probably due to the rapid change in the client's functional status. As Wilson[33] points out, this is the group most likely to undergo treatment.

Most memory questionnaires do not address issues of rehabilitation; rather, they are simply a series of questions related to the client's everyday memory functioning. Few are standardized or normed. The major purpose of memory questionnaires is to serve as a structured interviewing instrument and to provide further diagnostic information.

Sunderland and colleagues[34] were among the first to examine reports of memory dysfunction via questionnaire. Much of the Rivermead battery, discussed earlier, is based on the review of these structured self-reports. In general, the research and literature describing everyday memory problems is not well developed. There is some recent work concerning memory for people,[35] everyday cognitive deficits,[36] and everyday memory for things to do.[37] In general, interest in the study of everyday memory is growing (as evidenced by a recent issue of the *American Psychologist*,[38] which was devoted entirely to this topic). Nevertheless, valid and reliable scales for measuring memory are not generally available. We recommend the following ones.

1. The Brief Cognitive Rating Scale[39] is a battery developed for clinical use and relates the questions on the test to Axes I–V of the *Diagnostic and Statistical Manual* (3rd ed., DSM-III). It is therefore especially helpful for interviewing clients who will later require structured diagnosis.

2. Mateer and colleagues[40] developed a functional memory scale that breaks memory down into four distinct components: attention and prospective memory, retrograde memory, anterograde memory, and biographic memory. The purpose of the scale is to describe deficit processes, not specifically to diagnose using the revised DSM-III, on the basis of the client's responses.

Both these questionnaires have a different intent and purpose, and we recommend using both during the assessment. Each one is short and easy to fill out. The items are easy for the client to understand, and both questionnaires are well validated. The information can then be summarized or averaged to yield a picture of the client that is not readily discerned during a one-shot evaluation. Repeated surveys of the client and family with these instruments are recommended to determine changes in factors over time as well as changes in possible diagnoses as the client improves.

Therapist Subjective Observations

Christensen[41] has long argued the merits of clinical observations during the assessment phase of any neuropsychological battery. Wheatley and Rein[42] recently formalized a Learning Style Assessment that is specifically applicable for summarizing clinical observations of the person with TBI. It is our belief that much of our assessment of memory deficits must be based upon observation, which is often more useful than test results.

During the memory assessment, the client's ability to remember, latency of memory retrieval, ability to attend and to maintain vigilance, and fatigue caused by extended effort are crucial observations, as are the issues of motivation, use of medications, drug or alcohol use and abuse, etc. It is also necessary to examine whether the client is using any systems (strategies) for remembering that may not have been assessed earlier. The client may not use any particular memory strategy other than simple rehearsal. It is important to assess which types of information are most easily learned and retained. Latency of retrieval provides information about the seriousness of the memory impairment. If the client can retrieve novel information even though it takes a while, then the storage system is intact but the mechanism for retrieval is inefficient. Therapy would then emphasize search operations. If the client cannot recall information even with unlimited time, then therapy should focus on rehearsal and simple encoding techniques.

Often, what seems to be a memory impairment is really the result of an attention deficit. If performance improves markedly when the client is wearing earplugs or is intensely interested in the material, then defects in the memory system may be secondary to the attentional disorder. Therapy should then focus on the attention process rather than on memory training. It is also necessary to assess the fatigue factor during the testing. If the client fatigues rapidly, then it may be necessary to limit treatment sessions to accommodate for this.

NOTES

1. R.A. Bornstein, "Report of the Division 40 Task Force on Education, Accreditation and Credentialing: Recommendations for Education and Training of Nondoctoral Personnel in Clinical Neuropsychology," *Journal of Clinical and Experimental Neuropsychology* (January 1991): 20–23.

2. D. Wechsler, *Wechsler Memory Scale–Revised,* in The Psychological Corporation (New York: Harcourt Brace Jovanovich, 1987).

3. A. Rey, "Auditory-Verbal Learning Test," in *Neuropsychological Assessment,* ed. Muriel Lezak (New York: Oxford University Press, 1983), 422–429.

4. T. Hart and M. Hayden, "The Ecological Validity of Neuropsychological Assessment and Remediation," in *Clinical Neuropsychology of Intervention,* eds. Y. Gross and B. Uzell (Boston: Nijhoff, 1986).

5. M. Acker, "Relationship between Test Scores and Everyday Life Functioning," in *Clinical Neuropsychology of Intervention,* eds. Y. Gross and B. Uzell (Boston: Nijhoff, 1986).

6. F. Parenté and J. Anderson, "Use of the Wechsler Memory Scale for Predicting Success in Cognitive Rehabilitation," *Cognitive Rehabilitation* 2 (1984): 12–16.

7. K.D. Cicerone and D. Tupper, "Cognitive Assessment in the Neuropsychological Rehabilitation of Head-Injured Adults," in *Clinical Neuropsychology of Intervention,* eds. Y. Gross and B. Uzell (Boston: Nijhoff, 1986), 65–70.

8. H. Ellis and R. Hunt, *Fundamentals of Human Learning, Memory, and Cognition* (Dubuque, Iowa: W.C. Brown, 1988), 4–5.

9. E. Miller, *Recovery and Management of Neuropsychological Impairments* (New York: John Wiley & Sons, 1984), 78–89.

10. A. Schultz, "Client Information and Interest Form," *Communication Skills Builders* 1 (1989): 9–14.

11. L. Poon, ed. *Clinical Memory Assessment* (Washington, D.C.: American Psychological Association, 1986), 417.

12. D. Wechsler and C.P. Stone, *Wechsler Memory Scale* The Psychological Corporation (New York: Harcourt Brace Jovanovich, 1973).

13. D. Wechsler, *Wechsler Memory Scale–Revised,* The Psychological Corporation (New York: Harcourt Brace Jovanovich, 1987).

14. B. Wilson, *Rehabilitation of Memory* (New York: Guilford Press, 1987), 89–103.

15. D. Ross, "Ross Information Processing Assessment," *PRO-ED* 1 (1991).

16. C. Randt, E. Brown, and D. Osborne, "A Memory Test for Longitudinal Measurement of Mild to Moderate Deficits," *Clinical Neuropsychiatry* 2 (1980): 184–194.

17. *California Verbal Learning Test,* (San Antonio, Tx: The Psychological Corporation, 1988).

18. A. Rey, "Auditory-Verbal Learning Test," in *Neuropsychological Assessment,* ed. Muriel Lezak (New York: Oxford University Press, 1983), 422–429.

19. M. Lezak, ed. *Neuropsychological Assessment* (New York: Oxford University Press, 1983).

20. A.L. Benton, *The Revised Visual Retention Test,* 4th ed. (New York: The Psychological Corporation, 1974).

21. J. Webster, R. Parenté, and L. Bowersox, "A Multifunction Memory Scale for Clinical Use," *Cognitive Rehabilitation* 4 (January-February 1986): 32–37.

22. J. Williams, *Memory Assessment Scales* (Odessa, Fla.: Psychological Assessment Resources, 1990).

23. H. Buschke and P. Fuld, "Evaluating Storage, Retention, and Retrieval in Disordered Memory and Learning," *Neurology* 24 (1974): 1019–1025.

24. H. Hannay and S. Levin, "Scoring and Interpretation of the Buschke Selective Reminding Procedure," *Journal of Consulting and Clinical Psychology* 2 (1985): 185–193.

25. R. Parenté and T. DiCesare, "Retraining Memory: Theory, Evaluation, and Application," in *Cognitive Rehabilitation for Persons with Traumatic Brain Injury,* eds. J. Kreutzer and P. Wehman (Baltimore: Paul Brooks, 1991), 147–162.

26. R. Mohs, K. Youngjai, A. Celeste, D. Johns, D. Dunn, and L. Davis, "Assessing Changes in Alzheimer's Disease: Memory and Language," in *Clinical Memory Assessment,* ed. L. Poon (Washington, D.C.: American Psychological Association, 1986), 151.

27. B. Reisberg, S. Ferris, M. DeLeon, and T. Crook, "The Global Deterioration Scale for Assessment of Primary Degenerative Dementia," *American Journal of Psychiatry* 139 (1982): 1136–1139.

28. T. Jernigan, "Anatomical Validators: Issues in the Use of Computed Tomography," in *Clinical Memory Assessment,* ed. L. Poon (Washington, D.C.: American Psychological Association, 1986), 353–358.

29. P. Fuld, "Guaranteed Stimulus Processing in the Evaluation of Memory and Learning," *Cortex* 16 (1980): 255–271.

30. R. Parenté and J.K. Anderson-Parenté, *Retraining Memory: Techniques and Applications* (Houston: CSY Publishers, 1991).

31. C. O'Hara and M. Harrell, *Rehabilitation with Brain Injury Survivors: An Empowerment Approach* (Gaithersburg, Md.: Aspen Publishers, 1990).

32. T. Crook, "Instruments for the Evaluation of Symptoms and Complaints of Memory Dysfunction," in *Clinical Memory Assessment,* ed. L. Poon (Washington, D.C.: American Psychological Association, 1986), 91–197.

33. B. Wilson, *Rehabilitation of Memory,* 90.

34. A. Sunderland, J. Harris, and A. Baddeley, "Assessing Everyday Memory after Severe Head Injury," in *Everyday Memory, Actions and Absentmindedness,* eds. J. Harris and P. Morris (London: Academic Press, 1984).

35. A. Sunderland, J. Harris, and A. Baddeley, "Do Laboratory Tests Predict Everyday Memory? A Neuropsychological Study," *Journal of Verbal Learning and Verbal Behavior* 22 (1983): 341–357.

36. M. Gilewski and E. Zelinski, "Questionnaire Assessment of Memory Complaints," in *Clinical Memory Assessment,* ed. L. Poon (Washington, D.C.: American Psychological Association, 1986), 93–97.

37. D. Broadbent, P. Cooper, P. Fitzgerald, and K. Parks, "The Cognitive Failures Questionnaire (CFQ) and Its Correlates," *British Journal of Clinical Psychology* 21 (1982): 7–16.

38. *American Psychologist* 46 (1991).

39. B. Reisberg, M. Schneck, S. Ferris, G. Schwartz, and M. DeLeon, "The Brief Cognitive Rating Scale (BCRS): Findings in Primary Degenerative Dementia (PDD)," *Psychopharmacology Bulletin* 19 (1983): 734–739.

40. C. Mateer, M. Sohlberg, and J. Crinean, "Focus on Clinical Research: Perceptions of Memory Functioning in Individuals with Closed-Head Injury," *Journal of Head Trauma Rehabilitation* 2 (1987): 74–84.

41. A. Christensen, "Applying Luria's Theory to the Rehabilitation Process of Brain Damage," in *Clinical Neuropsychology of Intervention,* eds. Y. Gross and B. Uzell, (Boston: Nijhoff, 1986), 169–178.

42. C. Wheatley and J. Rein, "Intervention in Traumatic Head Injury: Learning Style Assessment," in *Work in Progress: Occupational Therapy in Work Programs,* eds. S. Hertfelder and C. Gwin, (AOTA Press, 1990), 197–212.

Appendix 3A
Testing Materials

This appendix contains the following exhibit:

- **Exhibit 3A-1** Vendors for Testing Materials

Exhibit 3A-1

Vendors for Testing Materials

Benton Visual Retention Test
The Psychological Corporation
Order Service Center
P.O. Box 839954
San Antonio, Texas 78283-3954
(800) 228-2722
Price: $73.00

Buschke Selective Reminding Procedure
See: H. Buschke and P. Fuld, "Evaluating Storage, Retention, and Retrieval in
Disordered Memory and Learning," *Neurology* 24 (1974): 1019–1025.

California Verbal Learning Test
The Psychological Corporation
Order Service Center
P.O. Box 839954
San Antonio, Texas 78283-3954
(800) 228-2722
Price: $82.50

Memory Assessment Scales, Wide Range Assessment of Memory and Learning
Psychological Assessment Resources
P.O. Box 998
Odessa, Florida 33558
(800) 331-8378
Price: $180.00

Rey-Auditory Verbal Learning Test
See: R. Berg, M. Franzen, and D. Wedding
Screening for Brain Impairment
(New York: Springer Publishing Company, 1987), 139–140.

Rey-Osterreith Complex Figure Test
See: R. Berg, M. Franzen, and D. Wedding
Screening for Brain Impairment
(New York: Springer Publishing Company, 1987), 101–103.

Exhibit 3A-1 continued

Randt Memory Test
See: C.T. Randt and E.R. Brown
Randt Memory Test
(Bayport, New York: Life Sciences Associates, 1983).

Rivermead Behavioural Memory Assessment
See: Barbara Wilson, *Rehabilitation of Memory*
(New York: Guilford Press, 1987).

Ross Information Processing Assessment
Pro-Ed
8700 Shoal Creek Boulevard
Austin, Texas 78758-9965
(512) 451-3246
Price: $64.00

Webster Memory Scale
Dr. John Webster
Psychology Department
Towson State University
Towson, Maryland 21204
(301) 830-3080
Price: $50.00

Wechsler Memory Scale, Forms I and II
The Psychological Corporation
Order Service Center
P.O. Box 839954
San Antonio, Texas 78283-3954
(800) 228-2722
Price: $32.50

Wechsler Memory Scale–Revised
The Psychological Corporation
Order Service Center
P.O. Box 839954
San Antonio, Texas 78283-3954
(800) 228-2722
Price: $220.00

Note: Some vendors require licensure information from purchasers.

4
Goal Setting and Treatment Planning

Effective treatment planning begins the first day a client is seen in treatment and extends throughout rehabilitation, and beyond. This process involves setting goals (both long- and short-term) across physical, cognitive, emotional, and interpersonal areas of the client's life; and planning treatment by developing initial treatment plans, treatment and discharge summaries, and follow along.

GOAL SETTING

The establishment of goals is the first step in planning and continuing effective treatment. Goals are set at the beginning of treatment, and revised as necessary based on measurements obtained throughout rehabilitation. Successful rehabilitation is measured by the client's goal attainment.

Establishment of goals is essential for effective treatment planning. Goals work best when they are established in small increments, as small steps toward a larger goal. Therapists who do not have experience in behavioral therapy and goal-setting techniques may need assistance in writing measurable specific goals.

The Empowerment Rehabilitation Model

Goal setting is a multifaceted process, and involves all members of the treatment team working together to establish measurable and attainable goals with the client. This process is sometimes a difficult one and we have found it helpful to use a model to assist in this process. The Empowerment Rehabilitation Model[1] consists of several components, each of which is important in the process of setting goals. These components are discussed in the sections that follow. Therapists can teach this model to their clients so they can successfully identify goals for themselves in future situations (See Chapter 5 for a further discussion of this model).

Structure

Structure is the framework within which the client can build and achieve goals. Structure involves identifying the supportive information necessary in the attainment of goals. Included are the development of goals written in behavioral terms, determination of how progress will be measured, setting of time frames, and development of contracts.

Goals must be written in clear, concise behavioral terms, e.g., "By the end of two weeks, I wish to remember a minimum of 80 percent of the information covered in my CRT therapy sessions, as measured by a test given to me by my therapist." This example provides a goal that is clearly stated and can be easily measured. A goal such as "I want to remember what happens in my therapy sessions" is not measurable.

It should be noted, however, that some goals in rehabilitation will be more vague, particularly during the beginning stages of treatment when minimal information is available about strengths, limitations, and prognosis for recovery. For example, a client may state, "I want to go back to work," but may not be able to set a more definitive goal until more data are available. In this situation, the therapist can teach strategies and set goals that can be applied across a variety of employment situations. For example, the therapist can teach the client the strategy of note taking to remember information, and then set goals on a weekly basis. This strategy can be used later, regardless of the client's eventual employment situation.

Another element of structure is a determination of how progress will be measured, for instance, as a percentage of total information remembered. The client and therapist can decide upon appropriate ways to measure performance together. Other possibilities include the time it takes the client to complete the task, the percentage of items correctly remembered, the number of trials to achieve success, and so forth. The most important consideration is whether the task can be measured in an objective manner.

Once a determination of how to measure performance has been made, structure then focuses on taking a baseline of the client's present level of functioning. This provides a starting point in the goal setting process. Baseline data include formalized objective test data, as well as information gained during sessions (see Chapter 3 for a discussion on assessment techniques). Following training, a postpractice measure is taken so that the client can compare performance after training to performance before training. Postpractice measures may also include formalized assessments, therapy tasks, and real-life situation assessments.

Time frames are also considerations in structuring the goal setting process. The client and therapist must decide whether the goal is to be a short- or long-term one, then they need to determine the desired amount of time needed to achieve it. The amount and intensity of work needed to achieve the goal are also identified. For example, the client could work on a particular goal on a daily basis or only occasionally; or, work can occur several times per day or just once per day.

Another part of structure is the development of contracts between the therapist and client. Contracts formalize the goal setting process and clearly state information. Typical contracts delineate goals, ways they will be measured, and delineate the responsibilities of the therapist and the client. While contracts are not essential in the goal setting process, they can be helpful, particularly in the development and achievement of long-term goals.

Contracts also typically include reinforcements for success and consequences for non-compliance. Writing the contract is the last stage in the goal setting process, and is preceded by the structural elements discussed above, as well as the identification of motivation, information, acceptance, and skills-assessment.

Motivation

Motivation includes identifying the client's interests, intents, wishes, and dreams. It also involves an assumption that the client is ready to begin treatment and participate in the goal setting process. The therapist must identify the positive motivators which then can be used as reinforcers when writing goal contracts.

It is also important to identify any maladaptive motivators that may adversely influence goal setting and attainment. For example, clients who have been in a liferole of providing and caring for others may, after an accident, find themselves in the position of others caring for them. In some cases, this can be a motivation to continue in the "patient role" so that the attention and caretaking continue. This may become a maladaptive motivator that hinders movement through rehabilitation. Clients may be aware of this process but, more typically, it occurs on a subconscious level. These clients may verbalize the goal of return to their previous lifestyles, but may inadvertently undermine this process if the maladaptive motivator is not recognized and addressed.

Information

Without information, clients cannot set achievable goals. Clients may set unrealistic goals that either over- or under-estimate their abilities. Therapists can also set unrealistic goals, either expecting too much or too little, based on experiences with previous clients.

For goals to be realistic and reachable, the therapist must gather as much information about the client as possible, involving not only cognitive spheres, but also emotional, physical, and interpersonal ones. This includes a psychosocial history, objective assessments of cognitive strengths and limitations, and medical and health status evaluations, financial and legal considerations, and the amount of family support available. Information must be gathered on the client's previous lifestyle and future wishes and dreams. Other important information factors include the client's readiness and motivation to participate in treatment.

Information is gathered at the beginning of treatment and throughout the treatment process. As information is obtained, goals are revised, deleted, and added; and treatment becomes a flexible process.

As the therapist gains information, it must be shared with the client. Many clients remain unaware of their strengths and limitations. The therapist will need to respectfully share this information so that data used in the goal setting process are as truthful, honest, and accurate as possible.

Information is the data obtained through which the client measures performance and sets goals. As treatment progresses, information must also be obtained so that long-term goals can be revised. For example, in the beginning of treatment, the client may wish to return to work but may not know whether this is possible. As treatment progresses and the client learns memory and other cognitive strategies, and achieves goal levels on tasks, it becomes apparent that return to the previous job may be possible. As this point, information about the availability of the job must be obtained, along with information about the employer's willingness and ability to adapt the work environment to accommodate any special needs the client may have.

Acceptance

Acceptance involves two parts: the respect demonstrated by the therapist toward the client, and the client's internal acceptance of his or her strengths and limitations.

Crucial to the process of goal setting is the therapist's demonstration of respect. Goals must be set *with* the client not *for* the client. It is the responsibility of the therapist to ensure that the client participates in the goal setting process and that all members of the treatment team (including the family) are in accord and working together.

Therapists can also demonstrate respect for clients by acknowledging their wishes in the goal setting process. At times, the therapist may think a goal to be frivolous or even ridiculous. However, if the client wishes to pursue the goal and there is a good chance of success, the therapist's responsibility is to support the client's decision.

Even when the therapist demonstrates respect for the client, provides structure and information, and teaches the skills necessary to set and achieve goals, the client may remain unrealistic. This may be related to his or her unwillingness to accept strengths and limitations following injury or may be related to organic denial. In either case, the denial of deficits can be an extremely frustrating experience, both for the client and for the therapist.

Therapists can work with clients to provide information so that opinions and views may gradually change. Videotaped feedback is particularly helpful in demonstrating observable behaviors. This information must be presented gently and respectfully; it is not the job of the therapist to break down a client's denial systems. Emotional denial is a defense mechanism and is there because the client is not ready to receive contrary information. It is a way for clients to protect their emotional beings from information too threatening to acknowledge.

Denial is not wrong or bad but it may interfere with treatment. Some clients can work with the denial and make progress in spite of it. Typically, denial does not occur across all modalities, but may be limited to small pockets of data. When clients become entrenched in denial, it can be addressed in psychotherapy, and it may become necessary to delay treatment until these emotional areas can be addressed.

Skills

The skills component is what we endeavor to teach clients throughout the rehabilitation process. Skills are what they carry with them into life after rehabilitation. A multitude of memory skills are discussed in the chapters that follow in this text. Another valuable skill therapists can teach clients is that of goal setting.

To teach this skill, therapists can simply address each of the components in the Empowerment Rehabilitation Model and teach the client to use these components in setting goals both inside and outside treatment. Therapists can provide written information or drawings of the model, and can also provide a list of questions for use in each of the component areas to help clients understand. For example, clients can ask themselves questions such as, "What is the goal I wish to achieve?", "How will I measure this goal?" (structure); "Do I really want to do this?", "What factors might stop me from reaching this goal?" (motivation); "Do I have the cognitive ability to reach this goal?", "How much information can I remember from what I hear?" (information); and "Do I know any strategies to use in remembering information I hear?" (skills).

The above questions are, of course, simply samples of questions to use in the goal setting process. Hundreds of others may be developed and the therapist can assist the client in structuring such questions.

Types of Goals

Goals are set across many areas of the client's life, i.e., cognitive, emotional, social, interpersonal, physical, behavioral, vocational, and academic. Goals need to be set for the long-term (accomplished at a point after discharge), and short-term (accomplished during treatment and in transition back into the real world).

Long-Term Goals

Long-term goals are those that the client wishes to attain following discharge. Long-term goals can be set in a variety of increments. For example, a client may set a one-year goal of return to work, a five-year goal of having children, and a 30-year goal of being financially stable upon retirement. Long-term goals are discussed first because they provide the framework within which the client and therapist will work in treatment. There must be an overall structure and direction to the treatment, otherwise treatment is done in a vacuum and is not effective.

If may be difficult for many clients to conceive of and set long-term goals as they embark upon a course of rehabilitation. This can be complicated by a lack of knowledge about present limitations or about how much recovery will occur. For example, if the client is having difficulty remembering what was eaten for breakfast, it will be hard to think about return to an academic setting where technical skills have to be learned. Even if specific long-term goals cannot be set, more general goals can, however. These goals may then be revised as new information becomes available. Periodic evaluations can assist in this process of goal setting and revision.

Clients will often have more than one long-term goal during treatment. For example, a client may wish to return to work, return to independent living, and build interpersonal relationships. If there are many goals, they may need to be prioritized so that treatment can focus on the top priority and include other goals as appropriate. In reality, therapists always work on several goals simultaneously. Many tasks and strategies introduced in sessions can be practiced in multiple areas of the client's life. We conceptualize these areas as "treatment tracks,"[2] and label them as vocational, academic, avocational, and maintenance.

Vocational. Vocational goals are those most frequently encountered in rehabilitation settings. Some clients will quickly state these as long-term goals, while others remain unsure. Even when specific vocational goals are not identified, therapists can begin teaching memory and other cognitive skills that can ultimately be generalized into the work environment.

In the early stages of rehabilitation, vocational goal setting may be general. Clients may wish to return to previous positions; change position, job descriptions, or employer; or change careers to an entirely new field. Short-term treatment goals can focus on areas that will be necessary in any job (e.g., remembering instructions and directions). Later, as goals become more defined, treatment goals can address these areas more specifically.

Periodic assessment can provide both client and therapist with information to fine-tune long-term goals. Memory areas that may affect success on the job can be identified along with those strengths upon which the client can build and capitalize. As the client improves to the point of returning to employment, assessment would include tests of interest as well as aptitude.

To set specific goals, clients and therapists need to consider the type of employment (full-time, part-time, competitive, noncompetitive, work simulations, etc.). The work environment will also need to be considered, i.e., the ability of the employer to accommodate any special needs the client may have. Financial concerns also need consideration, for example, amount of income needed and minimum insurance benefits required.

Identification of job tasks is a necessity. Tasks can be varied or repetitive; they may provide for much supervision or minimal supervision; they may be simple or complicated. Finally, the therapist will need to identify whether the employer is willing to work with persons who may need additional considerations due to their limitations.

Academic. In this area, the focus is on a return to an academic setting. Clients may return to or enter for the first time settings in school systems, colleges, vocational or trade schools, or short-term training programs.

To assist clients in the process of goal setting, several factors need consideration. The client's strengths and limitations need to be identified in all areas (cognitive, emotional, physical, and interpersonal). The type of academic environment the client will return to must also be identified, i.e., university, community college, vocational or technical school, graduate school, or noncredit courses. Other areas to consider in setting goals are what environments are available (large or small campus or city, accessibility of the campus and need for transportation, number of students in classes, etc.). Financial considerations are also important in goal setting (cost of the program, amount of money available to the client for living expenses, need for work, etc.).

Avocational. Avocational goals are important additions to long-term treatment goals and include noncareer oriented activities. The client's interests play the dominant role in determining which skills, hobbies, and equipment may be necessary to ensure that he or she will be able to pursue goals in these areas. Avocational goals can be divided into two main areas: life enhancement activities and activities of daily living.

Module 1: Life Enhancement: these activities are those that provide the client with a sense of personal accomplishment or achievement. In this area, the client seeks to identify options to enhance quality of life versus the primary purpose of producing income. Life-enhancing goals can be set across the areas of physical, intellectual, emotional, and social/interpersonal stimulation.

Any client can participate in a Life Enhancement Module. For those clients having a primary goal of return to work, for example, the areas of exercise and interpersonal relationships are still important considerations. Clients can focus on these long-term goals simultaneously with short-term goals. Clients who do not return to work or school settings may focus primarily on the area of life enhancement so that they can still maintain a good quality of life. For example, a long-term goal in this area might be for the client to participate in fund raising activities for a local charity. Short-term goals in treatment would then focus on assisting the client in learning strategies to remember information over the telephone, thus facilitating success in the avocational goal.

Module 2: Activities of Daily Living: this module includes all those activities that add structure to our daily lives. Such tasks include self-care and personal health, independent living, transportation, household maintenance, money management, dietary management, and safety. Regardless of other long-term goals, the client will likely need assistance in one or more activities of daily living. For example, the client may have difficulty remembering to turn off the stove or to finish all the steps involved in doing laundry and would need strategies designed to assist. Goals can be set in each area within this module and can be a primary focus of treatment or a supplement to other goals.

Maintenance. This area focuses on maintaining the skills learned during treatment. Clients pursuing these goals may be impaired such that they will not be able to participate in work, school, or high-level life enhancement activities. Maintenance ensures the maximum quality of life, given the extent of limitations these clients may have.

Maintenance provides structure and a continued source of support for clients. Goals focus heavily on the use of external aids to provide this structure, as well as teaching family members how to structure clients at home for the lifetime. Maintenance goals may be much lower than those set in other areas. For example, the long-term goal may be to ensure that the client remembers not to stand up out of a wheelchair independently.

Short-Term Goals

Short-term goals are those that the client and therapist initially may set upon entering treatment and those set to achieve long-term goals. Immediate goals may be improving memory functioning relative to the last session, reaching a goal level set on a particular task, or learning to use a particular strategy or prosthesis.

If the client is living in a rehabilitation center, there are certain functional memory skills that may be necessary to learn to adapt to the new environment. This type of memory training usually takes immediate priority to keep the client on schedule with rehabilitation, to foster independence, to limit missed appointments, and to assist clients in feeling more in control over their environments.

In setting short-term goals, therapists must continue to be sensitive to the needs of the clients versus their own goals. For instance, the therapist may focus on percentages of information remembered, whereas the client may want to remember the location of the cafeteria. As with any goal, short-term goals must be meaningful for the client.

Once long-term goals have been identified, short-term goals must be set within the framework of such goals. At that point, they become building blocks to reach the ultimate goals. Short-term goals are the heart of the rehabilitation process. They are the means to the end of rehabilitation, and ultimately, provide the framework and structure upon which the long-term success of the client rests.

The process of setting short-term goals is discussed in depth in Chapter 5 in the context of the Eight-Step Treatment Model. In addition, examples of goal setting within several types of tasks are given throughout the remainder of this book.

While the long-term goal provides the overall outline for the client and therapist, it is the short-term goal that provides the work and fills in the details of the outline. When short-term goals are set in context, the rehabilitation plan works more smoothly and potential for success is optimized. For example, if the client's long-term goal is to return to college level coursework, the therapist can set short-term goals within this framework in the area of memory strategies to assist in classroom situations. These strategies (note taking, repetition, and chunking) can be taught using pen and paper, three-dimensional and computerized tasks, and more functional materials such as textbooks. Aids, such as notebooks, calendars, or microcassette recorders, can be introduced to assist.

TREATMENT PLANNING

Once long-term goals have been established, the treatment planning process becomes a simple one that incorporates the long- and short-term goals of the clients. Tasks, strategies, and practice situations to learn strategies are designed. Finally, environments are provided so that the client can practice in real world situations.

There are undoubtedly many similarities among TBI survivors; however, there are also many differences. Clients differ in the location and severity of injury, amount and type of resulting cognitive deficits, and premorbid characteristics of personality, experiences, and dreams. Treatment plans must be developed to accommodate these individual differences. The preferences of the client must be taken into account in the choice of tasks, development of strategies, and setting of goals.

Treatment planning must also take into consideration factors that facilitate learning for the client. These factors include:[3]

- Empowerment of the client
- One-to-one treatment
- Structured individual sessions
- Provision of daily practice
- Multisensory encoding of information
- Selection of tasks at a level appropriate for the client
- Gradual increase in level of task difficulty
- Ensure successful experiences
- Maximized potential for generalization

- Provision of reinforcement
- Consideration of the client's level of endurance.

Treatment planning also takes into consideration the length of treatment, the involvement of family members, and group and individualized treatment modalities.

Treatment plans are developed with the client and therapist and work best when they are in written format. Treatment plans vary from facility to facility but minimally contain identifying client information (name, date of accident, date of the treatment plan, date of next written report); frequency and timing of treatment sessions (five times weekly, one-hour sessions); targeted treatment areas; description of treatment and long-term goals to be attained; treatment track area(s); and names of treating therapists. Upon development of a written treatment plan, a meeting of the team to review, edit (if necessary), and determine distribution is recommended. At that point, the next report and team meeting can be scheduled so the client knows the process will not continue indefinitely. Setting frequent report dates will also facilitate quality control in the provision of treatment.

As treatment progresses, the therapist must continually assess progress and assist the client in restructuring goals and planning different treatment interventions. Along with these session assessments of progress, therapists need to provide written summaries of treatment to clients at regular intervals. This documentation is important in providing information to the client, family members, other team members, insurers, and others.

The client can be asked to write a separate treatment summary that can be used as a comparison of his or her perceptions of progress with those of the therapist. If the client has kept records throughout the treatment process (a recommended strategy for memory), this becomes an easier task. However, the client's preparation of a written treatment summary can represent an enormous cognitive task requiring the ability to organize, sequence, remember, and honestly evaluate progress.

Measurement of outcome is an important component of planning treatment. This can occur only if baseline measures have been taken against which outcome can be measured. Therapists must document where the client begins on a task, set goals, teach strategies, provide practice and generalization, and then assess learning. Quality assurance of treatment can only be maintained in outcome that can be measured.

From the client's point of view, outcome is often subjective. Clients may feel they are getting better or worse, or may not have a sense of any change occurring. Therapists and family members may also experience similar feelings. It is not adequate to state that a client is "improving." The therapist must back up subjective impressions with concrete, objective, and measurable data. Such data are also important to third parties involved in the client's care, such as insurance companies who base payment on progress, or attorneys who base the value of litigation on the progress of the client.

Discharge planning occurs on the first day a client enters treatment and is facilitated by establishment of long-terms goals. The accurate and adequate documentation of progress throughout treatment is important in the process of planning for discharge from treatment. With measurable data, the therapist can better estimate the client's readiness for discharge and determine additional needs for the long-term following discharge. In addition to in-session measures of progress, it is appropriate to perform evaluations as the client nears discharge status. These objective evaluations (See Chapter 3) provide the client and therapist with additional information on strengths and any residual limitations. Based on the assessments and performances in sessions, the therapist can then make recommendations postdischarge.

Transition back into the real world is often a frightening and difficult process for clients, as they may either under- or over-estimate their readiness and ability to return. Therapists can ease this process by providing clients with accurate, honest, and realistic information about themselves.

Therapists can also assist the transition by projecting any future needs the client may have and providing recommendations for these. For example, in the case of the client returning to college, the therapist may recommend taking only one course (based on the client's measured continued distraction and slowed information processing). The therapist may also recommend taking tests in a separate classroom (to minimize distraction), and audiotaping lectures (to facilitate memory). As the client returns to the academic setting, the therapist may also recommend continued periodic follow-along sessions to trouble shoot any potential problems and to monitor use of strategies in the real-life situation of school. The therapist may also need to continue monitoring the client throughout the remainder of his or her coursework as courseload increases and as difficulty of courses increases.

Acute care and transitional living facilities represent only a small portion of the client's rehabilitation efforts. Typically, clients continue to experience difficulty long after discharge from such facilities, and many may need continued follow-along for years. Therapists must remain cognizant of the limitations of any particular facility, and provide resources for clients for the long-term. Rehabilitation or treatment planning does not end with discharge from a particular facility.

Follow-along is crucial for the client's success and involves monitoring progress and problems, and providing periodic reevaluations to assess changes over time. Clients and therapists are often unprepared for the difficulties that arise after discharge. At discharge, the therapist must again document treatment in written format and provide this information to the client. The discharge summary includes progress and recommendations for real-life situations. Additionally, recommendations are made for follow-along sessions and resources are provided to the client. Finally, a team meeting is held at discharge to review the written reports and provide a closure to the treatment process.

NOTES

1. C. O'Hara and M. Harrell, *Rehabilitation with Brain Injury Survivors: An Empowerment Approach* (Gaithersburg, Md: Aspen Publishers, 1991) 7-10.
2. Ibid., 133-153.
3. Ibid., 120-123.

Part III
Clinical Applications

5
Philosophy of Retraining Memory and Treatment Model

This chapter and the ones that follow are intended to provide the reader with practical, useful information that can be used in therapy sessions with clients.

As with any type of treatment, therapists must have a theoretical framework within which they address treatment issues with clients. This framework is often a combination of personal views and beliefs, theoretical positions, and administrative requirements of a particular facility.

Our philosophy of retraining memory (and cognition in general) is based upon several basic assumptions.

1. Empowerment of clients is a crucial ingredient in the rehabilitation process.

2. Optimally, treatment should consist of a combination of approaches, such as direct retraining, use of compensatory strategies, and use of prosthetic aids or orthotic devices.

3. Therapists who provide rehabilitation services should have appropriate training and experience and abide by the ethical guidelines of their profession.

4. Clients who participate in cognitive rehabilitation therapy (CRT) should be ready to do so, and

5. Clinicians who provide CRT should operate within a model of treatment.

EMPOWERMENT

To ensure a client's success in treatment as well as in the return to real-world functions, there are several crucial components to be considered. These components make up the Empowerment Rehabilitation Model[1] and include STRUCTURE, INFORMATION, MOTIVATION, ACCEPTANCE, and SKILLS. When any component is missing from treatment, the client may experience failure in the rehabilitation process. Each of the components of empowerment is discussed in the sections that follow.

It is our experience that the Empowerment Rehabilitation Model can be understood by most clients beyond the confused or agitated state as well as by most rehabilitation team and family members. Therefore, we advocate its use with all individuals beginning cognitive rehabilitation.

Structure

In the Empowerment Rehabilitation Model, structure is described as the "ability to set appropriate boundaries, controls, and rules upon one's life, and to effectively carry them out on a day-to-day basis."[2(p.15)] After brain injury, clients may be so traumatized that others are required to assume decision-making responsibilities regarding such issues as placement, assessment, and treatment. As a result, the client loses much internal control over external forces. It is these external forces that tend to disempower the individual. This loss of control should be considered only a temporary one, however, with the goal of treatment being to move the client toward resumption of internal structure (self-control) as soon as possible. Initially, the treatment team will provide external structure for the client, setting up schedules for him or her, making choices about types of treatment and assessments to engage in, and so forth. As the client progresses through treatment, however, these external structures should be gradually removed as the client resumes internal control. There are many ways in which the therapist can provide opportunities for the client to assume some measure of control over activities. The client can be involved in developing the treatment plan by identifying cognitive problems, prioritizing treatment areas, developing schedules, and setting goals in treatment.

Information

The sharing of information among the client, the family, and the treatment team is an essential component of empowerment. This is a two-way sharing of information. The treatment team members obtain as much information as possible about the client so that they will be prepared to interact with the client in a respectful and appropriate manner. The treatment team also provides as much information as possible to the client and family members. Some treatment providers are hesitant to provide information to the client and family for fear that it will have a negative effect upon them. This belief reinforces the client's loss of control over his or her own life. It may be necessary to simplify the information, but it is essential to share with the client to facilitate equality among treatment team members. In some instances, for example, when a client does not totally understand information, it is still important for the treatment team to include the client in meetings. The length of time of the meeting (or the client's participation) may need to be shortened to accommodate any limitations in attention, concentration, etc. If information sharing is evident, the client will feel more in control of treatment and will be better able to participate in the goal-setting process.

There are many ways in which the therapist can provide information to the client. Clients can be given articles about the nature of their injury, and can participate in local or organizational support groups. They can meet with other survivors who have completed rehabilitation (mentors). They can keep independent records of their sessions, recording their performance on tasks. They can be given full explanations of tasks inside and outside therapy and of the rationale behind doing them. They can be given written treatment summaries of their progress on a regular basis and be given the opportunity to participate in discharge planning at the appropriate time.

Motivation

Although motivation is generally considered an internal process, it can be generated and maintained by external reinforcers. Often, at the beginning of recovery, the therapist may need to provide such reinforcers to assist in maintaining the client's motivation. It is important at this level that the therapist take the time to explain to the client the purpose of the specific tasks because often the client is unable to see how a specific task in a therapy session relates to past experiences or current needs. It is difficult for the client to remain motivated when he or she is unsure of the nature of a task. Eventually, the client will need to motivate internally, but this process may not occur rapidly.

In efforts to maintain motivation, therapists can use appropriate reinforcers, establish reasonable goals and expectations *with* clients rather than *for* them, and address interpersonal relationship issues with clients. To ensure continued commitment, hope, and energy in pursuing goals, the clients must develop a sense of purpose, success, and progress at the same time. Therefore, the goals set with the client and therapist must reflect the goals, dreams, and successes of the client. It is this understanding that will enhance and reinforce motivation.

Acceptance

This component of the Empowerment Rehabilitation Model is twofold and includes both internal and external elements of acceptance. Internally, it reflects the necessity of the traumatic brain injury (TBI) survivor's coming to terms with the nature of the injury, the losses and changes it has produced, and the eventual consequences of those losses and changes to the client and family members. It involves issues of self-awareness, self-respect, and self-acceptance. Treatment should include work with a psychotherapist who can assist the client in confronting the injury on an emotional level, which involves a process of grieving and coming to terms with the old and new concepts of self.

Externally, acceptance reflects the client's need for acceptance and respect from the treatment team. There are many ways for the therapist to provide acceptance for the client. The client's rights to person, feelings, and privacy all deserve consideration. Other ways to demonstrate respect include providing information, structure, and skills. It is through acceptance and motivation that the client will develop feelings of confidence, competence, and empowerment.

Skills

The final element in the Empowerment Rehabilitation Model is skills building. The therapist must provide the client with instruction and practice in skills. These include areas such as cognitive and physical mastery, skills of independent living, academic and vocational skills, self-awareness, self-monitoring, and interpersonal skills. This skills training portion of treatment is an important one; it is here that the client learns strategies and techniques that can be applied to real-world settings after rehabilitation.

APPROACHES TO TREATMENT

Throughout this text, it is our purpose to present a variety of approaches that therapists can use in their individual settings. The ideal cognitive rehabilitation of memory program would include direct retraining, use of compensatory strategies, and use of prosthetic aids and/or orthotic devices.

There are many types of materials available to therapists to use in the cognitive rehabilitation of memory. These materials include pen-and-paper, and three-dimensional and computerized tasks. In addition, there are a number of prosthetic aids and orthotic devices designed to help clients perform some memory functions. These materials and types of tasks are discussed in detail in the chapters that follow, and the reader is directed there for more information.

We do want to emphasize that our philosophy of treatment is one that incorporates *all* the above materials. We use computer, pen-and-paper, and three-dimensional tasks as well as prosthetic and orthotic devices in all phases of memory rehabilitation. Depending on the client's strengths, weaknesses, and needs, one or more areas may receive extra focus. For example, if a client has difficulty concentrating for several minutes at a time, treatment may focus more on computerized tasks of concentration. Or, if the person is ready to return to school, therapy sessions may focus on note taking as a compensatory strategy or the use of a spelling checker as an aid. We strongly recommend the approach of incorporating a variety of tasks as a guideline in the cognitive rehabilitation of memory.

THERAPIST TRAINING

Therapists who provide cognitive rehabilitation services to clients come from a variety of disciplines. It is our position that the discipline within which a clinician operates does not matter, but whether or not the therapist can provide adequate services to TBI survivors does. The therapist must be both effective (providing what the client needs) and efficient (providing what the client needs in a timely manner).

CRT is not a formalized discipline but is rapidly moving toward being so, especially with the recent formation of the Society for Cognitive Rehabilitation, Inc. This multidisciplinary organization was incorporated in 1990 and is engaged in many activities related to cognitive rehabilitation, including development of standards, ethics, and certification requirements for providers of cognitive rehabilitation.[3]

At present, educational levels for persons providing CRT generally consist of training in the therapist's specific degree, which may contain a few courses specifically geared toward rehabilitation. However, most clinicians obtain the majority of their training through practical experience (supervised) and continuing education experiences.

It is our belief that therapists providing CRT to clients should have a basic understanding of brain-behavior relationships, neuroanatomy, and the identification of cognitive strengths and limitations. Additionally, therapists must have skills sufficient to provide treatment in an empowering manner (providing the client with information, structure, and acceptance; enhancing motivation; and teaching skills). Therapists need good interpersonal skills so that they can interact with clients in an adult-to-adult manner in sessions (rather than a parent-to-child manner, where the therapist is in control).

Therapists providing CRT to survivors of brain injury should also have access to a qualified professional who is available for consultation regarding cognitive and emotional issues. Therapists should honestly assess their skills and ensure that they can provide what a particular client requires; if this is not possible, then a referral to another therapist may be appropriate. Therapists must be straightforward with themselves about their personal strengths and limitations and not treat clients when they are not qualified to do so.

Finally, many components of CRT can be provided across disciplines; thus there are overlapping areas, particularly with regard to psychotherapeutic issues such as self-awareness and social skills training. In efforts to provide these services, additional training in psychotherapeutic interventions may be required, or the therapist should have access to individuals who can provide these services directly to the client.

Levels of Training

We have found it helpful to view training on three levels: CRT supervisor, CRT therapist, and CRT technician. The required training and supervision elements that we propose here are only *suggestions* and are not meant to be the final word on credentials of those who provide CRT. It is assumed throughout this text that persons providing services have the appropriate education, training, and supervision to do so.

CRT Supervisor

Historically, individuals who specialize in the provision of CRT have come from many backgrounds, including neuropsychology, psychology, special education, speech, and occupational therapy. In our model, persons who supervise the provision of CRT services have either a doctoral or a master's degree in a related field (neuropsychology, psychology, counseling, education, speech, or occupational therapy) and maintain current licensure, certification, or registration in their field to ensure knowledge of ethical and legal responsibilities. In our model, CRT supervisors would have a minimum of 5,000 hours of direct provision of CRT and evaluation services to persons with neurological disorders. In addition, they would have received a minimum of 300 hours of individualized supervision in the provision of CRT services. Supervisors should have an understanding of brain-behavior relationships, knowledge-based skills, and the clinical skills to facilitate the empowerment process for clients. In addition, they should provide guidance and feedback to other therapists whom they supervise.

Additional responsibilities of the supervisor include interpretation of test data, development and supervision of targeted problem areas, maintenance of quality control of provision of services, and assessment of the "big picture" of the CRT process. CRT supervisors provide supervision to CRT therapists and technicians. They may also provide psychotherapy, case management, and direct CRT to clients, depending upon their training and experience.

CRT Therapist

The CRT therapist is the second level of training. This person would have a minimum educational level of a master's degree in a related field or hold a license, certification, or registration in his or her field. We suggest a minimum of 2,000 combined hours of direct provision of CRT and evaluation services for CRT therapists. We also suggest these individuals receive a minimum of 100 hours of individual supervision in the provision of CRT (there are noteworthy exceptions to these requirements, i.e., persons who may not hold the minimum educational requirements but who may be experienced clinicians).

Individuals at this level should have basic knowledge and skills in treatment of cognitive deficits after TBI. CRT therapists should also possess a basic understanding of brain-behavior relationships and data gained from assessment instruments and treatment interventions. They are responsible for providing direct treatment, targeting goals, selecting strategies, and assessing progress of clients. CRT therapists may also supervise CRT technicians in provision of treatment.

CRT Technician

The third level of training is the CRT technician, who typically holds a bachelor's degree in a field such as psychology, speech, occupational therapy, or education. We suggest in our model that CRT technicians have a minimum of 1,000 hours of direct provision of services to clients and a minimum of 50 hours of individual supervision in the provision of treatment to clients.

CRT technicians should possess a basic understanding of brain-behavior relationships and documentation procedures. In addition, they would assist the CRT therapist in providing direct services to clients. Duties of the CRT technician may include maintaining charts and graphs, monitoring clients' performance on computer tasks (after training), and monitoring CRT strategies used in other therapy settings to ensure consistency of treatment. Technicians require supervision from CRT therapists or supervisors on at least a weekly basis, and all notes should be co-signed by either the CRT therapist or the supervisor.

CLIENT READINESS

Another basic assumption in providing rehabilitation of memory services is that the client must be ready to begin treatment. Readiness depends upon the client's level of physical, cognitive, and emotional recovery. Clients who can benefit from memory retraining are assumed to be recovered sufficiently that attention can be focused and concentration sustained over time. If the client cannot concentrate or becomes distracted (either externally or internally), memory retraining may be ineffective.

Many clients traditionally have been placed in CRT before they are ready to benefit from such treatment. This can result in frustration for both the client and the therapist as well as decreased motivation, acting out or agitation, and possibly resistance. Ultimately, memory skills will not improve.

In determining when clients are ready to begin treatment, the following issues bear consideration. Clients can participate in therapy even with difficulties in many of these areas, but therapists will need to determine the extent of the deficit and the amount of difficulty the client may have in treatment because of one or more problems in these areas.

Medical and Physical Limitations

Clients may have various physical changes, pain, sleep disturbance, and so forth. If these interfere with the ability to concentrate, treatment may need to be delayed; some clients are able to work "through the pain" and can participate in treatment. Another issue that can affect readiness is the use of medications. Some medications (even prescriptions) interfere with memory. Clients who need drugs (such as in the case of seizures) and do not take them may also be affected and may be inappropriate candidates for memory retraining. Similarly, clients who abuse drugs cannot adequately concentrate in sessions.

Sensory and Motor Limitations

Areas to be assessed include: sensory (visual, auditory, gustatory, olfactory, tactile), proprioception, balance, ambulation, coordination, motor speed, range of motion, dexterity, ability to use hands and fingers, and so forth. If clients have difficulty seeing materials or hearing the therapist, treatment may be adversely affected. Similarly, if motor speed is slowed, reaction time and processing speed of memory functions may also be affected.

On many tasks, clients must possess basic visual and motor skills such that the nature of the task can be perceived and a response can be made by writing, moving an object, and so forth. With computer tasks, speed of motor response must be sufficient to respond accurately and quickly. If the client has limited use of arms, hands, or fingers, treatment may be initiated, but therapists will need to be creative and persistent in finding or developing tasks that can accommodate the difficulties (e.g., adaptive equipment for computers, see Chapter 6).

Cognitive Limitations

Areas to be addressed include arousal, attention and concentration, language (expressive: speech and writing; receptive: comprehension and reading), capacity for learning, status of memory across modalities (visual and verbal) and by types (recognition, recall, immediate, delayed, long term, and short term), and executive functions (ability to initiate and switch mental set).

In Chapter 2, memory was described as a multistep process. One of the key building blocks of memory is the capacity to attend to and concentrate on a stimulus for a sufficient amount of time so that the information can be encoded and stored. If the client cannot focus attention (i.e., is unable to orient and focus on a task) or sustain concentration (i.e., the client is repeatedly distracted by external noise), the ability to encode, store, and retrieve information will be impaired.

There are several ways to determine whether a client has achieved an optimal level of attention and concentration. These include psychometric measures (see Chapter 3), objective and subjective observations in sessions, and performance on CRT tasks designed to address attention and concentration.

Two sample computerized programs that address these basic building blocks (attention and concentration) are the *Foundations* and *Foundations II* software developed by Psychological Software Services, Inc.[4] These two disks provide practice on increasingly difficult tasks of attention and concentration, ranging from simple response to a simple stimulus to a rapid discriminatory response to complex stimuli. For example, on some of the simpler tasks the client responds (by pressing a button) when the stimulus item appears on the screen. In the more complex tasks, the client responds rapidly to only one specific stimulus in the presence of several distracting stimuli. If the client can achieve basic levels with the more simple tasks of attention, the therapist can then move into specific memory work. If the client experiences consistent difficulty with tasks of concentration, it is a strong indication that more preliminary work should be completed before focusing on memory tasks.

Emotional Limitations

Areas to be addressed include self-awareness and interpersonal awareness, self-care skills, affect (flatness, disinhibition, hyperirritability, indifference, or anosagnosia), social appropriateness, adjustment reaction (denial, depression, anger, social withdrawal, or anxiety), and agitation (confusion, loss of control, or aggressive or self-destructive behaviors). For example, if the client is experiencing anger about the accident, it may be extremely difficult for him or her to participate in therapy. Clients who are depressed may not have the energy to focus on treatment tasks, as they are dealing with massive losses. Some clients are able to participate in CRT while experiencing strong emotional reactions, particularly if they are simultaneously involved in psychotherapy to address the emotional issues. These clients can learn to "shelve" emotional issues and proceed with treatment. For other clients, CRT may need to be deferred.

THE EIGHT-STEP TREATMENT MODEL

In providing CRT to clients, therapists must have a structure within which to work; otherwise tasks are assigned in a vacuum and assessment of progress over time is difficult. There are many designs and models that can be useful in providing treatment. Some of these, adapted from experimental designs, are included in Appendix 5A at the end of this chapter, for those readers who wish to explore the issue further.

Over the last 10 years of providing CRT to clients, we have developed a clinical model that has been effective with our clients. It is applicable in all rehabilitation settings and with clients at various levels of recovery. It can also be used with various approaches to treatment, including focus on the direct retraining of memory using pen-and-paper tasks, three-dimensional tasks, and computerized tasks, and use of compensatory strategies and aids.

This model is implemented after assessments have been made, the client has been determined to be ready for treatment, and a treatment plan has been devised. The treatment plan (see Chapter 4) should include both short- and long-term goals. The client can assist the therapist in prioritizing needs and providing structure at the onset of the process; goals will need to be revised throughout the treatment process.

The Eight-Step Model (Exhibit 5-1) is presented in detail in the sections that follow.

Step 1: Select a Task or Strategy

In this initial step, the client and therapist review the treatment plan and select tasks and/or strategies to be used to address particular problems with memory.

Before determining what type of task or strategy to use with a client, the therapist must make a decision regarding whether to introduce a task as the starting point in the eight-step process or whether to use a strategy or aid as the starting point. For example, if the goal is to learn the strategy of *chunking,* the therapist may use a computer program or pen-and-paper tasks to teach the strategy, later moving into use of more real-life tasks for practice. Step 1 would be choosing which tasks to use. On the other hand, if the client is in school, step 1 would be teaching note taking strategies using texts or lectures.

Tasks or strategies are selected as means to an end, not ends in and of themselves. Thus, in the beginning phases of treatment, tasks may need to be introduced so that the client can learn a strategy; after strategies have been learned, however, it may

Exhibit 5-1 The Eight-Step Model

1. Select a task or strategy
2. Obtain a baseline measure
3. Set goals with the client
4. Choose and teach strategies
5. Practice strategies
6. Obtain a postpractice measure
7. Develop transfer and generalization of strategies for real-life situations
8. Practice transfer and generalization

then be appropriate to choose the implementation of a strategy or the use of a compensatory aid as the task with which to begin.

The type of task or strategy to be used is based upon many factors, including the client's cognitive level (see Chapter 3) and short- and long-term goals (see Chapter 4). Any tasks, strategies, or aids given need to begin at a level appropriate to the client's cognitive strengths and limitations, age, and problem areas. In addition, tasks must be interesting and applicable to the client's real world. Finally, tasks should also be clearly understandable and measurable.

Appropriate Level to Begin

Once criteria for the client's readiness to begin treatment have been met (see the section on client readiness in this chapter), tasks or strategies can be introduced. It is important to begin at a level where the client can experience success. The therapist can use the Eight-Step Model to measure performance and to build tasks and strategies in a hierarchical manner so that the client's short- and long-term goals are met. Tasks will need to be revised, depending on the client's ability to complete them. Therapists can strive to select tasks that are neither too easy nor too difficult for the client. If they are too easy, motivation may be affected, and the client may feel diminished; if they are too hard, the client may become frustrated, angry, and defensive.

Selection of tasks is done in a hierarchical manner. For example, basic attention and concentration skills must be addressed before immediate recall of information. The structure of a hierarchy is crucial to therapists working with clients after TBI. Without it, random tasks may be selected that may or may not target the individual client's particular needs. Tasks that are appropriate also take into consideration the elements that are discussed below.

Even when therapists use all available information and feel they have selected a task at a level that fits the client, this clinical judgment may still be in error. The selection of tasks at the appropriate level is often a hit-or-miss proposition. Even so, each trial or practice of a task can be used as learning experience for the client and therapist, who can flexibly shift to an easier or harder task.

Choose Tasks Appropriate to Client's Problem Area

This may seem unnecessary to discuss, but it is so obvious that it can become a problem. If a therapist is working on visual memory, for instance, the tendency may be to use all tasks available in this area and inundate the client with them. Therapists must first be clear about what particular problem the client is experiencing with visual memory. Where is the memory process breaking down? Does this mean the client is having trouble remembering all visual information (i.e., pictures and language) or just some? Is the deficit in encoding, storage, or retrieval? Is it a problem with recognition or recall?

If the above client is a student and the visual memory problem is actually in the ability to recall written information, the tasks chosen will be different from tasks chosen for a person who is having difficulty remembering where a car is parked in a shopping mall.

It is a disservice to clients to present them with an array of tasks in an area (e.g., visual) that may have nothing to do with their specific deficit area, and therapists must be sensitive to this issue. As rehabilitation funding is often inadequate to cover needs, therapists can assist in honoring these limited resources by ensuring that tasks are chosen on an individual basis and actually apply to the client.

Helpful questions for therapists to ask themselves in the selection of tasks include the following: Why am I using this task? What specifically do I hope to achieve by using this task versus another? What strategy will I teach with this task? How can this be applied to the client's real world?

Age Appropriateness of Task

In choosing tasks, the therapist must take into consideration the age of the client. Many materials used in rehabilitation settings are adapted from educational materials for children and do not translate well when working with adults. For example, many printed books have simple drawings or wording, large print, and age categories printed on them. Three-dimensional materials may be "games" designed for children, and computerized programs may have features such as Muppet Learning Keys or cartoonlike characters on the screen. These materials are obviously geared toward small children and may be insulting to some TBI survivors. Consider, for example, the reaction of a person with a Ph.D. in philosophy who is given a book with pictures of clowns on the cover that was originally intended for first-graders. Even clients without a Ph.D. may feel insulted by such materials. Therapists can endeavor to adapt materials and tasks for use with adults to promote respect and acceptance aspects of the relationship. Survivors of TBI who are already feeling in a "one-down" position as a result of an injury may feel even worse when given simple material obviously designed for children. This may make the client feel impaired or believe that the therapist thinks of him or her as stupid.

Creative therapists can redo materials, search for different ones to address the same area, create their own, and adapt those already on the market for use with their clients (e.g., obvious references to age levels can be deleted, wording rearranged, and so forth). Even with age-appropriate materials, however, clients will often feel "dumb," and therapists will need to practice caution and care in presenting tasks and materials to clients.

Interest and Applicability

For clients to maintain motivation, the tasks must hold some interest and applicability for them. This should not be a problem if therapists have accurately and adequately discussed goals with the client and established these goals in a mutual and respectful manner. If the client is working on personal goals (versus those of the therapist), then motivation will be higher. If the therapist is clear about the goals, then the likelihood of choosing materials that will be of interest to the client increases.

Related to interest in tasks and materials is their applicability to the client's real-world setting. For example, consider the client whose long-term goal is to return to work as an inventory clerk, where he must remember various sequences of number codes. Therapists can introduce tasks (pen-and-paper, three-dimensional, or computerized) for this client such that they address this area. That is, instead of giving meaningless numbers repeatedly to teach a strategy, actual numbers used on the job can be incorporated into the therapy sessions. For a client whose job is working with word processing systems, the therapist can design tasks of memory in this area (e.g., remembering the steps involved in editing a letter) versus a meaningless sequence of instructions. These concrete tasks are specific and interesting to the client and will apply in the real world after rehabilitation. They make sense to the client, and motivation will be higher.

Understandable Tasks

To ensure success in therapy sessions or in practice at home, therapists must choose tasks that are clearly understandable. If instructions are written, the print must be easy to read, and drawings should be clearly represented. Clients are often struggling with other cognitive deficits as well as memory, and giving unclear, fuzzy, or incomplete materials can create unnecessary frustration. With pen-and-paper tasks, these problems can occur when materials are torn from workbooks (pieces of a page may be missing) or when materials are photocopied from other sources (copy may be too dark or too light, portions of the page may not be visible or only parts may be visible, and so forth). With computerized tasks, graphics can be confusing, instructions may not be clear, and printouts may be illegible or not understandable. Three-dimensional tasks may have pieces missing or otherwise be unclear.

Prosthetics and orthotics can be complicated and confusing. Therapists can assist in explaining and demonstrating the use of materials and strategies as well as giving the client repeated practice trials to ensure comprehension.

Another component of comprehension is the client's knowledge and understanding of the use of certain tasks and strategies. The client must be familiar with the reasons behind the tasks as well as the expected outcome. Therapists can assist in this process by setting clear and concrete objectives with the client.

Measurable Tasks

This is one of the crucial components of task selection. The therapist and client must have some way to measure how the client is doing on a particular task. There are many ways to measure performance, including:

- time it takes the client to complete the task
- percentage of items correctly remembered (e.g., from a list of seven numbers, the client remembers four in any order)
- percentage of items correctly remembered and remembered in the correct sequence (e.g., from a list of seven numbers, the client remembers four in the correct sequence)
- number of trials it takes the client to achieve success on a task; this could be compared to number of trials on a similar task to measure transfer
- number (percentage) of strategies used independently in completing a task
- percentage of time that the strategy is independently used by client within a treatment session or in the real world

There are, of course, many variations on these, and therapists can adapt measures to fit particular tasks and client needs.

The important consideration is that the client and therapist understand the goal of the task and then determine a manner in which to measure performance. For example, if the goal is to increase the immediate span of memory, then the measurement could be the longest sequence of numbers a client can remember over a set number of trials; if the goal is to remember a sequence of instructions, then the measure could be the percentage of steps accurately remembered in correct sequence; and so forth.

If tasks are scorable, then the therapist and clients can document progress in a concrete way. Otherwise, both may have a sense that memory is getting better, but there will be no adequate way concretely (or correctly) to verify this.

Step 2: Obtain Baseline Measure

A baseline measure is the first measurement taken of a client's performance. This initial performance is measured without any assistance, and its purpose is to determine where the client is at the present moment in time. In this way, the therapist and client know where to begin and have information to assist in setting realistic goals. It provides a measure to which all future performance of tasks can be compared.

Baseline measures are ratings and can be done in many ways, depending upon what the client and therapist wish to measure (see the section above on measurement of tasks selected). The particular measurement will be different if the client is working on speed (in which case the baseline may be the amount of time required to complete a task) than if the goal is to improve accuracy (in which case the percentage of correct answers may be the measurement chosen). In addition to objective data such as time of completion and accuracy rates, therapists in this phase can gain much additional information of value by observing not only the score achieved on a task but the manner in which the task was performed. The therapist can observe approach to the task, independent generation of strategies, frustration and distraction levels, any contributing cognitive factors that affect performance, and so forth. We have found it helpful to use a form such as that in Exhibit 5-2, on which data can be recorded and shared with the client.

In addition, therapists and clients can record information visually on graphs such as the one in Figure 5-1, which can then be used throughout the therapy process. Figure 5-1 represents a baseline on a computerized number-sequencing task. The client was given a computer task in which he was able to recall three numbers in the sequence in which they were presented.

If clients are involved in their own charting and graphing process, the likelihood of continued motivation will be increased. After taking the baseline measure, the therapist and client can discuss the next step to take; that is, they can set a goal for a higher performance, return to a simpler level, discontinue the task, and so forth.

Step 3: Set Goals with Client

Once the therapist and client determine where the client's performance level is on a task, they can then determine where the client would like to be. This is an extremely important step, and accurate identification of goals at this point will assist in continuing motivation to achieve success. This is assuming that the client is capable of working with the therapist to select appropriate goals. Sometimes this is not possible in the early stages of rehabilitation. If the client is too impaired to set goals, or exhibits very poor judgment in selection of goals, the therapist may wish to set goals for him or her. As recovery progresses, the client may get more involved in the goal-setting process. With clients who have difficulty setting goals, the task

Exhibit 5-2 Baseline Reading

Name of client: _____

Date: _____

Therapist: _____

Task selected: Immediate recall of sequenced numbers presented by computer.

Baseline measure: Recalled three numbers in sequence.

Strategies used: None.

Comments: Experienced difficulty maintaining concentration during stimulus presentation. Twirled pencil during presentation.

Goal: Recall seven numbers in sequence using strategy of repetition.

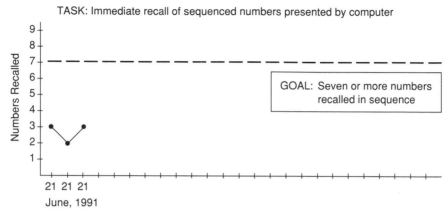

Figure 5-1 Immediate Recall of Sequenced Numbers: Baseline Graph

of the therapist becomes teaching this skill (which can be generalized to other areas of the client's life).

The goals must ultimately be the client's goals and not those of the therapist. The client must feel that the goal is worthwhile, has meaning, and is applicable to him or her (see the discussion in this chapter on selection of tasks). For example, if a client is someone who took copious notes before injury as a way to remember information (and this strategy worked well), this client may have no interest in working on remembering information using repetition and rehearsal, even though the therapist may think this is a wonderful idea. The goals set by the therapist and client should be worthwhile in the sense that they reflect the long-term and short-term needs of the client. The goals of a client who is returning to an academic setting will differ from those of one returning to a manual labor position. The goals of a client living independently will differ from those of a client in an acute care facility.

As previously discussed, goals must also be achievable. This involves striking a balance between what the client or therapist perceives as optimal performance and what is actually feasible.

Often, computer programs and other therapy materials will provide normative data for desired levels of performance. This standard can easily be applied or modified to fit the client's performance. Other tasks may require the therapist to generate criteria for performance. Depending upon difficulty level, the client may need to break a larger long-term goal into several smaller short-term goals. For example, if a client wishes to retain 80% of the material presented to him or her orally but the baseline measure indicates that recall is 10%, it may be necessary to initiate several short-term goals, such as retaining 40% of the information. When this goal is reached, the client and therapist can reassess the long-term goal and set a new goal of recalling, for example, 60% of the information. Sometimes it may be necessary to revise the original long-term goal when it is felt that peak performance has been achieved or a plateau has been reached. Or, it may be necessary to revise the strategies used to attain the goal (e.g., notetaking rather than repetition).

Step 4: Choose and Teach Strategies

A strategy is a way to approach a task. This may involve learning a different way to perform an old task or a new way to approach tasks altogether. Strategies are skills that therapists can teach clients to enable them to feel more empowered in their worlds.

Learning strategies is one of the most important steps in our treatment model. If tasks are designed according to the long-term goal, then strategies become the primary focus to reach this goal. Selection of tasks is an important step, but many varied tasks can be used to teach one strategy. For example, if the strategy to be taught is repetition, therapists can use tasks such as recall of digits, words, or sentences, and materials can be three-dimensional, pen and paper, or computerized. The focus is learning strategies that can be applied to real-world settings.

Most persons use some type of strategy (often not consciously) in completing tasks, and this is valuable information for therapists and clients. Therapists need to be vigilant in observing and maximizing strategies with clients. Some clients use strategies that are readily noticeable, such as using a finger as a pacer when reading or moving the lips as material is read. Other strategies may require the therapist to ask questions such as "How did you do the task? Were you aware of using a strategy?"

In choosing strategies, it is important to choose ones with the most potential applicability to the client's real world. This sometimes involves identifying a variety of strategies and teaching a menu of these from which the client can pick and choose, such as those listed in Exhibit 5-3, depending on various situations. Information regarding the client's most efficient channel of information processing is also incorporated into the process of choosing appropriate strategies.

Exhibit 5-3 Task and Strategy Sheet

Task	Strategy
Recall of short paragraph	1. Rehearsal
	2. Chunking
	3. Highlighting
	4. Notetaking
	5. Outlining

On the basis of assessments completed before the start of treatment, the therapist can identify whether verbal or visual memory is relatively stronger and emphasize this in choosing strategies for long-term use. If visual is stronger than verbal memory, emphasis can be placed on strategies that employ the visual channel; likewise, if the verbal channel is stronger, emphasis can be placed on strategies in the verbal channel. Ideally, as many sensory channels as possible would be used in encoding information (that is, visual, auditory, tactile, and so forth). In this way, the client is maximizing potential for encoding to occur.

There are many types of memory strategies, each of which can be used in various real-life situations. Some examples include repetition and rehearsal of information, chunking, association, story building, rhythm, rhyming, active listening, and so forth. These and other strategies are discussed in depth in Chapter 7.

Once a particular strategy is chosen, the therapist must discuss how the strategy can be used both inside and outside sessions. Depending upon the strategy, the therapist may need to model its use and then lead the client through the first learning trial. Most clients will need several trials to learn the specifics of the strategy and how to perform it.

Step 5: Practice Strategies

This is the skills acquisition phase of treatment and is an extremely crucial element of any retraining program. It is essential that the client be given the opportunity to practice the new learning on a regular basis until goal levels are achieved. In fact, it is recommended that the client practice until strategies are overlearned (i.e., practice to the point that use becomes automatic). For example, overlearning is generally the way in which we learn the alphabet or basic number facts to such a degree that we can respond without seeming to think about it.

Practicing strategies in rehabilitation of memory is similar to the process of learning to play tennis. If a person learns to serve a tennis ball and then does not pick up a tennis ball or racket for several months, the tennis serve may not show much improvement. On the other hand, if the person practices the serve daily for several weeks, the serve will probably improve and eventually become an automatic function. Similarly, when a client and therapist develop a strategy and that strategy is accompanied by extended practice, the learning is enhanced.

It is the responsibility of the therapist to ensure that sufficient amounts of practice time are available for the client to learn, enhance, and reinforce skills. This practice is originally performed in therapy sessions with the therapist present. In this way, any problems encountered with using the strategy can be addressed (for example, a client may understand the strategy as the therapist explained or performed it but does not know how to implement it independently). This is the phase where the client does the task independently rather than watching the therapist do it or having the therapist do it with him or her. The therapist is available for assistance and structure while the client learns and performs the skill.

In addition to work done in sessions, the therapist can assign practice to be done outside sessions, thus maximizing the potential for learning and overlearning the strategy. The therapist may wish to be available (possibly during set office hours) or provide a resource person whom the client can consult if difficulty is encountered during the out-of-session practices. This resource person could be an aide, a more experienced client, a family member, or someone else. If feasible, the therapist may bring family members into the therapy session to familiarize them with the nature of the assignments so that they can provide assistance if needed during out-of-session practice.

Regardless of where the practice sessions occur, it is essential that they be held on a regular basis and that clients are aware of the purpose of the sessions and their relative performance. One way to keep track of performance is to record it on a graph or chart, as previously discussed.

Step 6: Obtain a Postpractice Measure

When the client has mastered the strategy or has reached a plateau level, some form of postpractice measurement should be taken. Depending upon the client, the task, and the amount of practice time available, the client may reach this phase within a matter of days or weeks.

This postpractice measure can be either the same material used as the baseline or similar material. If using the same material for baseline and postpractice measures, and different materials for practice, the postpractice measurement is easier. If the same baseline task is used for practice, the therapist would then use a similar task for the postpractice measure. However, when using the same task, therapists will need to be sensitive to the potential effects that repeated practice may have on outcome.

A comparison of measurements before and after practice provides the client with an accurate picture of performance. Since many successes and achievements in rehabilitation can be slow in coming and minor in degree, it is particularly beneficial for the client to have a way to measure change over time. This can be presented graphically as shown in Figure 5-2 which depicts a task that required sequential recall of letters flashed on a computer screen. The primary strategy employed was repetition.

After a postpractice measurement is taken, a determination will need to be made with the client regarding whether more practice is needed, whether the goal should be revised upward or downward, or whether the task should be terminated temporarily because performance has plateaued or because the client has reached desired goal levels.

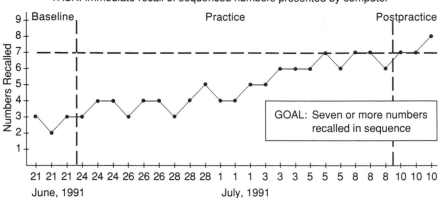

Figure 5-2 Immediate Recall of Sequenced Numbers: Postpractice Graph

Step 7: Develop Transfer and Generalization Tasks for Real-Life Situations

Once the client has achieved the goal level on a task and a postpractice measure has been taken (verifying that the strategy learned can be transferred to a similar task), the next step is one of developing situations in the real world where the strategy can be generalized. The client must be able to see some practical application of the strategies learned and practiced in sessions.

A useful way of tracking the variety and usefulness of strategies learned in sessions is by recording them on sheets such as the one shown in Exhibit 5-4. These sheets are maintained by the client, who completes them as new strategies are learned or as new information is learned about strategies already in use. In this way, the client has a running record of successful strategies and a ready resource that can be referenced in similar future situations. Ideally the client independently records performance on these sheets. If this is not feasible or possible, the therapist can assist the client in recording information.

Once situations for practice have been developed, the therapist and client can move through this process in a gradual hierarchical manner; they can design practices for transfer of strategies to a different task in therapy, transfer to the next therapy session, transfer to a similar therapy, transfer to a different type of therapy situation, or generalize to the real world in various situations (e.g., work, home, school, and so forth).

The development, practice, and generalization of strategies is the most important part of rehabilitation. Therapists are encouraged to spend as much time as necessary in this stage of treatment. Ultimately, it is the measure of successful rehabilitation.

Exhibit 5-4 Strategy and Generalization Sheet

Strategy	Generalization
Rehearsal/repetition	1. Use this technique at the office. For example, when the secretary reports the telephone number of a new client, repeat the number continuously as you dial or write the number down.
	2. Use the strategy when going out to the store for only a few items. Repeat the items until you arrive at the store.
	3. Use the strategy when obtaining instructions over the phone. For example, when instructed to press "1" for sales, "2" for personnel, and so forth, repeat the number continuously until it is time to press the correct number.

Step 8: Practice Transfer and Generalization

As many opportunities as possible should be provided for the client to practice the strategy learned. The client may need to learn his or her room number, therapists' names, social security numbers, phone numbers, work codes, and so forth and practice this information intensively with the therapist so that learning can be retained.

The ability to generalize strategies to the real world is one of the most essential elements of rehabilitation as it is the end result of all the time spent practicing and rehearsing strategies. If the opportunity to practice is not given to the client, there is a strong possibility that learning will decline.

To ensure long-term positive results, the therapist can include follow-up measures in the treatment plan. These follow-ups could occur several months or up to a year later, and would assist the therapist in estimating the most effective use of strategies and/or any deterioration of skills after discontinuation of practice.

NOTES

1. Christiane C. O'Hara and Minnie Harrell, *Rehabilitation with Brain Injury Survivors: An Empowerment Approach* (Gaithersburg, Md.: Aspen Publishers, 1991): 23–25.
2. Christiane C. O'Hara and Minnie Harrell, "The Empowerment Rehabilitation Model: Meeting the Unmet Needs of Survivors, Families, and Treatment Providers," *Cognitive Rehabilitation* (January–February 1991): 14–21.
3. Society for Cognitive Rehabilitation, Inc.; P.O. Box 33548; Decatur, Georgia 30033-0548.
4. Psychological Software Services, Inc.; 6555 Carrollton Avenue; Indianapolis, Indiana 46220.

Appendix 5A
Therapy Designs

This appendix contains the following figures:

- **Figure 5A-1** Withdrawal Design
- **Figure 5A-2** Changeover Design
- **Figure 5A-3** Multiple Baseline Design
- **Figure 5A-4** Rehabilitation Assessment Design

Clinicians must treat disorders of memory and document the client's progress in therapy. Documentation involves more than simply writing a narrative report at the end of treatment. It includes measures of performance that clearly show which of several treatment interventions actually improved the client's memory functioning.

There are well-developed procedures for recording the results of treatment. These are usually referred to as single-case experimental designs. The therapy designs presented in this appendix are not strictly experimental designs, particularly since most therapists will not always use therapy results for research or publication; therefore, in the context of this appendix, the models are referred to as therapy designs. Each is a structured treatment model that allows the therapist to evaluate systematically the results of treatment. Several designs are presented in this appendix to provide clinicians with additional models to use separately from, or in addition to, the Eight-Step Model presented in Chapter 5.

BASIC THERAPY DESIGNS

Withdrawal Design

The therapist begins by measuring baseline memory to determine how well the client will do independently. Next, the therapist teaches the client a strategy or skill or changes the environment to facilitate new learning. In any case, interventions can be designed. Finally, the intervention is removed to see if performance returns to baseline levels.

This process can be converted to a general step-by-step procedure (see Figure 5A-1).

1. Decide what behaviors need to improve, and determine how they will be measured.

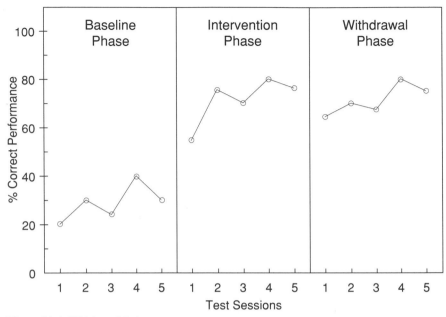

Figure 5A-1 Withdrawal design.

2. Measure the baseline performance and convert the scores to scaled units such as percentages. Plot the baseline data on a graph or chart.

3. Decide how to improve the behavior (e.g., teach one of the memory strategies) and train the client accordingly. Reassess performance after training.

4. Convert the scores obtained after training to percentages and plot them in the chart next to the scores obtained during baseline assessment.

5. Compare the two plots. If performance improves during the intervention phase, then training was successful. If there is no difference between the plots obtained during baseline assessment and intervention, then discontinue that treatment and try another.

6. Remove the treatment if successful (this is the withdrawal phase).

Measurement continues to determine whether memory performance returns to baseline levels. For example, if the task is to organize word lists semantically, the therapist assumes that the training was effective, and the client recalled substantially more words in the *B* phase after the semantic organization training. After the client is taught how to organize word lists semantically in the *B* phase, he or she learns another list without any specific instructions to organize (*A* phase). If performance returns to baseline levels, the client has not internalized the strategy to the point where it is used spontaneously. The design shows that the strategy was effective but that the client would probably require additional training. If recall is enhanced, then it is necessary to continue testing with new word lists to see if the client continues to use the strategy.

Obviously, the therapist does not want performance to return to baseline levels. This is one reason why this structured treatment procedure is termed therapy design as opposed to a single-case experimental design. The goal is to improve performance, not to demonstrate a cause-and-effect relationship between performance and the presence or absence of an intervention strategy. Therapy designs are not for testing formal hypotheses. They are for providing quantitative information about whether specific interventions will work with a given client.

Changeover Therapy Design

The *A-B-A* therapy design outlined above is useful for testing the effects of a certain intervention. It is limited, however, because only one intervention is tested. The changeover design permits the testing of many interventions at once. Its purpose is to compare the relative usefulness of any one strategy to any other. Consequently, it is not necessary to acquire a baseline measurement because performance after one intervention is compared to performance after another. The only goal is to see which one works best.

1. Define a set of strategies to be tested. For example, the client practices categorizing words into semantically related groups or, alternatively, uses mental imagery to learn a similar word list. Both techniques can improve memory functioning, but one may be more effective than the other with a particular client.

2. Alternate training between the two memory strategies. Begin by teaching one strategy (e.g., imagery) and then measuring the client's memory functioning using this strategy. Next, the client is taught to use a semantic organization strategy, and then performance is measured. Switch back to the imagery strategy, then back to semantic organization, then to imagery, and so forth.

3. Evaluate over training sessions which strategy produces the best performance.

The results of this hypothetical treatment regimen are presented in Figure 5A-2. Notice that performance on the various tasks is scaled in percentages. The *x* axis of the chart represents training under imagery (I) and organization (O) conditions. In this example, the imagery training seems to produce the highest overall level of

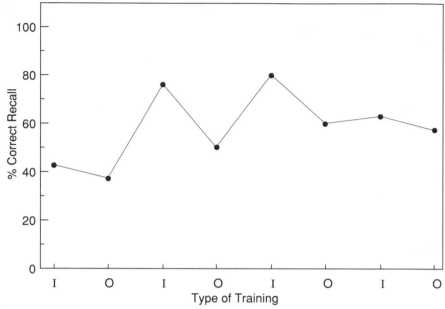

Figure 5A-2 Changeover design.

performance, although the client improved with practice across the therapy sequence regardless of which technique was used.

From this chart, it can be concluded that imagery was an effective intervention with this client. The therapist might then go on to try another strategy with the client, along with imagery, to determine if it might also prove effective.

In general, the idea is to evaluate several strategies to determine which ones produce the desired results and which ones do not. After a period of evaluation using this design, the therapist can eventually isolate those memory strategies that work best for that particular client.

The changeover design is efficient for several reasons. Conceivably, more than two strategies are testable. The therapist could test any number and eventually evaluate those that worked best with that client. There is no real need for baseline measurement since the goal is to evaluate several alternative therapies relative to one another. Finally, the design fits the confines of a conventional therapy session. The therapist can teach one strategy during one session and record the results, then teach another the next session and record the results. After several sessions, those that are effective become obvious. In addition, the design gives the therapist a tool to convey the results of treatment to the client and to justify why certain treatments were used.

Multiple Baseline Design

This design is similar to the changeover design. It differs primarily in terms of when the data are collected. In one use of the multiple baseline procedure, performance is measured in several different situations to determine where it occurs most frequently or where it occurs with highest quality. For example, suppose the therapist was interested in examining what types of training produce the most vigilant and attentive behavior.

1. Measure how long the client can maintain vigilance with one type of task and plot it (see Figure 5A-3). For example, measure how long the client can maintain vigilance while playing cards.
2. Change the situation and continue to measure and plot the client's vigilance in another baseline context. For example, measure the client's vigilance while watching videos on a VCR.

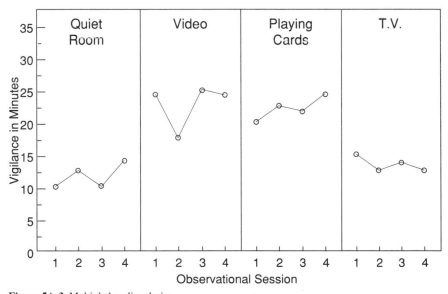

Figure 5A-3 Multiple baseline design.

3. Determine which context produces the highest level of vigilance. If the activity has an effect, then vigilance will increase in the one context relative to the others.

4. Once specific contexts have been isolated where vigilance is best, then treatment can be planned around these contexts as much as possible. For example, if the goal is to improve memory, interesting videos could be used and the client asked to recall the contents of the picture.

Another application of the multiple baseline design involves measuring several different behaviors simultaneously to determine which one is most affected by an intervention. For example, the therapist may measure vigilance, recall, and recognition at the same time, plot each one, and determine which was most affected after training in a certain memory strategy. The first application is called the multiple baseline across situations, and the second is a multiple baseline across behaviors.

Sometimes, it may be difficult to distinguish between the multiple baseline design across situations and the changeover design. In both designs, one treatment is provided, withdrawn, and replaced with another. In both designs, the goal is to see what works best. The changeover design is usually used with alternative treatment strategies, however, whereas the multiple baseline design is commonly used for examining when a desired behavior occurs most frequently. In some cases, it may be used without trying to manipulate the therapy technique per se.

Rehabilitation Assessment Design

This is a structured model of treatment that combines all the qualities discussed earlier. The procedure involves testing the client to see if performance on some memory task would improve spontaneously with practice and how long it takes before average levels are reached (learning phase). Next, the therapist assesses how much the client would profit from specific instructions or training procedures. Finally, the therapist evaluates how much the training transfers to some related activity. The design therefore includes three distinct qualities: learning potential, instructional profit, and transfer of learning (see Figure 5A-4).

1. Assess learning potential. Choose a memory task the client performs without any specific instructions (baseline). A measurement is taken of how long it takes before performance can improve to average levels (for example, the client is given messages in a simulated phone conversation, and the therapist assesses how many repetitions are necessary before the message is taken correctly).

2. Assess instructional profit. Provide a specific strategy and determine if the client remembers better with the strategy than without it (for example, the

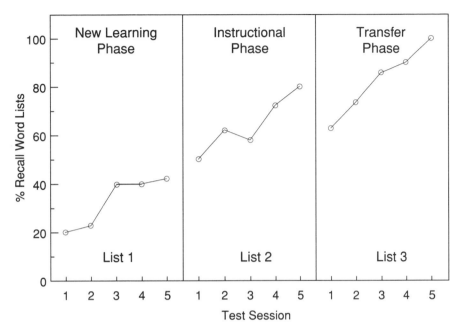

Figure 5A-4 Rehabilitation assessment design.

client is taught to use a small dictation tape recorder to record the message so that details can be written down later). At this point, the assessment design is no different from any other previously discussed design.

3. Continue training until the client can use the strategy or device effectively.

4. Define a relevant transfer task and set a criterion for acceptable performance. Ideally, this is a task that involves some activity of daily living (for example, taking a phone number or phone message is something the client may have to do on a daily basis).

5. Test the client to see if the training transfers to the task defined in step 4 (for example, see if the client can use this tape recorder or a chunking strategy [see Chapter 7] to improve memory for phone messages and phone numbers).

6
Direct Retraining of Memory

This chapter introduces our concepts and views of direct retraining of memory skills. It is intended to provide the reader with a basic approach to begin the direct retraining of memory as well as practical examples of tasks, materials, and strategies to be used in sessions with clients.

Also included in this chapter are sections that define direct retraining of memory and address how to select materials and determine where to begin tasks. Practical approaches to direct retraining of memory using pen-and-paper, three-dimensional, and computerized tasks are also included. Finally, appendixes at the end of the chapter provide listings of materials and manufacturers' information. The materials discussed in this chapter and in the appendixes can be used in any rehabilitation setting (inpatient, outpatient, or transitional living), with traumatic brain injury (TBI) clients in various stages of recovery (acute to chronic), and with clients across a broad spectrum of impairment levels (severe to mild).

DEFINITION OF DIRECT RETRAINING

Direct retraining of memory deficits (which has also been called restitution or restoration) is loosely based on the theory of anatomical reorganization.[1] This theory holds that continued external stimulation will facilitate internal reorganization of the brain, which involves a restitution or recovery of the function, and that this process occurs in some automatic way.[2] In clinical settings, this translates to therapists designing tasks with clients that can be practiced until they are mastered. While direct retraining is based on this theory, it should be noted that minimal hard evidence exists as to its efficacy. As previously stated, we are not attempting to prove or disprove efficacy; readers are encouraged to review research, participate in research, and form their own opinions regarding this extremely controversial issue (see the additional readings at the end of the text for information about this issue). Our purpose is to present a variety of approaches and materials that therapists can use in their individual settings.

The direct retraining approach to cognitive rehabilitation has been used extensively in acute care as well as outpatient facilities. In fact, there often appears to be an assumption by therapists entering the field that direct retraining is cognitive rehabilitation therapy, when in fact *it is not*. Because the methods used in direct retraining generally involve repeated practice trials or memorization of information, clients may not learn how to learn, but rather how to memorize. Thus transfer and generalization to applicable settings may not take place.

It is our opinion that there is a place for direct retraining techniques in the rehabilitation of memory, especially in the acute stages of recovery. Cognitive areas that are particularly amenable to this type of treatment include attention, concentration, short-term memory, visual-motor skills, and some aspects of visual-spatial skills. In addition, the act of repeatedly practicing tasks provides structure, engages the client in treatment, and can be used as an in-session compensatory strategy.

Even with the above areas, however, direct retraining in isolation can become a task of memorization and may not translate past the therapy setting. The ideal cognitive rehabilitation of memory program includes elements of direct retraining, use of compensatory strategies, and use of prosthetic and orthotic devices (see Chapters 7 and 8). Furthermore, if therapists use the Eight-Step Model discussed in Chapter 5, the rehabilitation process can naturally progress from direct retraining to teaching the use of compensatory strategies or aids; this is simply the next step (for more impaired clients it may be the only step).

TYPES OF MATERIALS: PEN-AND-PAPER, THREE-DIMENSIONAL, AND COMPUTERIZED

As previously stated, direct retraining can be done with a variety of materials, including pen-and-paper, three-dimensional, and computerized tasks. Each of these areas is presented separately in the sections that follow, with suggestions for tasks that therapists can use in sessions. Sample tasks in each area are presented using the Eight-Step Model introduced in Chapter 5; additional materials and task suggestions are included in the appendixes at the end of the chapter.

Pen-and-Paper Tasks

Pen-and-paper tasks can be defined as those that use paper and pen (or pencil) in some manner. This includes materials generated by the client or therapist and encompasses written, spoken, or figural material. Several examples of tasks that can be used are discussed in this section, but the possibilities for using pen-and-paper tasks are enormous, and therapists are encouraged to be creative and to expand tasks appropriate to their setting. Appendix 6A at the end of this chapter includes samples of tasks and a listing of materials and manufacturers' information.

Getting Started

When introducing pen-and-paper tasks (as with any task), the therapist must provide sufficient instruction and examples, so that the client understands the nature of the task, its purpose, how it will be measured, and its applicability to the real world. Pen-and-paper tasks can be performed in sessions and are also easily adapted for use at home. Before assigning such tasks for out-of-session practice, however, therapists must explain the task in session and give clients adequate practice. Giving a client a task to do independently without explanation or purpose is not rehabilitation practice; it is homework or "busywork."

As tasks are presented, we encourage therapists to use a model similar to the Eight-Step Model (see Chapter 5). This provides structure to the therapy session for both the therapist and the client and provides a "big picture" overview of treatment. It also serves as a quality control mechanism to ensure that tasks and strategies are being presented in a hierarchical manner and that they are actually addressing areas applicable to the client.

Sample Task

A sample pen-and-paper task is presented below that demonstrates how the therapist can approach tasks and strategies. The sample also incorporates the Eight-Step Model so that therapists will have a structure within which to work. It is only representative of the many tasks therapists can devise. Therapists would likely use this task in conjunction with other therapy tasks; it would rarely, if ever, be used in isolation.

Step 1: Select a task or strategy. Suppose the client has difficulty remembering information he or she reads (visual-verbal memory) and has a particular interest in world events. The therapist and client can select materials such as articles from newspapers, journals, or magazines to use in sessions. In the selection phase, the therapist and client can talk about different options for tasks and choose those with the most applicability. The therapist in this phase explains to the client the rationale for the task, the specific cognitive area that the task will cover, how performance will be measured, and the long-term applicability.

Step 2: Obtain baseline measure. In this step, the therapist determines how the task will be measured (e.g., percentage of information, such as main ideas, remembered from the newspaper article) and then measures the client's performance before teaching any strategy or giving any assistance on the task. Continuing the sample task of a newspaper article, assume that the client silently reads this article and summarizes (aloud) the information contained therein, recalling 5 of 10 main ideas (50%).

During this baseline phase, the therapist observes the client's performance on the task, measures it, and identifies any strategies the client independently used in the performance. This is also a phase where the therapist and client can identify any maladaptive strategies that may hinder performance (e.g., rereading one sentence repeatedly while losing the rest of the text). The therapist can also attend to other aspects such as speed, recognition of errors, frustration level, and so forth.

Step 3: Set goals with client. Once the therapist and client know where the performance level is, they can discuss where the client would like to be. The goals must be stated in measurable terms and must be the client's versus the therapist's goals. For example, the therapist may feel that the client needs to remember 100% of the newspaper article, but the client may not have the same need and may be comfortable with 80%. If the therapist imposes goals on the client, potential for failure increases.

In addition to the short-term goal of achieving 80% accuracy on this task, the client and therapist can also discuss long-term goals. For instance, later the client may want to add remembering information from textbooks, novels, and so forth. This ultimately becomes the reason for teaching tasks and strategies and can guide the rehabilitation process.

Step 4: Choose and teach strategies. After the goal level has been set on the task, the therapist and client can discuss strategies to be introduced. If independent strategies were observed in step 2 (see above), these may provide a base on which to capitalize and expand. For example, if the client used rereading a sentence several times (a maladaptive strategy), the therapist can use this strategy of repetition but adapt it such that the client reads all the information once before rereading a particular sentence repeatedly. Alternatively, the therapist can teach the repetition strategy of reading information three times (first to preview, second to encode, and third to incorporate into personal knowledge; see Chapter 7 for further discussion of this strategy).

Repetition is often the strategy of choice for persons to remember what they read (repetition and rehearsal can be done either aloud or silently). There are other possible strategies for remembering a newspaper article, however, including chunking and grouping information, highlighting important aspects of the text, taking notes on the information as it is read, or writing an outline of the material (refer to Chapter 7 for more detailed information about these strategies).

The therapist can teach all these strategies, and the client can determine which ones (perhaps none or a combination of one or more) fit best. Each person will have different preferences, prejudices, and motivations to use these different strategies, and therapists must be sensitive to these issues. Clients often need to practice using various strategies in real-life settings before deciding which ones fit, and they may often switch back and forth between strategies, depending on the specific situation.

In teaching a strategy, the therapist can explain how it is used and may also need to perform the strategy for the client and then assist the client in actually performing the strategy.

Step 5: Practice strategies. This is an important part of the rehabilitation process. The client must be given ample opportunity to practice the strategies taught in session. Initial practices should occur inside the therapy session with the therapist. In this way, any problems encountered with using the strategy can be addressed. This is the phase where the client does the task independently versus watching the therapist do it or doing it with the therapist. In addition to work done in sessions, the therapist can assign practice to be done outside sessions, which maximizes the potential for learning and overlearning the strategy.

Practicing the strategy of repetition can be done using the same newspaper article in several trials or using similar articles in several trials. For example, one article can be used for the baseline and postpractice measure, while a similar article is used for practicing the strategy. In this way, the therapist can measure performance on the same article after instruction in a strategy. Alternatively, the baseline article can be the same article on which the client practices, and the postpractice article can be a similar one.

There is no set number of times a client must practice to ensure encoding; this process must be individualized. Some clients can learn to use a strategy after 4 or 5 practices, while some may need 20; others may not be able to use the strategy at all.

In the example of using the strategy of repetition to remember the newspaper article, assume that it takes the client 6 times to achieve 80% accuracy on the task. At this point, the therapist and client can reevaluate and decide whether a new goal level (e.g., 100%) needs to be established or whether this 80% level feels appropriate to the client.

Step 6: Obtain postpractice measure. After the client has practiced for a reasonable amount of time (when a certain level has been reached constantly, for example), a postpractice measure is taken. As discussed in step 4, this measure can be either the same material used as the baseline or similar material. In using the same material for the baseline and postpractice measures and different material for practice, the postpractice measurement is easier. That is, with a similar newspaper article on which the client achieves 80% accuracy, the therapist can then posttest knowledge of the strategy by using the original article presented as baseline to determine if the client's original score (50%) has now improved (80%). If the score has improved, the client has demonstrated knowledge of the strategy and ability to transfer the strategy to another similar material. The possibility should be considered, however, that it is the result of the practice-effect.

If on the postpractice measure the client does not achieve the goal level (e.g., 80%), a decision can be made to provide more practice, revise the goal, or develop different tasks and strategies altogether.

Step 7: Develop transfer and generalization tasks for real-life situations. After the client has achieved goal level on the task and has been able to transfer the strategy learned to a similar therapy task, the next step is one of developing situations in the real world where the strategy can be generalized. In the instance of the repetition strategy used for the newspaper article, the client may at this point want to try this strategy in a classroom setting to remember text from a book, or he or she may use it to read magazine articles or novels. The client may also want to practice the strategy in other areas of memory; for example, repetition can be used to remember spoken information (e.g., church sermons, lectures, and conversations). Therapists can encourage clients to use the strategies learned in as many situations as possible and to be vigilant in searching for such situations in the real world.

Step 8: Practice transfer and generalization. Once real-life situations have been devised, the therapist then redefines the task and takes a baseline measurement. For example, using the strategy of repetition learned with the newspaper task, suppose the client now wishes to practice this strategy on magazine articles. The therapist could again take a baseline measure of memory before practicing the strategy on this task, set a goal with the client, provide practice both in and out of sessions, and then take a postpractice measure.

When the client has achieved goal levels, can transfer strategies to other similar tasks, and can generalize strategies to other situations, the task can then be discontinued.

Although this step may seem like a final one, it is not. Rehabilitation of memory is a fluid process; once the client achieves success in one area, additional situations may continue to arise where work will need to be done. Clients may also need continuing assistance in developing and practicing new strategies and new situations in which to practice. Therapists can assist in this process by periodically assigning practice tasks and checking with clients to determine whether new problems have arisen.

Three-Dimensional Tasks

In this section, three-dimensional tasks are defined, various types of three-dimensional tasks are presented, and a sample application of the Eight-Step Model is made to one of these tasks. Appendix 6B gives sample three-dimensional tasks and information about manufacturers.

A three-dimensional task is any concrete material such as a game, toy, instrument, and so forth that can be used as a therapy tool. Some obvious tasks are games such as Concentration®, Memory®, and Simon®. Concentration®[3] is an adaptation of a television show that requires the player to match two numbers or prizes on a board and to solve a rebus puzzle as he or she uncovers matched pairs. Memory®[4] is a game played with pairs of cards that are placed face down on the table. The player selects two cards at a time with the goal of uncovering matching pairs. Simon®[5] is a game that requires the player to duplicate a sequence of sounds paired with patterns of light. There are many other tasks that can be used to practice memory skills. These include pegboards, blocks, playing cards, games that employ a game board or other highly visual elements, and so forth. Therapists are encouraged to create their own tasks and to modify or adapt existing materials to suit their clients' needs.

Getting Started

When introducing a three-dimensional task, the therapist must provide sufficient instruction and examples so that the client understands the nature of the task, its purpose, how it will be measured, and its applicability to the real world. Assigning a task to a client without explaining the purpose or application is an injustice to the client. The therapist may need to explain to the client that although some of these items are designed as "games," they will be used in therapy as treatment interventions with measures of progress being recorded. These items are not meant to diminish the client's self-esteem or to suggest that the therapist perceives the client as limited to using toys or games. One way to circumvent this somewhat is to repackage the materials into a clear plastic box or container.

It is also important to ensure that the client is able to use the three-dimensional material. For example, a certain amount of manual dexterity is needed to pick up a peg and place it in a hole in a pegboard. The therapist can work with the client's particular needs and choose tasks appropriate for the client in this respect.

Three-dimensional tasks can be introduced and performed in session and, if possible, can be adapted for use at home or in out-of-session practice. Before assigning such tasks for out-of-session practice, the therapist must explain the task in session, give the client adequate practice to ensure that he or she is performing the task correctly, and make sure that instructions are adequate for completing the practice activity without the therapist's supervision.

Ideally, therapists can use three-dimensional tasks to complement pen-and-paper and computer tasks that the client may also be using. This increases the possibility of carryover and transfer of strategies learned from one modality to another and also allows the therapist to assess the effectiveness with which the client can transfer the strategy to comparable situations or problems (i.e., whether the client uses the repetition strategy learned on a computer task when working with the pen-and-paper and/or three-dimensional tasks).

The Eight-Step Model described in Chapter 5 can be applied to this type of task. An example of its application to a task involving use of a pegboard follows. This task was selected as it involves a highly visual element (placement of pegs on a board), allows for varying degrees of difficulty, and has several generalized applications that may be appropriate for the client.

Sample Task

The sample task that is presented in this section uses three-dimensional materials. The presentation is a static one and in actuality, the therapist would not use this task in isolation. It would be used in combination with other tasks, strategies, and aids.

Step 1: Select a task or strategy. If a client in an in-patient facility has difficulty remembering locations in the hospital or locating items in his or her room, therapy tasks can be designed to focus on visual memory for location of items. In this selection phase, the therapist and client can discuss various types of tasks that would address this issue and choose an appropriate one. It is the responsibility of the therapist to explain to the client the rationale for the task, the specific cognitive area that will be addressed, the method of measuring performance, and the long-term applicability of the task.

One possible task involves use of a pegboard. A pegboard is a rectangular-shaped board that has several holes punched into its surface. It is used with pegs (soft wooden or plastic "nails") that can be placed into the holes, and designs can be reproduced. This task also addresses other cognitive areas, such as eye-hand coordination, visual-spatial synthesis, analysis, and organization, and the client's ability in these areas will need to be assessed before initiation.

Step 2: Obtain baseline measure. This involves the therapist's obtaining a baseline reading of performance without any direction or assistance to the client. The pegboard task can be designed so that the pattern can be built with the model as a guide before the client recreates the design from memory, or the task can begin with the memory phase of the task. Variables that can be controlled are the number of pegs in the design, the number of colors in the design, the length of exposure to the stimulus design, and so forth. It is usually easier to begin with a simple design employing only one color.

Once the model design has been removed, the client is then asked to duplicate the design on the pegboard. The time and accuracy with which he or she completes this design become the baseline readings for this task. For example, the client may attempt a one-color design that uses 20 pegs, and the task would be timed. The accuracy would be the percentage of pegs placed correctly. If a two-color design is used, two accuracy scores might be recorded: the percentage of pegs placed in the correct location, and the percentage of pegs of the correct color placed in the correct location. In this example, assume that the client accurately places 10 of 20 pegs (50%) in 2 minutes.

While the client is completing the task, the therapist observes performance, measures it, and attempts to identify any strategies the client is using independently to complete the task. For example, the client may use verbal mediation such as counting (aloud) the number of holes from the top before the first peg is placed. If the therapist does not notice any particular strategy being employed, it is appropriate to ask the client how he or she completed the task (using questions such as "How did you complete that design?" or "Did you use any strategies?"). This provides useful information to the therapist in that it identifies strategies in use and gives the therapist an opportunity to assess the effectiveness of the strategy, encouraging those that are successful and identifying any that are counterproductive to the effective completion of the task.

In addition to taking the baseline measure, the therapist also has the opportunity to observe other aspects of performance such as speed, recognition of errors, tolerance for frustration, coping strategies, and so forth. These behavioral observations can provide valuable information for designing future tasks and determining where problem areas may arise in the future.

Step 3: Set goals with client. With the baseline measure as the indicator of performance, the client and the therapist can discuss what the desired level of performance might be. It is important for the client to participate in this process because, as stated throughout this book, accurate identification of goals by the client will contribute to continuing motivation and enhance the possibility of success.

On the pegboard task, the client may at first set a short-term goal of recalling a 15-peg design of one color only. If success is achieved at this level, the next short-term goal of 20 pegs may be set. Building upon the reason for initiating the task in the first place, the long-term goal of remembering a specific location in the building may be generated.

Step 4: Choose and teach strategies. These may include *counting* the number of pegs, *verbalizing* the shape of the design (e.g., five-point star, six-sided figure, house-shaped figure, and so forth), *noticing the placement* of the design with respect to the four sides of the pegboard, *planning an overall approach* to the task, and *taking notes* while viewing the design (this would be an appropriate strategy in a real-world activity or situation). The client can also keep a written record of the various strategies that are employed in completing these tasks.

In teaching strategies, the therapist will need initially to demonstrate the use of the strategy for the client and may also need to model it. The client can then perform the strategy with the therapist watching to ensure understanding and carryover to therapy session tasks.

In the pegboard example, assume that the client chooses the strategy of verbalizing placement of the pegs in relation to the overall shape. For example, the client may say "The first row of pegs has two pegs, and the design begins four spaces from the right side of the pegboard."

Step 5: Practice strategies. The therapist needs to provide ample opportunity to practice so that the client can reach the agreed-upon goal level (this practice step is in itself a strategy of repetition). Initially, the client may need to consult strategy sheets and notes frequently; with practice, however, the likelihood that these strategies will be incorporated into memory is increased.

This practice phase should continue until the client is consistently able to perform at goal level, that is, until he or she can demonstrate performance at goal level in two or three (or more) consecutive therapy sessions. In this manner, the therapist and client can be reasonably confident that the appropriate strategies have been learned. There is no set amount of time that a client must practice before the posttest measure can be taken. With some clients or tasks it may occur after three or four sessions; with other clients or tasks it may require considerably more practice time.

In the example of the pegboard, assume that the client needs 10 trials to place correctly 20 pegs of one color.

Step 6: Obtain postpractice measure. The postpractice measure is the same type of task as completed in the baseline phase described above. The therapist may use the same pegboard designed for the baseline or a different one of similar difficulty level. The baseline on this task was 10 of 20 pegs (50%); with the strategy described above, performance at the postpractice measure increased to 20 of 20 pegs (100%). At completion of step 6, the client and therapist may decide to set a more difficult goal or may proceed to the next step.

Step 7: Develop transfer and generalization tasks for real-life situations. In this step, the client and therapist design transfer and generalization tasks so that the client can practice strategies in alternative situations. For instance, using the pegboard example, one possible generalization would be to assist the client in remembering the placement of various articles in a dresser. The strategy of verbalizing items in relation to the placement of other items is used as the client identifies the various items in the drawers and verbalizes their placement (e.g., "Beginning with the left side of the drawer and moving to the right side of the drawer are socks, underwear, handkerchiefs, and ties").

Some other possible generalizations to real-life settings include placement of items in a room, placement of items on a dinner table, and locating various parts of the treatment facility (nurse's station, solarium, workshop, and so forth). The client may generalize the strategy of counting the pegs to counting the number of doors in a corridor to reach his or her room. The strategy of verbalizing can assist in correctly hooking up a speaker to a stereo or a VCR to a television.

Step 8: Practice transfer and generalization. Once strategies have been learned, the next step is to assist the client in practicing them in various real-life situations. This may involve setting new goal levels. This is one of the most important steps in the process of rehabilitation of memory in that clients must have ample situations and opportunities to practice strategies.

As previously stated, this is a fluid process, and once success is achieved on one task and one strategy, there may need to be other tasks, strategies, or generalizations developed, depending on the client's situation (e.g., work, school, or avocation).

Computerized Tasks

Microcomputers are commonly used in the cognitive rehabilitation of memory. Sections to follow focus on computerized treatment, selection of hardware and software, how to use computerized tasks, and a sample task using the Eight-Step-Model presented in Chapter 5. Additionally, listings of computer programs that address memory functions as well as manufacturers' information can be found in Appendix 6C at the end of this chapter.

A Word about Effectiveness

The effectiveness of using computers in cognitive rehabilitation has been the subject of much controversy in the rehabilitation community. Recently, Matthews and colleagues[6] have been addressing the issue, and they have prepared a document for review by Division 40 (Clinical Neuropsychology) of the American Psychological Association. This document proposes two resolutions:

> 1.1 Computer-assisted rehabilitation procedures appear to have a sufficient number of practical advantages and potential benefits to encourage their continued experimental investigation, further development, and empirical validation.
>
> 1.2 Appropriate clinical use of computer software in rehabilitation is dependent upon maintaining a clear distinction between software being properly viewed as a component in an organized treatment program versus being improperly viewed as treatment itself.

These investigators also describe many advantages for both the client and the therapist of using computers. For the client, these advantages include:

- engaging interest
- minimizing frustration when working on tasks
- providing an opportunity to learn a new skill (operating a computer)

For the therapist, computers are useful in:

- providing automatic collection of data
- providing multiple measures of performance on specific tasks

- reducing preparation time
- providing a standardized presentation of stimuli

Some disadvantages of using computers focus on the tendency of the therapist to assign "busywork" rather than selecting specific tasks that are appropriate for the client. Also, some clients may experience difficulty learning functions or operating the computer independently. Some may not feel comfortable with computers. Computers do not automatically teach strategies the client can use in the real world. Finally, computers only measure the final performance or score on a task and do not measure how the task was approached by the client.

It is our opinion that the use of computers in direct retraining of memory is appropriate if the therapist uses it as a treatment *tool* rather than as the treatment itself. Computers can enhance treatment, but therapists must be careful to avoid using them to the exclusion of other types of therapy. When using computers or any material or task, the therapist must constantly keep in mind that any task or material is a means to an end. The end is the client's learning a skill that can be applied in real-life settings. The goal of therapy is not to become proficient at running a particular computer program.

Selection of Hardware

There are several avenues through which therapists and clients can obtain computer hardware (the computer, disk drives, printers, monitors, joysticks, adaptive aids, and so forth). Computers can be rented, leased, or purchased from a previous owner. They can be leased or purchased new from a local computer store, mail-order houses, or other stores such as those that sell toys or electronic equipment, or users can find used computers by reviewing the classified ad sections of newspapers, computer magazines, and electronic bulletin boards.

The obvious advantage to buying used equipment is that the price will be substantially lower (as much as 30% to 40%) than the price of a new machine. The disadvantage of this route is that often there is no support system available after purchase to assist the therapist in setting up and operating the equipment efficiently.

If the therapist is not familiar with computers and their use, the best option may be to visit a local computer store for assistance. Usually the personnel in these stores are quite knowledgeable and can assist in identifying needs and planning the purchase of appropriate equipment. If the purchase is a sizable one, some type of discounting may be available. The value of using a local computer store is that, if problems arise, there is someone available to assist in identifying the problem and dealing with it appropriately. For example, if a specific program requires a certain joystick or other optional equipment, the salesperson can usually give good information about how to purchase and/or install the equipment.

The above procedure and comments apply also to clients who purchase a computer for use at home. It is particularly beneficial that clients have a resource person to assist in the phases of purchasing and setting up the equipment. If a therapist feels that the client's rehabilitation will be enhanced by computer practice at home, insurers will on occasion cover the cost of a computer in the home (either by purchasing it outright or by arranging for the rental of equipment while the client is in treatment), and this is an option therapists can explore to defer costs.

IBM's National Support Center for Persons with Disabilities offers assistance in purchasing computer hardware and software.[7] It has also compiled an excellent directory of support programs and services throughout the United States, many of which will assist clients in obtaining discounts when purchasing or renting computers. Some organizations will provide computers to individuals and organizations free of charge.[8]

Regardless of where the computer purchase is made, the following equipment is required at a minimum: computer, disk drive, monitor, printer, and joystick. Occasionally there will be a need for additional optional equipment to operate specific software, and this can be purchased on an as-needed basis. One piece of optional equipment that we have found helpful in our practice is the Thumbprint option for Apple computers. This is a thin strip that attaches to the inside of the computer and has a red thumbprint exposed on the keyboard. When used, this option prints whatever appears on the screen. It is especially useful for recording performance on programs that do not provide an automatic printout. Other computers employ similar mechanisms.

Other types of adaptive equipment may also be needed, based on the client's limitations in various areas. Areas to be considered include the following.

1. *Visual:* It is not uncommon for TBI survivors to encounter visual disturbances as a result of their recent trauma. Specifically, such problems include total or partial blindness, diminished acuity, double or blurred vision, and light sensitivity. In addition, there may be left or right neglect, where the client is not aware of a particular side, or a visual field cut, where the client does not see past a particular point in the visual field. In any of these cases, diminished vision can complicate the use of computer hardware and software, particularly since the computer relies heavily upon visual precision.

2. *Motor:* With various therapy tasks, the client must possess basic motor skills. It is these skills that allow clients to perceive the nature of the task as well as to respond appropriately by using the keyboard, manipulating a joystick, moving an object, writing, and so forth. Physical limitations often include paresis or paralysis in one or many areas of the body; diminished sensitivity to touch; slowed motor responses; limited range of motion; and spasticity. Any of these can limit ability to perform computer tasks as well as many other tasks.

With computer activities in particular, the speed of motor response must be sufficient to perform tasks.

3. *Hearing:* Hearing impairment can be a direct result of brain trauma. Hearing limitations range from loss in certain frequencies to total deafness. Many computer programs reinforce performance in an auditory manner (musical notes for a correct response or a buzz for an incorrect response).

4. *Speech:* Difficulties in this area occur in articulation, voice production, rhythm, and aphasia.

There is a large variety of adaptive equipment available for most computers. DLM has published an excellent listing of adaptive equipment that is available for Apple computers[9] and IBM has published similar lists for their computers.[10–13] In a broad sense, available adaptations include the following general categories.

1. Pointing and typing aids. Included in this category are headsticks, mouth-sticks, light beam pointers, and so forth, which can be used with a client who has little or no use of the hands.

2. Keyboard modifications. This category includes keyboard covers that help reduce damage to the keyboard, converters that facilitate using one hand by enabling the client to perform two and three keyboard functions with assistance, keyguards that prevent more than one key from being pressed at a time or one key stroke from being repeated unintentionally, and foot operated shift keys.

3. Alternative input systems for standard and special software. These are innumerable systems designed to control software in the input phase of computer usage. They include voice synthesizers, adaptive cards, game paddles, large print, and alternative keyboards.

4. Switches and adapters. These are devices that assist the user in operating equipment by pressing with the finger, elbow, chin, or knee, or by puffing. They include special joysticks, air-bellows switches, bite switches, tongue switches, and eyebrow switches.

5. Alternative output systems for software. These devices provide alternative options in the computer output phase. They include large print, Braille, tactile displays, voice output, and Morse code.

6. Braille and tactile devices. These devices allow the computer to receive and send information in Braille.

7. Voice synthesizers. This category consists of both hardware and software voice synthesizers. Some have music and sound effects capabilities as well. They are designed to be used with other programs.

8. Other hardware. This category includes electronic communication and writing systems, environmental controls (such as page turners), remote control appli-

ance switches, telephone dialers, input adaptors (which allow equipment to be plugged into a computer), and other adaptations especially for the disabled user.

Consultation with a computer supplier or specialized computer center such as IBM's will assist therapists and clients in wading through the hundreds of available options and choosing ones appropriate for the client.

With respect to which type of computer to purchase, therapists will need to determine the types of programs that will be used with particular client populations. As we go to press, Apple computers are being phased out in favor of the Apple Macintosh® computers. For those therapists with an inventory of Apple programs, it is possible to purchase an emulator card that will enable Apple programs to be run on Macintosh computers (consult local dealers for additional information). Industry sources indicate that existing Apple software will continue to be available over the next several years;[14] however, very little new material will be forthcoming as development will shift to the more flexible Macintosh.

Selection of Software

The choice of computer software is based on the needs of clients. Some software is basic and may be appropriate for more severely injured persons, while more sophisticated and complex programs will be needed for higher-level individuals. Software with overly complex visuals may cause difficulty for clients as they try to concentrate on the task initially. As cognitive level increases, however, it may be appropriate to introduce these types of programs to some clients.

Software selection also depends on any physical limitations the client may have. For example, a client with impaired motor function cannot use a program that requires rapid pressing of a joystick button. Before the development of software specifically for cognitive rehabilitation, therapists adapted programs from education-oriented software. Some of these are still valuable, and therapists can adapt them as necessary and appropriate. In general, however, the software specifically designed for cognitive rehabilitation will meet the needs of most clinicians.

Some companies allow examination of their software for a period of time, typically 30 days, during which the therapist can review it for appropriateness. If the material is not useful, the therapist can return it at no obligation. Some companies, however, will not allow the 30-day trial, and the therapist takes a risk in purchasing the programs.

In general, any software purchased for use with clients should meet many of the following criteria: meaningful, user friendly, flexible, and scorable (preferably with criterion-based or normed data). It should be meaningful for the client and worth doing. The software should be user friendly; that is, the client should be able to run the program independently after minimal instruction from and practice with the therapist. There should be some flexibility within the program that enables the therapist and client to control the degree of difficulty. It should also be scorable in some manner, so that goals can be set and the client and therapist can measure and review performance on a regular basis. It is ideal if the program automatically prints out the score at the end of each trial.

Getting Started

It is generally helpful to begin all computerized retraining at a rudimentary level for several reasons. Often the client has had little or no experience with computers of any kind. Elementary tasks such as Psychological Software's Foundations programs for attention can serve as an introduction to computer usage while simultaneously allowing the therapist to assess basic skills of attention, concentration, and so forth that are crucial to success with most of the memory programs.

Depending on the client's level of computer sophistication, the entire first session may be spent on instruction in the use of the computer: identifying the various components (keyboard, monitor, disk drives, printer, joysticks, and so forth). The client should be given the opportunity to practice putting a disk in the appropriate disk drive, turning the computer on (a power pack on the floor that turns on all equipment is especially useful), booting up the disk, and following instructions (recording name and date, selecting a program from the menu, selecting program parameters such as degree of difficulty, speed, and so forth). It is essential that the therapist assist the client in learning these procedures, both to boost the client's morale and ensure correct use of the equipment. Providing the client with a labeled picture or sketch of the computer and its parts will allow the client additional rehearsal prior to the next session. Success on this task will provide the client with a new skill that has broad applications throughout the treatment period and, perhaps, life after treatment.

Prior to using any software with the client, the therapist should thoroughly review and test it to determine its correct operation, assess its appropriateness for the client, and decide on strategies that may be selected for successful completion of the task. As a result, the client's therapy time will not be wasted by the therapist learning the task and the therapist will be better prepared to anticipate any difficulties that may arise.

Sample Task

A sample computerized task is presented below that demonstrates how the therapist and client can approach tasks and strategies. The sample also incorporates the Eight-Step Model presented in Chapter 5 so that therapists have a structure within which to work. This sample only uses computerized tasks. In actual therapy sessions, therapists would generally not use this computer task in isolation. Other types of tasks and strategies would be incorporated, such as pen-and-paper, three-dimensional tasks, and prosthetics or orthotics.

Step 1: Select a task or strategy. If the client is having difficulty remembering phone numbers, therapy tasks can be designed to facilitate verbal recall for sequenced numbers. In the selection phase, the therapist and the client can discuss and choose an appropriate task. It is the responsibility of the therapist to provide complete explanations to the client regarding the rationale for the task as well as the specific cognitive area that will be addressed. In addition, the therapist should provide information regarding the method of measuring performance and the long-term applicability of the task. One possible task involves using the Memory program disk of Psychological Software Services, which includes a series of memory tests.[15] The second of these tasks is Verbal Memory–Sequenced. In this task, letters of the alphabet are presented one at a time in the center of the computer screen. After the last letter, the entire alphabet appears at the bottom of the screen, and the client is asked to type on the keyboard the letters he or she has seen in the same order that they were displayed on the screen. If the client types in the letters successfully, one letter is added to the next trial. If he or she is unsuccessful, a second chance is given at each level. If both trials at a level are failed, the program is terminated, and performance is printed on the screen.

Step 2: Obtain baseline measure. Step 2 involves the therapist obtaining a baseline reading of performance. To accomplish this, the client completes the task with no assistance from the therapist (other than mechanical information about operating the equipment). The performance (the number of letters recalled as well as the number of second chances) is printed on the screen once the program is terminated, and this becomes the baseline score for this task. For example, the client may recall four letters given two second chances.

While the client is completing the task, the therapist can observe performance, speed, and level of frustration as well as identify any strategies the client may use independently to complete the task. For example, the client may recite the letters aloud (repetition strategy) as they are presented on the screen and as he or she is typing them on the keyboard. If the client does not use any obvious strategy, the therapist may want to pursue whether one was used by asking the client how he or she completed the task. Identification of strategies in use provides valuable information for the therapist as it provides an opportunity to evaluate the effectiveness of the strategy. The information also allows the therapist to encourage the use of those strategies that are successful and to identify any that are counterproductive to the effective completion of the task.

Step 3: Set goals with client. At this point, the therapist and the client decide on an appropriate goal. It is essential that the client participate in this decision. On the Verbal Memory–Sequenced task above, the client who can recall four letters may set a short-term goal of recalling five letters. The client who can recall five letters may set a goal of recalling seven or eight letters, thus working on achieving the goal of remembering telephone numbers.

Step 4: Choose and teach strategies. Once the goal is decided on, the therapist and client can then begin the process of identifying strategies that may help improve performance on the task. With Verbal Memory–Sequenced, the primary strategy may be one of repetition. The client repeats the letters shown on the screen until he or she has finished recording the answers on the keyboard. This strategy may need to be supplemented by chunking strategies (repeating groups of letters presented on the screen), recording strategies (having the therapist record responses if the client is unfamiliar with the keyboard or is impeded by slowed motor skills), and so forth. See Chapter 7 for discussion of compensatory strategies.

The therapist may initially need to demonstrate the use of the strategy for the client as well as model it when teaching it. To ensure understanding and carryover to the therapy session, the client is then asked to perform the strategy with the therapist watching. In the Verbal Memory–Sequenced example, assume that the client chooses the repetition strategy. Therefore, the client may repeat the letters in the complete sequence continuously as additional letters are presented on the screen.

Step 5: Practice strategies. Ample opportunities to practice the strategies need to be provided so that the client can reach the stated goal. Performance on each practice trial can be recorded on a graph or chart. This graph should be individualized for the client by specifying the client's name, date, task initiated, and agreed-upon goal.

As the client continues to practice the task, client and therapist record the performance on this task. This practice phase should continue until the client consistently performs at goal level (criterion: performance at goal level in two or three consecutive therapy sessions) and until the therapist and client are in agreement that the strategies have been learned. It should be noted here that there is no set amount of practice time established before the postpractice measure can be taken; as some clients may grasp the strategy after only three or four practice sessions, while others may require considerably more practice time.

In the example of the Verbal Memory–Sequenced task, assume that the client needs seven trials to recall a sequence of seven letters.

Step 6: Obtain postpractice measure. In this step, the postpractice measure is recorded with the same type of task as was completed in the baseline phase described above. When the goal has been reached, it is recorded on the graph. The baseline on this task was four letters. Performance at postpractice measure increased to seven letters. Upon completion of step 6, the client and therapist may decide to change the goal or proceed to step 7.

Step 7: Develop transfer and generalization tasks for real-life situations. Often this is the point at which much direct retraining ends. However, this is one of the most important steps in the rehabilitation process. It is at this step that transfer and generalization tasks are designed by the client and therapist, so that the client can practice strategies in alternative settings in the real world. This ensures that relearning is not taking place in a vacuum. For example, having learned the strategy of repetition, the client may decide to apply this strategy to learning his or her social security number. Some other possible generalizations to real-life settings include the phone number of the outpatient facility, a bank code for the automatic teller, and so forth.

Step 8: Practice transfer and generalization. Once the strategy has been learned and applied, the final step is to provide the client with additional real-life situations and scenarios in which to practice and enhance these skills to ensure that learning is maintained. This may require setting new goals and is one of the most important steps in the process of the rehabilitation of memory.

In the sample of the client learning repetition, this is the phase in which to practice real-life situations. This client generated several possibilities (i.e., social security number, phone numbers, and bank card number). In this final and extremely important stage, the client practices the strategy to learn this information. Practice can occur both inside and outside sessions.

This final phase also involves the therapist and client periodically reviewing strategies learned in sessions and real-life situations. These periodic checkups also provide the opportunity for the client and therapist to generate any additional options or to fine tune the use of the strategy.

As previously stated, this is a fluid process, and once success is achieved on one task and one strategy, there may need to be other tasks, strategies, or generalizations developed, depending upon the client's situation (e.g., work, school, or avocation).

NOTES

1. Edgar Miller, *Recovery and Management of Neuropsychological Impairments* (New York: John Wiley & Sons, 1984), 55–61.

2. Christiane C. O'Hara and Minnie Harrell, *Rehabilitation with Brain Injury Survivors: An Empowerment Approach* (Gaithersburg, Md.: Aspen Publishers, 1991), 128–129.

3. *Classic Concentration.* Pressman Toy Corp. New York, N.Y.

4. *Memory.* Milton Bradley Co. Springfield, Mass.

5. *Simon.* Milton Bradley Co. Springfield, Mass.

6. Charles G. Matthews, J. Preston Harley , and James F. Malec, "Guidelines for Computer-Assisted Neuropsychological Rehabilitation and Cognitive Remediation (Division 40, American Psychological Association)," *The Clinical Neuropsychologist* 5 (January 1991): 3–19.

7. IBM National Support Center for Persons with Disabilities, Atlanta, GA.

8. IBM National Support Center for Persons with Disabilities, *Support Organizations* (Atlanta: IBM, 1991).

9. DLM Teaching Resources, *Apple Computer Resources in Special Education and Rehabilitation* (Allen, Tex.: DLM Teaching Resources, 1988), 35–136.

10. IBM National Support Center for Persons with Disabilities, *Resource Guide for Persons with Mobility Impairments,* (Atlanta: IBM, August 12, 1991).

11. IBM National Support Center for Persons with Disabilities, *Resource Guide for Persons with Hearing Impairments,* (Atlanta: IBM, August 1, 1991).

12. IBM National Support Center for Persons with Disabilities, *Resource Guide for Persons with Speech or Language Impairments,* (Atlanta: IBM, August 1, 1991).

13. IBM National Support Center for Persons with Disabilities, *Resource Guide for Persons with Vision Impairments,* (Atlanta: IBM, August 12, 1991).

14. Sunburst Communications, Pleasantville, NY, and Odie Bracy Personal Communications, 1991.

15. Psychological Software Services, Indianapolis, Ind. 46220.

Appendix 6A
Pen-and-Paper Tasks

This appendix contains the following exhibits:

- **Exhibit 6A-1** Sample Pen-and-Paper Tasks
- **Exhibit 6A-2** Lists of Materials and Manufacturers' Information

INTRODUCTION

Before using the material contained in this appendix, it is recommended that clinicians read this introduction section to obtain an overview of what is included and how to use the materials. The sample tasks are based upon the Eight-Step Model discussed in Chapter 5, and therapists are encouraged to read and review the model as the materials in this section are used.

This section contains two exhibits: Exhibit 6A-1 is a listing of sample tasks, and Exhibit 6A-2 is a listing of materials and manufacturers.

In Exhibit 6A-1, Sample Pen-and-Paper Tasks, samples of tasks are presented, all of which can be adapted and varied for different client populations. Samples are organized into four sections.

1. *Visual-verbal*. These are tasks that consist of verbal content (e.g., words, numbers, and sentences) and are presented to the client visually (i.e., the client reads the information to be remembered).
2. *Visual-figural*. These are tasks that consist of nonverbal content (e.g., figures, drawings, and photographs) and are presented to the client visually (i.e., the client looks at the information to be remembered).
3. *Auditory-verbal*. These are tasks that consist of verbal content (e.g., words, numbers, and sentences) and are presented to the client orally (i.e., the client listens to the information that is to be remembered).
4. *Auditory-nonverbal*. These tasks consist of nonverbal content (e.g., tones, noises, and music without words). The client listens to the information.

Within each of the above-listed sections, sample tasks are organized in the following way.

1. *Task*. This is a broad, general statement regarding what the client is being asked to remember. Even though this item is listed first, therapists are

reminded that the primary emphasis in our treatment model is the acquisition and generalization of skills. Tasks are simply provided as means to an end, not ends in and of themselves. In other words, if the task listed is Immediate Recall of Digits, therapists are cautioned not to think this is the goal. It is not. The client will set a goal to be reached, and the task is designed to reach that goal by use of various strategies.

2. *Description*. This section provides a brief description of the sample task presented. Each variation of a task can be altered in numerous ways, and therapists are encouraged to do so to fit the needs of the individual clients with whom they work.

3. *Materials*. This section describes materials that the therapist and/or client will need to perform the task. In general, all written materials can be altered by color, shape, size, and so forth. It is recommended that as a general rule therapists work from concrete to abstract stimuli and that materials be adjusted as necessary to meet the individual needs of their clients. Therapists can create materials or adapt ones from other sources. See the list of possible materials and manufacturers' information for ordering. Workbooks are particularly useful for memory tasks, and several are included in the list.

For almost all the pen-and-paper materials contained in this appendix, therapists can find parallel three-dimensional or computerized materials; these are discussed in Appendix 6B and Appendix 6C, respectively. These can be used together and can serve as a measure of transfer of skills from one type of task to another.

4. *Scoring*. One sample of scoring is given for each task and is based on the individual task given. There are, of course, many ways to score performances, and therapists can choose ones that meet the individual needs of their clients (see Chapter 5 for more detail on scoring techniques).

5. *Baseline*. Once the method of scoring is determined, then a baseline measure can be taken (e.g., the highest trial of a task before errors are made). Baseline measures are taken before teaching any strategies, so that the client's performance can be assessed before skills building. As with scoring possibilities, the specific baseline measures will vary with different clients and different types of problem areas.

6. *Strategies*. Numerous types of strategies that can be taught using the particular task are included, and therapists can work with clients to determine which will best fit (for details on strategies, see Chapter 7).

7. *Example*. For each task an example is given of a strategy that can be used. There are many ways to alter tasks, and the samples given are representative of the types of tasks that can be used. See Chapter 7 for information on teaching strategies.

8. *Variations.* We have listed a few of the many possible variations of these tasks. Most can be altered by number and type of stimuli presented, length of exposure, and other aspects of the task. They can also be used for recall, recognition, and delayed recall.

9. *Generalizations.* This section provides possible situations to which the skills (strategies) learned can be generalized. Therapists and clients can generate additional possibilities, depending on the needs of individual clients.

Exhibit 6A-2 is a listing of materials and manufacturers. It includes lists of possible materials to be used in therapy sessions and their manufacturers. Addresses are included as well as phone numbers (where appropriate) to assist therapists in locating materials. The listings included are the most up-to-date available as this book goes to press; as companies frequently move, change names, or disappear altogether, however, we cannot take responsibility for the continued accuracy of the information.

This section provides a listing of available resources and is not intended as a recommendation for any particular manufacturer. Therapists are encouraged to write or call companies and to obtain catalogs of materials from which to choose ones most applicable to individual settings and for use with particular client populations.

Exhibit 6A-1

Sample Pen-and-Paper Tasks

VISUAL-VERBAL TASKS

1. Task: Immediate recall of digits.

   Description: The client is given several written sequences of numbers. Each presentation of numbers increases in length of sequence (e.g., from two to nine), with each sequence being exposed for the same length of time (e.g., 10 to 30 seconds). Length of time can be varied with subsequent trials of the task. After presentation, the client can respond by writing, pointing, or reciting orally.

   Materials: Digits can be prewritten on cards or paper, or therapists can produce them in sessions with clients. Digits can be typed, printed, or hand written. Therapists can vary the size of digits, paper, print face, and color.

   Scoring: Highest number of digits recalled in sequence.

   Baseline: Highest correct sequence recalled before the first error.

   Strategies: Repetition, rehearsal, association, chunking.

   Example:

   >   2 5
   >   6 2 9
   >   8 4 2 7
   >   5 7 9 2 8
   >   1 0 6 3 5 8
   >   9 4 1 7 3 8 6
   >   3 0 6 9 5 1 8 4
   >   9 1 2 5 8 6 3 0 7

   Variations:

   - Can be used as a recognition task. For example, the client can be given a written list of numbers that includes the original list of numbers along with others. The number of choices can be varied as well. The client must choose the correct numbers. For example, using the same numbers listed above, the variation task could be as follows (original numbers are underlined for the therapist's use but would not be presented this way to clients). This task also provides interference.

     >   6 2 5 3
     >   8 0 6 2 9
     >   8 4 6 2 7 1

Exhibit 6A-1 continued

4 5 7 9 6 2 8
1 2 0 6 3 7 5 8
0 2 9 4 1 7 3 8 6
3 0 6 9 2 5 1 8 4
9 1 2 5 8 6 3 0 7 4

- Another variation of a recognition task is to provide the client with choices. The number of choices can be varied, e.g., from two to nine items. For example, using the same numbers as above, the variation task could be as follows.

— Identify the first two numbers given (2 5) from the following options:

6 1
2 5
5 2

— Identify the first three numbers given (6 2 9) from the following options:

6 2 9
7 0 1
6 9 7

— Identify the first four numbers given (8 4 2 7) from the following options:

9 0 8 7
4 8 1 7
8 4 2 7

— Identify the first five numbers given (5 7 9 2 8) from the following options:

2 7 1 0 6
5 7 9 2 8
8 2 9 7 5

— Identify the first six numbers given (1 0 6 3 5 8) from the following options:

1 0 5 6 3 8
1 0 8 6 3 5
1 0 6 3 5 8

— Identify the first seven numbers given (9 4 1 7 3 8 6) from the following options:

1 7 3 9 6 8 4

Exhibit 6A-1 continued

       9 4 1 7 3 8 6

       9 4 1 3 7 6 8

— Identify the first eight numbers given (3 0 6 9 5 1 8 4) from the following
options:

       3 0 6 9 5 1 8 4

       3 0 9 6 5 1 8 4

       3 0 6 9 1 5 8 4

— Identify the first nine numbers given (9 1 2 5 8 6 3 0 7) from the
following options:

       9 1 2 5 8 6 3 0 7

       9 7 8 6 4 3 2 0 7

       9 7 1 0 2 3 5 6 8

- Can be used as a delayed recall task by asking the client to remember numbers at various time intervals after initial learning (e.g., 10 minutes to weeks).
- Scoring can be done with the highest number of correct responses regardless of whether or not they are in sequence. For example, if the sequence to be remembered is

       7 4 8 1

and the client remembers 8 4 1, he or she has remembered three of four digits (75%) but out of sequence. The next task could then be designed to assist in remembering the numbers in sequence.

    Overall scores can also be taken (i.e., percentage of correct numbers out of the total numbers given). For example, if eight sequences are given ranging from two to nine numbers, the total possible numbers to be remembered is 44. If the client remembers 30 of these, the score would be 82%.

Generalizations: Phone numbers, social security numbers, bank automatic teller numbers, bank account numbers, driver's license numbers, birthdays, anniversaries, date of accident, security system codes.

2. Task: Immediate recall of letters.

Description: The client is given several written sequences of unrelated letters (i.e., letters that do not form words). Each presentation of letters increases in length of sequence (e.g., from two to nine), with each sequence being exposed for the same length of time (e.g., 10 to 30 seconds). Length of time can be varied with subsequent trials of the task. After presentation, the client can respond by either writing, pointing, or reciting orally.

Exhibit 6A-1 continued

Materials: Letters can be prewritten on cards or paper, or therapists can prepare them in sessions with clients. Letters can be typed, printed, or hand written. Therapists can vary letters by size, color, or type (e.g., italics, hand written, or typed).

Scoring: Highest number of letters recalled in sequence.

Baseline: Highest correct sequence recalled before the first error.

Strategies: Repetition, rehearsal, association, chunking.

Example:

M R
A E G
S L Q T
C X B W N
D O Z U F H
K I V J P Y B
N T Z E A C F G
X R W O P M U L K

Variations:

- Related letters (i.e., those that form words) can be used, and the number of letters contained in the words can be gradually increased. In this task, the therapist would present stimuli as simply letters and would not inform the client that they form words.

  D O
  G E T
  F I R E
  B A T C H
  N U M B E R
  R E L A T E D
  C A L E N D A R
  C O N T A I N E D

- Can be used as a recognition task. For example, the client can be given a written list of letters that includes the original list of letters along with others. The client must choose the correct letters. This task also provides interference.

- Another variation of a recognition task is to provide the client with choices (e.g., using the same letters with several choices; see task 1 above).

Exhibit 6A-1 continued

- Can be used as a delayed recall task by asking the client to remember letters at various time intervals (e.g., 10 minutes to weeks).
- Scoring can be done with the highest number of correct responses regardless of whether or not they are in sequence (see task 1 above).
  Overall scores can also be taken, i.e., percentage of correct letters remembered out of total letters given (see task 1 above).

Generalizations: Addresses, work identification numbers, word processing file codes, license tag numbers, car identification plates.

3. Task: Immediate recall of related words.

Description: The client is given a written sequence of related words (i.e., those that have some characteristic in common). Each presentation of words increases in length of sequence (e.g., from two to nine), with each sequence being exposed for the same length of time (e.g., 10 to 30 seconds). Length of time can be varied with subsequent trials of the task. After presentation, the client can respond by writing, pointing, or reciting orally.

Materials: Therapists can use preprinted materials or make their own. Words can vary by size, shape, and color.

Scoring: Highest number of words recalled in sequence.

Baseline: Highest correct sequence recalled before the first error.

Strategies: Repetition, rehearsal, chunking, association.

Example: Using the category of animals, the following words could be given:

> dog
>
> cat, rat
>
> monkey, rabbit, horse
>
> tiger, elephant, snake, zebra
>
> pig, cow, goat, mule, duck
>
> goose, turkey, chicken, dove, ox, lion
>
> bear, whale, peacock, fox, beaver, alligator, shark
>
> chipmunk, squirrel, sloth, lizard, turtle, penguin, ape, snail
>
> rhinoceros, giraffe, panther, leopard, buffalo, lamb, camel, llama, wolf

Variations:

- Related words can be given within categories with similar properties, parts, functions, and so forth.
- Initially, words given can be concrete (e.g., category of animals) and increase to more abstract concepts (e.g., category of words dealing with the concept of freedom).

Exhibit 6A-1 continued

- Can be used as a recognition task. For example, the client can be given a written list of related words that include the original list along with others (which would need to be in the same category). The client would then choose the correct words. The number of items in the list from which the client chooses can be varied, e.g., 12–50 words. This task also provides interference.
- Another variation of a recognition task is to provide the client with several options from which to choose the correct words.
- Can be used as a delayed recall task by asking the client to remember words at various time intervals.
- Scoring can be done with the highest number of correct responses regardless of whether or not they are in the correct sequence. Overall scores can also be taken (e.g., percentage of correct words remembered out of the total words given).

Generalizations: Lists (things to do, appointments, chores, and shopping), names of persons, names of medications, work-related items, academic information (e.g., biology texts).

4. Task: Immediate recall of sentences.

Description: The client is given several written sequences of sentences. Each presentation of a sentence increases in length of words (e.g., from two to nine), with each sequence being exposed for the same length of time (e.g., 10 to 60 seconds). Length of time can be varied with subsequent trials of the task. After presentation, the client can respond by writing, pointing, or reciting orally.

Materials: Sentences can be written on large or small sheets of paper or on cards. They can also come from magazines, newspapers, and other printed materials.

Scoring: Highest number of words recalled in correct sequence within the sentences.

Baseline: Highest number of correct sequences before the first error.

Strategies: Repetition, rehearsal, chunking.

Example:

I go.
He will help.
The baby is crying.
She will run very fast.
His dog is still a puppy.

Exhibit 6A-1 continued

Her dad works for a big company.

Yesterday, we went swimming in the late afternoon.

My husband loves to play softball, tennis, and golf.

Variations:

- The client can generate sentences to be used.
- Sentences can be presented with scrambled words.
- Sentence sequence can be varied, i.e., trials given in which the client must remember correct order. Sentences can flow or can be unrelated.
- Can be used as a recognition task. For example, the client can be given a written list of sentences that include the original sentences along with others. The client must choose the correct sentences. This task also provides interference (see task 1 above).
- Another variation of a recognition task is to provide the client with several options of sentences from which the correct answers must be chosen (see task 1 above).
- Scoring can be done with the highest number of correct sentences regardless of whether or not they are in sequence. Scoring can also be by "gist" of sentences versus a word-for-word recall. Overall scores can be obtained (e.g., percentage of sentences remembered out of the total number given).

Generalizations:

- Instructions: Cooking (ingredients for recipes, how to use a microwave), cleaning, safety (appliances, chemicals, emergencies), assembly (bookcases, storage boxes), installation (hanging pictures, installing an answering machine or VCR), driving (car maintenance, car wash, maps), money management (income tax returns), personal health (medications).
- Directions: Operating computers and automatic teller machines, driving to new locations.

5. Task: Immediate recall of paragraph-length material.

  Description: The client is given a written paragraph. Each presentation of a paragraph increases in length (i.e., number of sentences, such as from two to nine), with each paragraph being exposed for the same length of time (e.g., 10 seconds to 2 minutes). Length of time can be varied with subsequent trials of the task. After presentation, the client can respond by writing, pointing, or reciting orally.

  Materials: Paragraphs can be designed by the therapist or can be taken from workbooks, newspapers, magazines, and so forth. They can also be generated from work-related or school materials. Print size can be varied, as can the number of words in each sentence.

Exhibit 6A-1 continued

Scoring: Highest number of sentences recalled in a paragraph in sequence.

Baseline: Highest number of sentences recalled in a paragraph in sequence before the first error.

Strategies: Repetition, chunking, highlighting, outlining, note taking.

Example:

Paragraph 1 (two sentences): Yesterday we went to the zoo. We saw many animals.

Paragraph 2 (three sentences): On Monday we were involved in a car accident. It was a two-car collision. No one was injured in either car.

Paragraph 3 (four sentences): My favorite restaurant is the Chinese Palace. It is located in downtown Atlanta. It serves wonderful soup, eggrolls, and garlic chicken. The lunch specials are the best deals in town.

Paragraph 4 (five sentences): George Bush is the president of the United States. He lives in the White House located in Washington, D.C. He is the leader of our country. He was recently elected by the people. His term in office is four years.

Paragraph 5 (six sentences): Our house has been on the market for several months. We own a three bedroom, two bath, split level home. We have a large greatroom as well as a separate dining room. In addition, we have a two car garage and a stone fireplace. As of today, no offers have been made. We do, however, hope to have it sold by the end of the year.

Paragraph 6 (seven sentences): Across from my house there is a park. The park has recently been remodeled. In the remodeling, they replaced the swingset, sliding board, and jungle gym. In their place is shiny new equipment. There is also a picnic area and water fountain. Plans for next fall include restrooms and softball diamonds. By next year we hope to have a beautiful new facility for everyone to enjoy.

Paragraph 7 (eight sentences): On Friday night, my husband and I like to go to the movies. We usually try to make it to the early show, which usually starts around 8:00 P.M. If we are running late, however, we can almost always make it to a later showing. The box office opens around 5:00 P.M. Reserved seating is not available. Seating is first come, first served. Therefore, we always try and make it to the show a few minutes ahead of time. By arriving early, we are able to get good seats, popcorn, and soda before the movie starts.

Paragraph 8 (nine sentences): The amusement park will open this Saturday, May 14th, for weekends only. Opening hours will be from 9:00 A.M. to midnight on Saturdays. On Sunday, the park will not open until noon and

Exhibit 6A-1 continued

will close at 11:00 P.M. Beginning June 1st, the park will be open Monday through Sunday. Hours will be 9:00 A.M. to midnight daily. Because of the new rides, a large crowd is expected for the summer. Therefore, parking will be difficult. To alleviate this problem, the park has opened up lots off the immediate park grounds. Shuttles to transport you back and forth will be available during park hours.

Variations:

- Length of words within the paragraph can be varied to increase complexity.
- Types of material covered in the paragraphs can be increased in complexity. For example, paragraphs could move from personal to factual to abstract data (e.g., the above example has personal information; factual information could include a paragraph from a biographical novel; abstract material could contain information such as theories on the origin of the universe).
- Can be used as a recognition task. For example, the client can be given questions to answer about the paragraph using multiple-choice, fill-in-the-blank, or matching test items.
- Can be used as a recall task. For example, the client can be asked to write essay questions about the material.
- Can be used as a delayed recall (or recognition) task by asking the client to remember information at various time intervals (e.g., 10 minutes to weeks).
- Scoring can include percentage of information remembered in the paragraph (verbatim or gist).

Generalizations:

- Instructions: Cooking (ingredients for recipes, how to use a microwave), cleaning, safety (appliances, chemicals, emergencies), assembly (bookcases, storage boxes), installation (hanging pictures, installing an answering machine or VCR), driving (car maintenance, car wash, maps), money management (income tax returns), personal health (medications).
- Directions: Operating computers or automatic teller machines, driving to new locations.

6. Task: Immediate recall of short articles.

  Description: The client and therapist choose a short article to read. Each presentation increases in length (e.g., from 2 to 20 paragraphs), each article being exposed for the same length of time (e.g., 3 to 5 minutes). After presentation, the client can respond by writing, pointing, or reciting orally.

Exhibit 6A-1 continued

Materials: Therapists can use articles from magazines, newspapers, short stories, books, essays, poems, and so forth.

Scoring: Percentage of information remembered from the article.

Baseline: Highest percentage of material recalled from the article.

Strategies: Chunking, highlighting, note taking, outlining, reading aloud (and audiotaping for repetition).

Example: Short newspaper or magazine article.

Variations:

- Types of articles can be varied from concrete to abstract, from old information that the client already knows to entirely new information, and so forth.
- Can be used as a recognition task by giving the client multiple-choice questions to answer at the end; the client can also recall information independent of cues.
- The task can be used for delayed recall by asking the client to remember information several minutes, days, or weeks later.
- Scoring can be done with the highest percentage of information recalled (either verbatim or gist).

Generalizations: Manuals (car, appliances, computer), speeches, materials for class or work.

7. Task: Immediate recall of complex, lengthy information.

Description: The client chooses or is given a book to read. Upon completion of the book, the client summarizes the book by either a written or oral summary. The therapist may also present a written set of questions for the client to respond to by writing, pointing, or reciting orally.

Materials: Books of all types (novels, textbooks).

Scoring: Percentage of information remembered from the book.

Baseline: Highest percentage of information recalled correctly.

Strategies: Note taking, highlighting, outlining, chunking, repetition.

Example: Client is given a text on computer use to read and remember (reading for main points versus detail).

Variations:

- The task can be designed to remember details versus main points; the client can be given a particular question that he or she must read the text in order to answer; the client makes up his or her own questions after reading the text.

Exhibit 6A-1 continued

- Can be used as a recognition task by using multiple-choice questions.
- Can be used as a measure of delayed recall by testing memory after time intervals (minutes to months).

Generalizations: Classroom situations where information must be remembered, activities of daily living such as reading a novel for enjoyment, work activities such as learning information contained in a policy manual, and so forth.

VISUAL-FIGURAL TASKS

1. Task: Immediate recall of objects.

Description: The client is given several pictures of concrete objects. Each presentation of the objects increases in length of sequence (e.g., from two to nine), with each set being exposed for the same length of time (e.g., 10 to 30 seconds). Length of time can be varied with subsequent trials of the task. After presentation, the client names (either aloud or by written response) as many objects as possible.

Materials: Objects can be photographed or drawn. Materials can be presented in real-life color, black and white, or other mixtures of colors. Size can be varied.

Scoring: Highest number of objects remembered in each trial.

Baseline: Highest number of objects remembered before the first error.

Strategies: Repetition, rehearsal, visual imagery, categorization, association, loci.

Example: The following pictured objects could be presented.

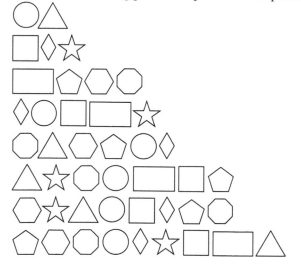

Exhibit 6A-1 continued

Variations:

- The pictured objects can increase in difficulty from concrete to abstract, related (i.e., easily categorized) to unrelated, and so forth.
- The task can be used to measure recognition (i.e., the client can be given choices from which to pick the correct objects).
- The task can be used as a delayed recall task by asking the client to remember objects at various time intervals.
- The client can be required to remember items in each trial in sequence or by placement in sequence. Using the example

the client could be asked to remember in which position the ◇ was located (first, second, or third). The location of objects can also be altered, and objects can be presented vertically, horizontally, or randomly on the page:

Two objects:

Three objects:

Four objects:

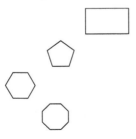

and so forth.

Exhibit 6A-1 continued

- Scoring can be done in various ways: total number of objects remembered over several trials, percentage of correct overall trials, and so forth.

Generalizations: Location of objects in the home such as keys, purse, wallet, checkbook; sequence of objects contained in stores such as location of soup in a particular grocery store aisle.

2. Task: Immediate recall of names and faces.

Description: The client is given photographs of real persons to remember. Each presentation increases in length of sequence and is exposed for the same length of time. Length of time can be varied with subsequent trials of the task. After presentation, the client recalls by either writing or reciting orally as many names as possible.

Materials: The therapist can use photographs of persons whom the client does not know; pictures can also be cut from magazines. Abstract (cartoonlike) characters can also be used. The therapist can generate these or use comic strips and similar materials.

Scoring: Highest number of names recalled in any order.

Baseline: Highest number of names recalled before the first error.

Strategies: Pegging, visual imagery, repetition, rehearsal.

Examples: Give the client one set of photographs at a time, increasing the number of photographs in each trial. Names should be varied.

Variations:

- Faces can be presented via photographs, line drawings, or pictures from magazines.
- Stimulus items can be presented with just a face or with names printed beneath the faces.
- Can be used as a recognition task (i.e., the client matches faces and names from an array of faces and names).
- The client can be given faces to recall names, or the client can be given names to recall faces (verbal description or drawing).
- Can be used as a delayed recall task by asking the client to remember names and faces at various timed intervals.

Generalizations: Remembering names of new persons or persons from the past whose names have been forgotten.

3. Task: Immediate recall of events or actions.

Description: The client is given pictures of events or actions to remember. The number of actions occurring in each picture is increased in subsequent trials,

Exhibit 6A-1 continued

with each trial being exposed for the same length of time. The client responds by initially describing the actions in the pictures and then by recalling as many details as possible.

Materials: Pictures of events such as appear in newspapers, magazines, and so forth.

Scoring: Highest amount of information recalled.

Baseline: Highest number of pieces of information recalled in each presentation.

Strategies: Association, repetition and rehearsal, visual imagery.

Example: The client is given pictures with:

- two actions: Two men are standing face to face and talking
- three actions: A man is getting out of a car, a woman is opening a door, and a child is riding a bicycle

and so forth (i.e., with number of actions increasing in subsequent trials).

Variations:

- Types of pictures can be varied from concrete to abstract; actions can be given in sequential order.
- The task can be given with or without verbal content (i.e., a newspaper article can be given with a picture describing the action that the client must remember, or a picture alone can be given for the client to interpret and remember the action).
- Can be used as a recognition task by giving the client multiple-choice questions to answer after exposure to the stimulus; the therapist can also give cues to assist in free recall (e.g., fill-in-the-blank questions).
- Can be used as a delayed recall task by asking the client to recall information at various intervals.

Generalizations: Personal events (either past or present), visual instructions (e.g., assembly of a bookcase), interpretation and memory of unknown events (e.g., seeing a bank robbery in progress).

AUDITORY-VERBAL TASKS

1. Task: Immediate recall of digits.

Description: The therapist reads several sequences of numbers to the client. Each presentation increases in length of sequence, with each sequence being exposed for the same length of time. Length of time can be varied with subsequent trials of the task. After presentation, the client can respond by writing, pointing, or reciting orally.

Exhibit 6A-1 continued

Materials: The client is not given materials; the therapist can use preprinted numbers or numbers from phone books, can create number sequences, and so forth.

Scoring: Highest number of digits recalled correctly in sequence.

Baseline: Highest correct sequence recalled before the first error.

Strategies: Repetition, rehearsal, chunking.

Example: See visual-verbal task 1 (information is presented orally versus visually).

Variations: See visual-verbal task 1 (information is presented orally versus visually).

Generalizations: See visual-verbal task 1.

2. Task: Immediate recall of letters.

Description: See visual-verbal task 2.

Materials: The therapist can use preprinted information or can create his or her own materials.

Scoring: Highest number of letters recalled in sequence.

Baseline: Highest correct sequence recalled before the first error.

Strategies: Repetition, rehearsal, chunking, note taking.

Example: See visual-verbal task 2 (information is presented orally versus visually).

Variations: See visual-verbal task 2 (information is presented orally versus visually).

Generalizations: See visual-verbal task 2.

3. Task: Immediate recall of related words.

Description: See visual-verbal task 3 (the therapist reads words rather than the client being given written information).

Materials: The therapist can use preprinted materials (workbooks, etc.) or create his or her own.

Scoring: Highest number of words recalled in sequence.

Baseline: Highest correct sequence recalled before the first error.

Strategies: Repetition, rehearsal, chunking, story making, association.

Example: See visual-verbal task 3.

Variations: See visual-verbal task 3.

Generalizations: See visual-verbal task 3.

Exhibit 6A-1 continued

4. Task: Immediate recall of sentences.
   Description: See visual-verbal task 4.
   Materials: See task 3 above.
   Scoring: Highest number of words within the sentence recalled in sequence.
   Baseline: See task 3 above.
   Strategies: See task 3 above.
   Example: See visual-verbal task 4.
   Variations: See visual-verbal task 4.
   Generalizations: See visual-verbal task 4.

5. Task: Immediate recall of paragraph-length material.
   Description: See visual-verbal task 5 (information is presented orally versus visually).
   Materials: See visual-verbal task 5.
   Scoring: See visual-verbal task 5.
   Baseline: See visual-verbal task 5.
   Strategies: Repetition, chunking, outlining, notetaking.
   Example: See visual-verbal task 5.
   Variations: See visual-verbal task 5.
   Generalizations: See visual-verbal task 5.

6. Task: Immediate recall of short articles.
   Description: See visual-verbal task 6 (information is presented orally versus visually).
   Materials: See visual-verbal task 6.
   Scoring: See visual-verbal task 6.
   Baseline: See visual-verbal task 6.
   Strategies: Chunking, note taking, audio taping, repetition, and rehearsal.
   Example: See visual-verbal task 6.
   Variations: See visual-verbal task 6.
   Generalizations: See visual-verbal task 6.

7. Task: Immediate recall of complex, lengthy information.
   Description: See visual-verbal task 7 (information is presented orally versus visually).

Exhibit 6A-1 continued

Materials: See visual-verbal task 7.
Scoring: See visual-verbal task 7.
Baseline: See visual-verbal task 7.
Strategies: Note taking, repetition, outlining, chunking.
Example: See visual-verbal task 7.
Variations: See visual-verbal task 7.
Generalizations: See visual-verbal task 7.

AUDITORY-NONVERBAL TASKS

1. Task: Immediate recall of rhythm or tones.
    Description: The client is presented a sequence of rhythm or tones. Each trial increases in length of sequence, with each trial being exposed for the same amount of time. The time sequence can be varied on subsequent presentations. After presentation, the client reproduces the tones (by humming, tapping, or playing on a musical instrument).
    Materials: The therapist can hum a sequence, tap it on a table, and so forth.
    Scoring: Highest number of tones recalled in sequence.
    Baseline: Highest number of tones recalled in sequence before the first error.
    Strategies: Repetition, rehearsal, rhythm, association.
    Example: The therapist hums sequences of notes such as:
    >high, low
    >high, high, low
    >low, high, low, high
    >low, low, high, high, low
    >high, low, low, high, high
    >high, high, low, high, high, low
    >low, low, high, high, low, low, low
    >high, low, low, high, low, low, high, high
    >high, low, high, low, high, low, high, high, high

    Variations:
    - Tones can be varied by pitch, loudness, length of note, and so forth.
    - Tones can be presented via various mediums, such as musical instruments, voice, or other sounds.

Exhibit 6A-1 continued

- Tones can be meaningful (e.g., forming phrases from a song) or nonmeaningful (random).
- Various sounds can be used (e.g., dog barking, water running, etc.).
- Can be used as a recognition task by giving the client several alternative sequences of tones from which to choose the ones originally given.
- Can be used as a delayed recall task at various time intervals.

Generalizations: Code sequences such as telephone numbers, microwave, security systems, different rings of a telephone to identify different callers, clock chimes.

2. Task: Immediate recall of songs.

   Description: The client is given songs (without words) with increasing sequences of notes to remember.

   Materials: See task 1 above.

   Scoring: Highest number of notes recalled in sequence.

   Baseline: Highest number of notes recalled in sequence before the first error.

   Strategies: Repetition, rehearsal, chunking, rhythm.

   Example: The client is given a song (no words) with two, three, four, and so forth phrases to reproduce.

   Variations: See task 1 above.

   Generalizations: See task 1 above.

Exhibit 6A-2

Listing of Materials and Manufacturers

GENERAL MATERIALS

Calendars
Comic Strips
Directions (cooking, to a location, etc.)
Essays
Flashcards (letters, numbers, words)
Instructions
Lists
Magazines
Manuals
Newspapers
Novels
Phone book
Photographs
Pictures
Poems
Recipes
Short stories
Social security cards
Songs
Textbooks
Workbooks

MANUFACTURERS

Anderson, Kathleen, and Pamela Crowe Miller. *Lessons for the Right Brain: Memory Workbook.* Austin: PRO-ED, 1985.

Anderson, Kathleen, and Pamela Crowe Miller. *Lessons for the Right Brain: Reading and Writing Workbook.* Austin: PRO-ED, 1985.

Brubaker, Susan Howell. *Workbook for Aphasia: Exercises for the Redevelopment of Higher Level Language Function.* Rev. ed. Detroit: Wayne State University Press, 1985.

Brubaker, Susan Howell. *Workbook for Language Skills: Exercises for Written and Verbal Expression.* Detroit: Wayne State University Press, 1983.

Brubaker, Susan Howell. *Workbook for Reasoning Skills: Exercises for Cognitive Rehabilitation.* Detroit: Wayne State University Press, 1983.

Exhibit 6A-2 continued

Craine, James F., and Howard E. Gudeman. *The Rehabilitation of Brain Functions: Principles, Procedures, and Techniques of Neurotraining.* Springfield, Ill.: Charles C. Thomas, 1981.

Goldstein, Edith, and Ann Ivins. *Go: Level EA.* Huntington, N.Y.: McGraw-Hill, 1966.

Goldstein, Edith, and Jane Lecht. *Go: Level DA.* Huntington, N.Y.: McGraw-Hill, 1966.

Goldstein, Edith, and George Riemer. *Go: Level FA.* Huntington, N.Y.: McGraw-Hill, 1966.

Goldstein, Edith, and George D. Spache. *Go: Level CA.* Huntington, N.Y.: McGraw-Hill, 1966.

Goldstein, Edith, and George D. Spache. *Go: Levels RA and AA.* Huntington, N.Y.: McGraw-Hill, 1965.

Granowsky, Alvin, and Stephen Tompkins. *Building Reading Rate: Speed with Comprehension.* Cleveland: Modern Curriculum Press, 1983.

Haradek, Anita. *Critical Thinking: Book One.* Pacific Grove, Calif.: Midwest Publications, 1980.

Haradek, Anita. *Critical Thinking: Book Two.* Pacific Grove, Calif.: Midwest Publications, 1980.

Hulloran, Sharon, and Elizabeth Bressler. *Cognitive Reorganization: A Stimulus Handbook.* Austin: PRO-ED, 1983.

Keith, Robert L. *Speech and Language Rehabilitation.* Danville, Ill.: Interstate Printers and Publishers, 1987.

Keith, Robert L. *Speech and Language Rehabilitation.* Vol. 2. Danville, Ill.: Interstate Printers and Publishers, 1987.

Kilpatrick, Katherine. *Therapy Guide for the Adult with Language and Speech Disorders.* Vol. 2. Akron, Ohio: Visiting Nurse Service, 1979.

Kilpatrick, Katherine, and Cynthia L. Jones. *Therapy Guide for the Adult with Language and Speech Disorders.* Vol. 1. Akron, Ohio: Visiting Nurse Service, 1977.

Martinoff, James T., Rosemary Martinoff, and Virginia Stokke. *Language Rehabilitation: Auditory Comprehension.* Austin: PRO-ED, 1981.

Martinoff, James T., Rosemary Martinoff, and Virginia Stokke. *Language Rehabilitation: Verbal Expression.* Austin: PRO-ED, 1981.

Morganstein, Shirley, and Marilyn Certner Smith. *Thematic Language Stimulation: A Workbook for Aphasics and Their Clinicians.* Tucson: Communication Skill Builders, 1982.

Reitan Neuropsychology Laboratory. *REHABIT* 1338 E. Edison Street, Tucson, AZ 85719.

Strickland, Dorothy S. *Language for Daily Use.* New York: Harcourt Brace Jovanovich, 1983.

Tomlin, Kathryn J. *Workbook of Activities for Language and Cognition.* Moline, Ill.: Linguisystems, 1984.

Wright, Josephine L., Edith Goldstein, and George D. Spache. *Go: Level BA.* Huntington, N.Y.: McGraw-Hill, 1966.

Appendix 6B
Three-Dimensional Tasks

This appendix contains the following exhibits:

- **Exhibit 6B-1** Sample Three-Dimensional Tasks
- **Exhibit 6B-2** Lists of Materials and Manufacturers

INTRODUCTION

Appendix 6B closely follows the format established in Appendix 6A. It contains two exhibits: a listing of sample three-dimensional tasks, and a listing of materials and manufacturers.

The sample tasks listed in Exhibit 6B-1 are designed to follow the Eight-Step Model presented and discussed in Chapter 5. The tasks are organized into four sections: visual-verbal, visual-figural, auditory-verbal, and auditory-nonverbal. Within each section, tasks are listed in a hierarchical manner, moving from simple to more complex tasks.

1. *Visual-verbal.* These are tasks that consist of verbal content (e.g., words, numbers, and sentences) and are presented to the client visually (that is, the client reads the information to be remembered).

2. *Visual-figural.* These are tasks that consist of nonverbal content (e.g., figures, drawings, photographs, faces, maps, and designs) and are presented to the client visually (that is, the client looks at the information to be remembered).

3. *Auditory-Verbal.* These are tasks that consist of verbal content (e.g., words, numbers, and sentences) and are presented to the client orally (that is, the therapist uses a tape recorder, videotape, or some similar format to present the information aloud that the client is to remember). Virtually any task listed in the auditory-verbal section of Appendix 6A can be adapted to a three-dimensional task by employing a tape recorder or similar aid to present the auditory stimulus.

4. *Auditory-nonverbal.* These are tasks that consist of nonverbal content (e.g., tones, noises, and instrumental music). The therapist presents the stimulus and the client listens (via musical instrument, tape recorder, game, and so forth), and the client is asked to remember it.

Within each of the sections described above, the sample tasks are organized in a manner similar to that in the beginning of Appendix 6A (Exhibit 6A-1). To review:

1. *Task.* This is a broad, general statement describing what the client is being asked to remember. Even though this is listed first, therapists are reminded that the primary emphasis in our treatment model is the acquisition and generalization of skills. Tasks are simply provided as means to an end, not ends in and of themselves. The client may set a short-term goal of acquiring a certain amount of proficiency with this task; the long-term goal, however, may be to enhance recall of verbal information or to enhance the ability to recall a social security card number.

2. *Description.* The description provides brief information about how the task is executed (that is, how it is presented to the client). These are only suggested methods; therapists are encouraged to modify and adapt procedures as needed for individual clients.

3. *Materials.* All the tasks in this section employ some type of three-dimensional object (blocks, puzzles, designs, game boards, tape recorders, videotapes, playing cards, and so forth). Materials needed to complete a task are listed. Again, the therapist may feel free to adapt available materials to suit client needs. Exhibit 6B-2 lists resources to obtain the materials described.

   As stated previously, it is recommended that the therapist proceed from concrete materials to abstract materials. It is also recommended that the therapist consider parallel forms of the same task. Almost every task described in Appendix 6B has a parallel task employing pencil and paper or computer materials. This work on parallel tasks enables the therapist to assess the extent to which the client is transferring information from one milieu to another and to assist the client in practicing this transference.

4. *Scoring.* Samples are given for scoring each task. The therapist may choose to vary the method of scoring to suit the needs of individual clients.

5. *Baseline.* The baseline score provides a reference point from which the client and therapist can measure progress. The therapist and client should decide on the nature of the measure to be taken and then proceed to establish the baseline using this measure. Examples of baseline measures include the highest performance on trials before errors are made.

6. *Strategies.* A number of strategies appropriate to each task are given; this list is not, however, comprehensive. Working together, the client and therapist may select one (or more) of these strategies or develop some other strategy that is more appropriate. Refer to Chapter 7 for more complete information about teaching strategies.

7. *Example.* Where appropriate, some sample task items have been given. Again, these examples serve as models for the therapist.

8. *Variations*. Virtually every task listed can be varied in innumerable ways: The length of exposure can be shortened or lengthened; the number of stimuli can be increased or decreased; a delay or interference material can be introduced between stimulus and response; the nature of the response can be varied (recall versus recognition); and so forth.

9. *Generalizations*. In this section, a number of appropriate generalizations to real-life situations are suggested. The therapist and particularly the client may develop several more generalizations on the basis of specific needs. This generalization is the ultimate goal of working on the task. While the short-term goal may have been to increase the number of digits that could be recalled in sequence, the long-term goal is generalizing this information to real-life situations, such as recalling a phone number, a social security number, and so forth.

Exhibit 6B-2 includes a list of materials cited for use in the three-dimensional tasks as well as information about their manufacturers or suppliers (including addresses and phone numbers where appropriate). The information listed is current at the time this book went to press; because companies may change ownership, addresses, or phone numbers or go out of business completely, we cannot ensure that the information will remain current.

Therapists are encouraged to write or call companies and to obtain catalogs from which to choose materials most applicable to individual settings and for use with particular client populations.

Exhibit 6B-1

Sample Three-Dimensional Tasks

VISUAL-VERBAL TASKS

1. Task: Immediate recall of digits.

   Description: A series of cards or blocks is placed in front of the client. Each presentation of numbers increases in length of sequence (e.g., from two to nine) and in length of presentation (10 to 30 seconds). After presentation, the client responds by either writing or reciting the sequence orally.

   Materials: Flash cards or blocks with numbers on them, or a deck of cards.

   Scoring: Highest number of digits recalled in sequence.

   Baseline: Highest number of digits recalled before the first error.

   Strategies: Repetition, rehearsal, chunking.

   Example: The following numbers can be represented.

   7 4
   6 1 5
   3 7 9 4
   6 3 0 2 8
   8 2 1 5 7 4
   1 9 4 8 2 7 3
   5 0 2 1 8 3 9 4
   2 8 1 9 3 6 7 5 4

   Variations:

   - A deck of cards (or some portion of a deck) can be placed on the table. The client is asked to recognize individual pairs by turning over two cards at a time.

   - The client can be asked to recall the previous card or block after the next one is shown.

   - The client can be asked to create the same sequence using blocks, cards, or other materials.

   - Can be used as a recognition task by giving the client a written list of numbers that includes the original numbers along with others. The client is then asked to choose the correct numbers.

   - Can be used as a delayed recall task by asking the client to recall the numbers at various time intervals (e.g., 10 minutes to weeks).

   - Scoring can be done with the highest number of correct responses, whether or not they are in the correct sequence.

Exhibit 6B-1 continued

Generalizations: Recall of phone numbers, social security card numbers, automatic teller machine numbers, birthdays, anniversaries, date of accident, security system codes.

2. Task: Immediate recall of letters.

Description: See task 1 above.

Materials: Alphabet flash cards or Scrabble® tiles.

Scoring: See task 1.

Baseline: See task 1.

Strategies: See task 1.

Example:

E G

R L B

N P Q W

O S L T E

J A C O X P

V E Y N K W L

P R Q B N I O V

D I F O G H U Z R

Variations:

- Use Scrabble® tiles to create words of increasing length (e.g., *go, hit, cart,* and so forth).
- Present flash cards or Scrabble® tiles in mixed-up order. Ask the client to recall the letters and to unscramble them to create a word.

Generalizations: Addresses, license plates, word processing file codes, car registration plate information.

3. Task: Immediate recall of related words.

Description: The client is given cards with various words printed on them. Each presentation of words increases in length of sequence (e.g., from two to nine) and in length of presentation (e.g., 10 to 30 seconds). After presentation, the client can respond by writing, pointing, or reciting orally.

Materials: Set of cards with common words printed on them (can be made by the therapist) or Scrabble® tiles.

Scoring: See task 1.

Baseline: See task 1.

Strategies: Repetition, rehearsal, chunking/categorizing, association.

Exhibit 6B-1 continued

Example: Using the category of food, the following words could be given.

ketchup, mustard

bread, muffins, rolls

milk, butter, eggs, yogurt

ice cream, pie, cake, cookies, candy

chips, dip, crackers, cheese, peanuts, popcorn

flour, salt, pepper, sugar, oil, vinegar, syrup

cherries, oranges, bananas, peaches, pears, apricots, tangerines, grapefruit

potatoes, lettuce, tomatoes, carrots, onions, cucumbers, radishes, mushrooms, beans

Variations:

- The client can be asked to group words within categories (e.g., by function, physical property, and so forth).
- The client can be given a set of word cards, some of which belong to a category and some of which do not, and then asked to recall the words that belong in the category or the words that do not belong in the category.
- The client can be asked to recall the words randomly rather than sequentially.
- Can be used as a recognition task. The client is given a written list of related words that include the original list and extra words (from the same category) and is asked to choose the correct words. This task also provides interference.
- Another variation of a recognition task is to provide the client with several options from which to choose the correct words.
- Can be used as a delayed recall task by asking the client to recall the words at various time intervals (e.g., 10 minutes to weeks).
- Scoring can be done with the highest number of correct responses, whether or not they are recalled in sequence. Overall scores can also be given (e.g., the percentage of correct words recalled out of the total words presented).

Generalizations: Recall of lists (to-do lists, appointments, chores, shopping), names of people, medications.

VISUAL-FIGURAL TASKS

1. Task: Immediate recall of concrete objects.

Exhibit 6B-1 continued

Description: The client is shown a specific number of items (e.g., from two to nine) for a specific amount of time and is then asked to recall as many of the objects as possible.

Materials: Blocks of different colors and/or different shapes (such as those used in the game Perfection®); concrete objects such as pencil, book, comb.

Scoring: Highest number of objects recalled.

Baseline: Highest number of objects recalled before the first error.

Strategies: Repetition, rehearsal, visual imagery, association, loci.

Example: The following objects could be presented.

> comb, pencil
>
> pen, button, paper
>
> paper clip, rubber band, stapler, eraser
>
> highlighter, calculator, tape, note pad, brush
>
> keys, appointment card, folder, pencil, pen, comb
>
> book, feather, leaf, wallet, coin, glasses, key
>
> pencil, comb, brush, key, wallet, calculator, note pad, eraser
>
> computer disk, calendar, note pad, comb, pencil, stapler, book, flashlight, folder

Variations:

- Can be used as a visual sequential memory task, i.e., the client can recall shapes in a sequence. For example, a number of colored blocks (e.g., two to nine) are placed in a row in front of the client. After a set period of time (e.g., five to 60 seconds), the blocks are removed and the client reproduces the colors of the blocks in sequence.

- Can be used as a recognition task. The therapist can present an array of objects for a brief period of time (e.g., 10 to 60 seconds), then add several objects and ask the client to identify those that originally had been shown. For example, using four shapes from the Perfection® game for the stimulus, four other Perfection® game shapes can be added, and the client asked to identify the original four shapes shown.

- Can be used as a visual-spatial task. The therapist places various objects around the room and after a set interval (one to 10 minutes) asks the client to remember the locations of each object in the room.

- Can be used as a delayed recall task by asking the client to recall the items at various time intervals (e.g., 10 minutes to weeks).

- The client can be required to remember items in each trial in the sequence that were placed on the table (e.g., which was the first item placed on the

Exhibit 6B-1 continued

table, the second, and so forth). The client can also be asked to identify the location of each object on the table (e.g., the comb in the upper right corner, the pen in the lower left corner, and so forth).

Generalizations: Identifying the location of items such as keys, wallet, checkbook; correct sequencing of visual items such as the location of the dairy, produce, and meat sections of a grocery store.

2. Task: Immediate recall of events or actions.

Description: The client is shown a sequence of actions using slides. Presentation may vary by the number of events or actions (from two to nine) and by length of exposure (10 to 60 seconds). After presentation, the client is asked to recall as many actions as possible.

Materials: Slides, videotapes of events or actions, picture cards.

Scoring: Highest number of actions recalled.

Baseline: Highest number of actions recalled before the first error.

Strategies: Visual imagery, association, loci, note taking, repetition.

Example: The client is shown a slide, picture, or videotape with two actions occurring (perhaps a man and woman talking and a child playing on a swing). The next presentation would be with three actions occurring (perhaps a picture of a picnic with people eating, playing ball, and swimming).

Variations:

- Can be used for delayed recall of the content of a videotape of daily news.
- The content of slides can be varied to include places, people, and can include concrete or abstract information.
- The client may recall events or actions in sequence.
- Can be used as a recognition task by giving the client a written list of actions that include the actions from the slides as well as other actions. The client is asked to select those actions that were shown on the slide.
- Can be used for delayed recall by asking the client to recall the actions shown at various time intervals (e.g., 10 minutes to weeks).

Generalizations: Preparation for return to classroom setting, recall of daily news and weather, recall of personal events (either past or present).

3. Task: Immediate recall of figural or abstract information.

Description: The client is shown a concrete design for a set period of time (e.g., five to 15 seconds) and is then asked to reproduce the target design using pegs, blocks, etc.

Exhibit 6B-1 continued

Materials: Block designs and blocks, pegboards, checkers.

Scoring: Percentage of design accurately reproduced.

Baseline: Highest number of blocks or pegs correctly placed before the first error.

Strategies: Visual imagery, association, note taking, rehearsal, repetition.

Example: Using pegboard designs, the client is given a one-color, four-peg design to observe for 10 seconds. The client is then asked to recreate the design on the pegboard.

Variations:

- Can be used for a recall task. Use a checkerboard and checkers to create an increasingly lengthy pattern on a checkerboard (e.g., 2 to 12 checkers). The client views the pattern for a set period of time (e.g., 5 to 60 seconds), the checkers are removed, and the client duplicates the design. This same task could be done with a pegboard and pegs, with a Lite Brite® board and pegs, a Battleship® game board, or tangrams (a set of wooden or plastic shapes that can be used to create various designs).
- Can also be used as a recognition task by asking the client to choose the target design from several choices.
- The number of blocks or pegs can be varied, as can the complexity of the design.
- The design patterns can be concrete (e.g., large designs with black lines outlining each block in the design) or abstract (e.g., smaller than actual size designs and component parts are not outlined on the grid).
- The client can remember the design either by assembling it after exposure or by remembering it without assembly.
- Designs can be assembled from identical models or from two-dimensional representations.

Generalizations: Identifying places, names, locations, and so forth; locating objects (wallet, keys, calendar).

4. Task: Recall of locations of items.

   Description: The therapist traces a route on a simple map with the number of turns increasing (e.g., from two to nine). The client is asked to trace the route after a brief interval (e.g., 5 to 60 seconds).

   Materials: Map drawn by the therapist, three-dimensional relief map, atlas.

   Scoring: The number of turns completed successfully in sequence.

   Baseline: The number of turns correctly completed in sequence before the first error.

Exhibit 6B-1 continued

Strategies: Visual imagery, association, repetition, rehearsal, note taking, verbalization.

Example: Draw a simple map of two streets running east-west and intersected by two streets running north-south. Label each street. If desired, indicate north, south, east, and west on the map. The therapist draws, or asks the client to draw, a route. The client must then recreate the route from memory.

Variations:

- The type of information can be varied (i.e., streets, stores, addresses, highways).
- The complexity of the map can be increased from simple (e.g., four to eight streets) to complex (e.g., a regular city map).
- Can be combined with a verbal memory task by having the client take notes on more complicated routes and memorize them.

Generalizations: Finding directions within the treatment facility or around the home and neighborhood, following directions to various locations.

AUDITORY-VERBAL TASKS

Virtually every task included in the visual-verbal section above can be adapted to auditory-verbal tasks by the use of an audiotape or videotape for stimulus presentation. Some advantages of using audiotape and videotape are consistency of stimulus (the rate of presentation is always the same), provision of a practice tool for the client, and possibly increased ability to concentrate (sometimes the client may find it easier to focus on a television screen than to focus on a therapist's voice). See Chapters 7 and 8 for more information on audiotaping.

AUDITORY-NONVERBAL TASKS

1. Task: Immediate recall of tones.

Description: Using Simon® or a musical instrument, the client is presented a sequence of tones increasing in length (e.g., from two to nine) and time of exposure. After presentation, the client reproduces the sequence.

Materials: Simon®, musical instrument (such as piano, guitar, drum, or any instrument with which the client is familiar).

Scoring: Highest number of tones reproduced in sequence.

Baseline: Highest number of tones produced in sequence before the first error.

Exhibit 6B-1 continued

Strategies: Repetition, rehearsal, rhythm, association.

Example: Using a keyboard, the therapist can play a sequence of notes.

C G

G E C

C B A G

C E G C G

C D E D C E

G C A F E C G

C G E C E G C G

C E G C B A G E C

Variations:

- On the basis of the method of presentation, the therapist can vary the time interval between tone presentations and time to recall.
- The tones can be varied by pitch, loudness, length of note, and so forth.
- Tones can be meaningful (e.g., forming a tune or song) or nonmeaningful (random).
- Can be used as a recognition task by presenting the same or a slightly varied sequence and asking the client to identify whether the sequences are the same or different.
- Can be used for immediate (or delayed) recall of rhythm by using a tapping board or Morse code board to present a sequence of taps in rhythm. The client recreates the sequence either immediately or with delay.

Generalizations: Remembering code sequences such as phone numbers, security systems on home or car, different rings of the telephone to identify different recipients of the call, clock chimes.

Exhibit 6B-2

Listing of Materials and Manufacturers

GENERAL MATERIALS

Audiotape recorder and tapes
Battleship®
Blocks and designs
Checkers and checkerboard
Coins
Colored cubes
Computer and programs
Concrete objects (pens, comb, books, etc.)
Designs (abstract)
Flash cards (numbers, letters, words)
Lite Brite®
Magic Mosaics®
Maps
Mastermind®
Memory®
Modeling clay
Musical instruments
Pegboard (pegs, designs)
Perfection®
Playing cards
Puzzles
Scrabble®
Simon®
Slides and slide projector
Superfection®
Tangrams (blocks and cards)
Television and VCR (videotapes)
Videocameras

MANUFACTURERS

1. Discovery Toys (Consult local phone books under *Discovery Toys* for the name
   and address of your local distributor).

Exhibit 6B-2 continued

- Magic Mosaics®. Consists of a six-sided plastic board; blue, green, yellow, and red trapezoid blocks; and a series of intricate designs that can be built within the board. Can be used as a visual memory task.

2. Developmental Leaning Materials (DLM)
   P.O. Box 4000
   One DLM Park
   Allen, TX 75002
   (800) 527-4747 [in Texas, (800) 442-4711]

- Animals in place (Pictures of animals and boards). Can be used for visual-figural memory tasks of recall and recognition.
- Associations (sets 1 and 2). Consists of 50 cards that can be combined to create 25 functional associations such as baby/crib. Can be used for practice in developing associations and for visual-figural memory tasks of recognition and recall.
- Auditory familiar sounds. Consists of 50 familiar sounds on a recording that can be matched with black-and-white drawings. Can be used for auditory-verbal memory practice.
- Categories. Three sets of cards: foods and animals (100 cards), clothing and household items (100 cards), and varied (70 cards). Can be used to teach classification and categorization; can be used for visual-figural memory tasks of recognition and recall.
- Functions. Consists of 14 sets of five cards each. Can be used to teach classification and categorization; can also be used for visual-figural memory tasks.
- Lite Brite®. Similar to a pegboard. Designs are created with plastic pegs on a black background. The board can be lit up, which creates greater visual impact. Can be used for visual-figural memory tasks of recognition and recall.
- Pegboard, pegs, designs, and blank peg pad. A board consisting of ten rows of ten holes each. Designs are created by placing pegs in holes according to a given design. Colors of pegs and complexity of designs vary. Can be used for visual-figural memory tasks of recognition and recall.
- Tangram designs and puzzle cards. Consists of seven varied shapes and 27 designs that can be made using the shapes. Can be used for more abstract visual memory tasks.
- Visual matching, memory, and sequencing exercises. A series of six books for practice in matching colors, shapes, designs, and so forth. Can be used as a visual recognition task.

Exhibit 6B-2 continued

- Visual memory cards, sets I (colors), II (objects), III (shapes), and IV (letters). Flash cards. Can be used for visual-verbal and visual-figural recall and recognition tasks.
- Visual sequential memory exercises. Thirty visual memory exercises progressing from shapes to letters. Can be used for visual-verbal and visual-figural recall and recognition tasks.

3. Lakeshore Learning Materials
   2695 E. Dominguez Street
   P.O. Box 6261
   Carson, CA 90749

   - Colored cubes and two-dimensional colored block designs. Can be used for visual-figural memory tasks of recognition and recall.

4. Milton Bradley
   443 Shaker Road
   East Long Meadow, MA 01101

   - Battleship®. Double board game. Players place plastic ships on their grids. The opposing player tries to locate his or her opponent's ships. Can be used as a visual memory task by having the client duplicate a design after brief exposure to the grid.
   - Memory®. Various games at different age levels. Consists of matched pairs of cards placed face down on the table. The player attempts to match pairs by turning two cards at a time. Can be used as a visual-figural memory task for location.
   - Perfection®. Game consisting of 25 small plastic shapes to be inserted in a game board under a time limit. The shapes, without the game board, can be used for visual-figural memory tasks of sequencing, recognition, and recall.
   - Puzzles of the United States, continents, the world, and so forth. Can be used for visual-figural memory tasks.
   - Scrabble®. Board game using letter tiles to create words. Game tiles can be used for visual-verbal memory tasks.
   - Simon®. Electronic game with several skill levels (battery operated) that produces a sequence of sounds. The player repeats the sequence by pressing the correct colored sections of the game board. Can be used as an auditory-nonverbal memory task.
   - Superfection®. Similar to Perfection® described above, but shapes are more complex.

Exhibit 6B-2 continued

5. Modern Educational Corporation
   P.O. Box 721
   Tulsa, Oklahoma 74101

   - PEP. Auditory Perceptual Enhancement Program Vol. 1. Consists of nine audio cassette tapes which provide exercises to develop memory through use of the chunking strategy.

6. Pressman Toy Corporation
   200 Fifth Avenue
   New York, NY 10012

   - Classic Concentration®. Board game based on a television game show in which players attempt to match pairs by uncovering two board locations at the same time. As matches are made, a rebus puzzle is revealed, which the player attempts to solve. Can be used as a visual-figural memory task.
   - Mastermind®. Player places pegs of specific colors in specific locations. Opposing player attempts to identify the color and location of the pegs by a trial-and-error deductive reasoning process. Can be used as a visual-figural memory task by having the client recreate the color sequence after brief exposure.

7. PRO-ED
   8700 Shoal Creek Boulevard
   Houston, TX 78758-9965
   (512) 451-3246

   - Photo resource kit. Consists of three sets of photographs: nouns, verbs, and prepositions. The noun/object set consists of photographs of common items (furniture, clothing, utensils, and so forth); the verb and preposition sets consist of photographs of children and adults in action settings. Can be used for visual-figural memory and for memory of actions or events.

Appendix 6C
Computerized Tasks

This appendix contains the following exhibits:

- **Exhibit 6C-1** Listing of Computer Programs
- **Exhibit 6C-2** Listing of Manufacturers

INTRODUCTION

Before using this appendix, it is recommended that clinicians read this section to obtain an overview of what is included and how to use the materials. Exhibit 6C-1 is a list of computer tasks and Exhibit 6C-2 is a list of computer manufacturers.

Exhibit 6C-1: Computer Tasks

The materials presented in this section are not organized in the same manner as those in Appendixes 6A and 6B. Rather, because of the large variety of software available, materials are listed in a more general fashion. When using these computer programs, therapists can use the sample tasks provided in Chapters 5 and 6 and in Appendixes 6A and 6B as models.

The various computer software programs presented can be adapted and varied for use with clients. The information presented in this section is the most up-to-date available as this book goes to press; however, because software companies frequently move, change names, or disappear altogether, we cannot take responsibility for the continued accuracy of the information (i.e., offerings, pricing, addresses, etc.).

We have surveyed the literature and attempted to provide as many software programs for memory as possible. This list is not all-inclusive, however, and therapists are encouraged to seek out additional resources. Also, we have purposely not recommended any particular programs; inclusion of a program does not constitute an endorsement. Therapists are encouraged to review programs and determine the appropriateness for their client populations.

The list of computerized task programs is organized in the following way.

1. *Title*. This is the name of the disk. In some cases, individual programs contained on disks are also presented and follow the main listing. Programs are listed alphabetically.

2. *Company*. This is the name of the manufacturer or distributor.

3. *Level*. There is no consistent rating system for various types of software. Some manufacturers list grade level, others list age appropriateness, and others list nothing at all. We have given the manufacturers' ratings, when available, but therapists should use caution in relying on these. Ratings may or may not be applicable and transferable to all rehabilitation settings. For example, a 30-year-old traumatic brain injury survivor may not possess the cognitive strength to perform a task that a manufacturer has rated at a third-grade level. Therapists are encouraged to explore various software and adapt programs as needed to meet the needs of their individual clients.

4. *Description*. We have used descriptions from the manufacturers. As will be noted, some of these are more elaborate than others, and some are virtually nonexistent. Descriptions are usually general rather than specific.

5. *Compatibility*. This information is provided by the manufacturers and describes what hardware will operate the software. See the discussion in Chap-ter 6 regarding availability of software for Apple computers.

6. *Requirements*. If any additional hardware is needed to operate programs, it is listed in this section. Examples include joystick, color monitor, and so forth. If manufacturers do not list any requirements, the section indicates "none listed." Clinicians who are considering purchase of any software listed in this section are encouraged to also explore additional hardware needed to operate the programs. Also, some clients may need special hardware adaptations. Therapists will need to contact manufacturers to determine compatibility issues.

7. *Price*. The most recent information available from manufacturers is listed. These data are subject to change but are current as this text goes to press. In some cases prices were not available, and this is indicated.

Exhibit 6C-2 includes a list of manufacturers or suppliers from whom the software presented in Exhibit 6C-1 can be purchased. Addresses are included as well as phone numbers where appropriate and available. The listings are the most up-to-date as this book goes to press.

Exhibit 6C-1

Listing of Computer Programs

1. Title: *Animal Hotel.*

   Company: Merit Software.

   Level: Not listed.

   Description: Memory game similar to Concentration®, uses animals staying in hotels.

   Compatibility: IBM and compatibles.

   Requirements: None listed.

   Price: Not available.

2. Title: *Best 100.*

   Company: Advantage Computing.

   Level: Older children and adults (age).

   Description: Various programs that address functional activities such as generation of shopping lists, calendars, and so forth.

   Compatibility: Apple II family, IBM PC, Macintosh, Commodore 64.

   Requirements: None listed.

   Price: $39.95 (plus shipping and handling). Slightly higher in Canada. Additional $5.00 for 3.5" disks.

3. Title: *Bounce.*

   Company: Sunburst Communications.

   Level: Mild to moderate (difficulty).

   Description: A series of balls bounce up into the air, and clients are expected to use recognition and memory skills to determine which ball will fall next.

   Compatibility: 64K Apple family, 128K IBM PC or PCjr, 256K IBM PS/2 model 25, 256K Tandy 1000.

   Requirements: Apple, operates with regular keyboard or Muppet learning keys; IBM, color graphics card required.

   Price: $65.00.

4. Title: *Brain Train.*

   Company: Rehabilitation Psychology Associates.

   Level: Not listed.

   Description: A series of 55 programs that address many cognitive limitations including visual and verbal memory. Available in Spanish and English.

   Compatibility: IBM PC with 3.5" or 5.25" disk drive.

Exhibit 6C-1 continued

Requirements: None listed.

Price: Not available.

5. Title: *Cognitive Disorders: disk 4: Memory for Pictures.*

   Company: Parrot Software.

   Level: Children and adults (age).

   Description: Addresses the basic skills for memory (i.e., improving concentration and increasing attention) as well as short-term memory.

   Compatibility: Apple II and IBM.

   Requirements: None listed.

   Price: $99.50.

6. Title: *Cognitive Rehabilitation Series.*

   Company: Hartley Courseware, Inc.

   Level: Not listed.

   Description: Consists of program disks in four areas: categorization, sequencing, association, and memory (as well as an authoring program disk in the licensed version for individualizing or expanding the four program areas). The memory disk ranges from simple recognition of two or three words to recall of paragraphs.

   Compatibility: Apple II+, IIe, IIe (48K); IBM PC (128K)

   Requirements: None listed.

   Price: $195.00 (nonlicensed), $595.00 (licensed).

7. Title: *Cogrehab,* volume 1.

   Company: Life Science Associates.

   Level: Not listed.

   Description: Focuses on memory and perception with eight tasks. The programs focus on speed reading of word lists, reaction time to visual stimuli, speed of shape matching, free memory recall, memory span capacity, mnemonic memory for word series, nonverbal sequenced memory.

   Compatibility: Apple family.

   Requirements: None listed.

   Price: Not listed.

8. Title: *Cogrehab,* volume 2.

   Company: Life Science Associates.

   Level: Not listed.

   Description: A training program for visual perception and memory. The program provides six tasks focusing on line bisection and vertical lines, eye

Exhibit 6C-1 continued

movement exercises with horizontal scanning, nonverbal shape matching, visual search for unusual shapes, and single and double simultaneous stimulation.

Compatibility: Apple family.

Requirements: None listed.

Price: Not listed.

9. Title: *Cogrehab,* volume 3.

Company: Life Science Associates

Level: Not listed.

Description: Consists of five tasks: immediate memory recall, associative memory recall, recall of block patterns, advanced verbal memory exercise, and reading memory exercises.

Compatibility: Apple family.

Requirements: None listed.

Price: Not listed.

10. Title: *CREATE.*

Company: CREATE.

Level: Not listed.

Description: Includes six areas: orientation, visual memory, visual discrimination, visual-motor integration, visual-spatial concepts, and visual organization. Visual memory provides practice in length of exposure time and complexity of figures and numbers as well as words for memory retention.

Compatibility: Apple family.

Requirements: None listed.

Price: Not listed.

11. Title: *The Einstein Memory Trainer.*

Company: The Einstein Corporation (distributed by Preface).

Level: Children to adults (age).

Description: Five lessons that present and give practice in various memory strategies, including pegging and loci.

Compatibility: Apple II, Atari.

Requirements: None listed.

Price: Not listed.

12. Title: *FASTREAD.*

Company: Life Science Associates.

Exhibit 6C-1 continued

> *Level:* Not listed.
>
> *Description:* Brief visual memory exercises. The computer flashes a word and asks the client to type it on the keyboard. Display time will speed up if the response is correct and will slow down if it is incorrect. The number of trials, number of words per trial, display time, and word lists can be input.
>
> *Compatibility:* Not listed.
>
> *Requirements:* None listed.
>
> *Price:* $50.00.

13. Title: *Figural Memory.*

    > *Company:* KLS Cognitive Educational System.
    >
    > *Level:* Not listed.
    >
    > *Description:* Consists of six programs addressing memory for figural units, classes, relations, systems transformations, and implications. Varying levels of difficulty for each program. Also includes immediate data analysis feedback for client.
    >
    > *Compatibility:* IBM PC.
    >
    > *Requirements:* None listed.
    >
    > *Price:* $100.00 (or $225.00 for set of three: *Figural Memory, Symbolic Memory,* and *Semantic Memory*).

14. Title: *FREEREC.*

    > *Company:* Life Science Associates.
    >
    > *Level:* Not listed.
    >
    > *Description:* Consists of 12 lists of 12 words each to measure short- and long-term retention of information. After each list is presented on the screen, the client is asked to recall the words on the list. On half the trials, the client reads an additional list of words before recall. On the other half there is an equal time delay, but no alternative list is given.
    >
    > *Compatibility:* Apple II, IIc, IIe, IIgs; IBM PC and compatibles.
    >
    > *Requirements:* None listed.
    >
    > *Price:* $40.00.

15. Title: *FRSELF.*

    > *Company:* Life Science Associates.
    >
    > *Level:* Not listed.
    >
    > *Description:* Similar to *FREEREC* above.
    >
    > *Compatibility:* Apple IIc, IIe, IIgs; IBM PC, XT, AT.
    >
    > *Requirements:* None listed.
    >
    > *Price:* $50.00.

Exhibit 6C-1 continued

16. Title: *Homework Coach.*

    Company: American Guidance Service.

    Level: School-age and above (age).

    Description: Provides memory tips for study skills.

    Compatibility: Not listed.

    Requirements: Optional: video, teacher's guide, student workbook.

    Price: kit, $125.00; teacher's guide, $12.95; student workbook, $9.95.

17. Title: *KLS disk 1.*

    Company: KLS Cognitive Educational System.

    Level: Young children to adults (age).

    Description: Several programs on various aspects of memory. This missing-number program displays oversized numbers (0 to 9) sequentially or randomly. The client must identify the missing number after the sequence is completed.

    Compatibility: Apple IIe.

    Requirements: None listed.

    Price: $65.00 ($50.00 if purchased with other disks).

18. Title: *KLS disk 2 (Traveling On).*

    Company: KLS Cognitive Educational System.

    Level: Young children to adults (age).

    Description: Computer and client alternately list items that are to be taken on a trip. The objective is to recall the entire list in order as each pair of items is added.

    Compatibility: Apple IIe.

    Requirements: None listed.

    Price: $65.00 ($50.00 if purchased with other disks).

19. Title: *KLS disk three (Gold Rush).*

    Company: KLS Cognitive Educational System.

    Level: Older children to adults (age).

    Description: Board game. The objective is to win $1 million by answering questions. The program taps long-term memory for math, sequencing, proverbs, and so forth. Files can be changed or added using the file manager program.

    Compatibility: Apple IIe.

    Requirements: None listed.

    Price: $65.00 ($50.00 if purchased with other disks).

Exhibit 6C-1 continued

20. Title: *KLS disk 4 (Yardstick).*

    Company: KLS Cognitive Educational System.

    Level: Older children to adults (age).

    Description: Memory challenge program displays two, four, six, or eight letters on the screen. The letters are then replaced by numbers, and the client must designate which letter will be found beneath each number.

    Compatibility: Not listed.

    Requirements: None listed.

    Price: $110.00

21. Title: *Listening to the World.*

    Company: American Guidance Service.

    Level: Young children (age).

    Description: Auditory memory activities.

    Compatibility: Not listed.

    Requirements: None listed.

    Price: Ten-part kit costs $225.00; available for a 30-day trial.

22. Title: *Memory.*

    Company: Hartley Courseware, Inc.

    Level: Not listed.

    Description: Variety of recognition and recall activities to facilitate development of compensatory memory skills. Thirteen different lessons are organized by complexity. Authoring program disk allows the therapist to create individual lessons.

    Compatibility: Apple II+, IIe, IIc

    Requirements: None listed.

    Price: $595.00 (licensing fee for five disks).

23. Title: *Memory I.*

    Company: Psychological Software Services.

    Level: Medium-high (difficulty).

    Description: Provides practice in immediate recall. The disk contains the following programs: *Auditory Memory, Spatial Memory, Verbal Memory (Sequenced Words),* and *Visual/Spatial Memory.* Individual programs are described below.

    Compatibility: Apple II+, IIe, IIgs; Atari 800XL, 1200XL, 130XE, 65XE; IBM PC, PCjr, PC XT.

Exhibit 6C-1 continued

Requirements: Apple, Atari-style joystick and PSS joystick adapter; Atari, Atari joystick; IBM, nothing additional.

Price: $110.00; programs may not be purchased separately.

- Title: *Auditory Memory.*

  Level: Medium (difficulty).

  Description: Beginning with one tone, a series of tones (that slide either up or down the musical scale) are presented for the client to mimic via the joystick or keyboard. Success at any level results in an increase in the number of tones presented.

- Title: *Spatial Memory.*

  Level: Mild-moderate (difficulty)

  Description: The computer randomly generates a trail through a maze of rooms. Through trial and error and with clues, the client must learn the trail. If an error is committed, the client starts over. Success is achieved by completion of the trail from beginning to end without error.

- Title: *Verbal Memory (Sequenced Words).*

  Level: Mild-moderate (difficulty).

  Description: The client is asked to recall a series of 3 four-letter words in the order presented. As the client experiences success, the computer adds one word to the next presentation. Because word order is random, a different set appears on every trial. Recall is by recognition from a list of 16 words.

- Title: *Visual/Spatial Memory.*

  Level: Mild-moderate (difficulty).

  Description: Objects are presented at random locations on the monitor. The client must recall which objects were displayed as well as the locations in which they were displayed.

24. Title: *Memory II.*

    Company: Psychological Software Services.

    Level: Mild-moderate (difficulty).

    Description: The programs found in the *Memory II* package are actually more basic than those in *Memory I,* thus allowing more practice in the areas of encoding, categorizing, and organization. When errors are made, correct choices are displayed. Graphics aid in strengthening and maintaining attention and concentration. The programs on this disk include: *Paired Associates Memory I; Recognition Recall 1, 2, 3; Spatial Memory; Verbal Memory;* and *Visual Memory.*

Exhibit 6C-1 continued

Compatibility: Apple II+, IIe, IIgs; Atari 800XL, 1200XL, 1300XE, 65XE; IBM PC, PCjr, PC XT.

Requirements: Apple, Apple joystick; Atari, Atari joystick; IBM, IBM joystick.

Price: $150.00, programs are not sold separately.

- Title: *Paired Associates Memory I*

  Level: Medium (difficulty)

  Description: Randomly generated colorful graphic designs are paired with digits 0 to 9 and presented as pairs on the screen, one pair at a time. After the last presentation, the graphic designs are placed on the screen, and the client is requested to indicate which number was paired with it.

- Title: *Recognition Recall 1, 2, 3*

  Level: Mild-moderate (difficulty).

  Description: A picture containing 19 commonly recognized items is displayed (the time is selected by the client and therapist). From a listing of 90 words, the client must indicate the items originally displayed. Options include a hard copy printout of all correct and incorrect choices for each trial.

- Title: *Spatial Memory.*

  Level: Mild-moderate (difficulty).

  Description: Thirty objects are presented. Starting with level 1, a high-lighted object is briefly presented. The client must indicate with the joystick cursor the item that was previously displayed. Success results in the addition of one object to the display.

- Title: *Verbal Memory.*

  Level: Mild-moderate (difficulty).

  Description: A list consisting of 20 words is displayed at the bottom of the screen. The client must divide these words into four categories. Upon completion, the client must recall the entire 20-word list. The program entitled *Listmaker* can be used to create a word list.

- Title: *Visual Memory.*

  Level: Mild-moderate (difficulty).

  Description: Starting with one block, the computer blackens boxes in the row one at a time. The client must reproduce the sequence via the joystick. With success, one block is added to subsequent trials. Each presentation is random; therefore, a new sequence is presented each time.

Exhibit 6C-1 continued

25. Title: *Memory.*
    Company: Sunburst.
    Level: K to adult (grade).
    Description: Consists of the following nine disks: *Memory Building Blocks; Memory Castle; Memory Machine; Now You See It, Now You Don't; Regrouping; Simon Says; Teddy and Iggy; The Test Taker's Edge;* and *What's in a Frame?* Each of these programs is discussed below.
    Compatibility: 64K Apple II family; 128K IBM PC or PCjr.
    Requirements: Individual programs vary. See descriptions that follow.
    Price: $299.00; programs can be purchased individually.

    - Title: *Memory Building Blocks.*
      Level: K to adult (grade).
      Description: Visual and auditory memory skills are targeted using concentration games.
      Compatibility: 64K Apple family, Macintosh Plus or later model, 128K IBM PC or PCjr, 256K IBM PS/2 model 25, 256K Tandy 1000, Commodore 64.
      Requirements: Apple, operates with regular keyboard, Muppet learning keys, or touch window; color monitor required.
      Price: $65.00; $99.00 for Macintosh Plus or later model.

    - Title: *Memory Castle.*
      Level: 5 to adult (grade).
      Description: Activities designed to assist in recall of instructions and directions.
      Compatibility: 48K Apple II family.
      Requirements: Color monitor.
      Price: $65.00.

    - Title: *Memory Machine.*
      Level: 5 to adult (grade).
      Description: Practice provided in the areas of visualization and awareness.
      Compatibility: 64K Apple II family.
      Requirements: None listed.
      Price: $65.00.

    - Title: *Now You See It, Now You Don't.*
      Level: 3 to 6 (grade).

Exhibit 6C-1 continued

> *Description:* The client is provided practice in finding missing puzzle parts.
>
> *Compatibility:* 64K Apple II family.
>
> *Requirements:* Color monitor (recommended).
>
> *Price:* $75.00.

- Title: *Regrouping.*

  > *Level:* 3 to 6 (grade).
  >
  > *Description:* Focuses on the strategy of regrouping. It introduces the technique and provides practice for the client.
  >
  > *Compatibility:* 64K Apple II family.
  >
  > *Requirements:* Color monitor.
  >
  > *Price:* $65.00.

- Title: *Simon Says.*

  > *Level:* K to adult (grade).
  >
  > *Description:* Provides practice in remembering color, number, and letter sequences.
  >
  > *Compatibility:* 64K Apple II family.
  >
  > *Requirements:* Color monitor.
  >
  > *Price:* $65.00.

- Title: *Teddy and Iggy.*

  > *Level:* K to 3 (grade).
  >
  > *Description:* A program focusing on memory as well as sequencing skills.
  >
  > *Compatibility:* 64K Apple II family.
  >
  > *Requirements:* Color monitor.
  >
  > *Price:* $65.00.

- Title: *The Test Taker's Edge.*

  > *Level:* 6 to adult (grade).
  >
  > *Description:* Multiple-choice, fill-in-the-blank, matching, and true/false practice tests are supplied in this program.
  >
  > *Compatibility:* 64K Apple II family, 128K IBM PC or PCjr.
  >
  > *Requirements:* None listed.
  >
  > *Price:* $75.00.

- Title: *What's in a Frame?*

  > *Level:* K to 6 (grade).

Exhibit 6C-1 continued

> *Description:* A group of objects is presented to the client to study. A new picture is then presented, and the client is asked to identify via the keyboard those objects that were not in the original presentation. The therapist controls the number of objects to be remembered.
>
> *Compatibility:* 64K Apple II family.
>
> *Requirements:* Color monitor.
>
> *Price:* $65.00.

26. Title: *Memory & Comprehension Development.*

> *Company:* Stoelting Company.
>
> *Level:* Young children (age).
>
> *Description:* Consists of a four-part kit of games and activities addressing visual sequential memory, auditory sequential memory, auditory direction memory, and auditory memory and listening comprehension.
>
> *Compatibility:* Not listed.
>
> *Requirements:* None listed.
>
> *Price:* $42.00.

27. Title: *Memory Master.*

> *Company:* KLS Cognitive Educational System.
>
> *Level:* Not listed.
>
> *Description:* Two to ten items are displayed on the screen for the client to remember. After the screen clears, locations are relabeled 0 to 9. An item is displayed, and the client is asked to identify the number of where it was located.
>
> *Compatibility:* Apple II.
>
> *Requirements:* None listed.
>
> *Price:* $65.00 ($50.00 if purchased with other disks).

28. Title: *Memory Match.*

> *Company:* Hartley Courseware.
>
> *Level:* Children (age).
>
> *Description:* Twenty-five exercises are provided in this program at three levels of difficulty in several categories. Involves matching words to an opposite, homonym, number, rhyme, and so forth. Can be modified.
>
> *Compatibility:* Apple II, IIe, IIc; IBM PC.
>
> *Requirements:* None listed.
>
> *Price:* Apple, $33.95; IBM, $39.95.

Exhibit 6C-1 continued

29. Title: *Memory Patterns.*

    Company: Brain-Link Software.

    Level: Not listed.

    Description: Designed for visual-spatial memory. The client must recreate a pattern of colored squares shown on the monitor.

    Compatibility: Apple IIe, II+.

    Requirements: Joystick, color monitor.

    Price: $79.00.

30. Title: *Money Bags.*

    Company: Slosson Educational Publishers.

    Level: Young children to adults (age).

    Description: Includes sequential memory, concentration, and listening skills. Each training session is self-instructional and lasts 10 to 20 minutes.

    Compatibility: Not listed.

    Requirements: None listed.

    Price: $17.00 for advanced and basic combination set.

31. Title: *Numeric Concepts/Memory Skills Module* (part of *Captain's Log*)

    Company: Brain Train.

    Level: Young children (age).

    Description: Memory training activities included with remedial work in understanding and working with memory.

    Compatibility: Apple, IBM PC.

    Requirements: None listed.

    Price: $495.00.

32. Title: *Ollie and Seymour.*

    Company: Hartley Courseware.

    Level: 2 to 4 (grade).

    Description: Challenges thinking skills, directionality, shape and color recognition, visual memory, and number concepts using the characters of Ollie the Balloon Man and Seymour the Monkey.

    Compatibility: Apple series.

    Requirements: None listed.

    Price: $49.95.

33. Title: *Olympic Decathlon.*

    Company: Microsoft Consumer Products.

Exhibit 6C-1 continued

Level: Not listed.

Description: Graphic simulation of Olympic events that requires serial memory, execution, and a sense of timing. Includes various activities of different length and complexity.

Compatibility: IBM Compatible.

Requirements: Need two hands on the keyboard.

Price: Not listed.

34. Title: *PAIRMEM*.

    Company: Life Science Associates.

    Level: Not listed.

    Description: Various exercises in associative verbal learning skills to assist the client in learning to transfer information to long-term storage. Pairs of unrelated words are displayed on the screen. When the computer gives the first word of a pair, the client must type in the second word of the pair. Interference, rehearsal, and final recall options can be input.

    Compatibility: Apple IIc, IIe, IIgs; IBM PC, XT, AT.

    Requirements: None listed.

    Price: $50.00.

35. Title: *Purposeful Patterns.*

    Company: Greentree Group.

    Level: Not listed.

    Description: Eight different tasks are presented using combinations of color, shape, and design. The client is required to match color and shape patterns. The tasks progressively increase in difficulty. Auditory and visual feedback is provided.

    Compatibility: Apple family.

    Requirements: None listed

    Price: Not listed.

36. Title: *Purposeful Symbols.*

    Company: Greentree Group.

    Level: Not listed.

    Description: Designed as a companion program to *Purposeful Patterns* (see above) to retrain similar visual-spatial and memory skills. The program includes *Letter Match, Number Match I* (basic), and *Number Match II* (advanced), which allow for a sequential building of cognitive skills in the areas of recognition, comparison, and recall of letters and numbers. Spatial

Exhibit 6C-1 continued

relationships can also be presented. Audio and visual feedback is also presented.

Compatibility: Apple family.

Requirements: None listed.

Price: Not listed.

37. Title: *Semantic Memory.*

Company: KLS Cognitive Educational System.

Level: Not listed.

Description: Consists of six programs for semantic units, classes, relations, systems, transformations, and implications. Varying levels of difficulty for each program. Also includes immediate data feedback for client.

Compatibility: IBM PC.

Requirements: None listed.

Price: $100.00 (or $225.00 for set of three: *Figural Memory, Symbolic Memory,* and *Semantic Memory*).

38. Title: *SOFT TOOLS '83.*

Company: Psychological Software Services.

Level: See individual program listings below.

Description: This disk contains *Color Match* and *Trail Trace.*

Compatibility: Apple II+, IIe, IIgs; Atari 800XL, 1220XL, 130XE, 65XE.

Requirements: Apple, Apple joystick; Atari, Atari joystick.

Price: $35.00.

- Title: *Color Match.*

  Level: Mild (difficulty).

  Description: A grid (eight by eight squares in size) is displayed. A color is hidden behind each square such that each color has a match on the board. There are 32 possible matches each time; the object is to match all 32 pairs using as few moves as possible.

- Title: *Trail Trace.*

  Level: Mild (difficulty).

  Description: The client specifies the number of steps to be randomly generated by the computer to form a pathway. By trial and error, the client must discover the correct path. Upon error, the client starts over in the center, and the path is erased. The client must recall and retrace already discovered moves before making a new choice. The grid depicting a square array of rooms is displayed in the size determined by the user.

Exhibit 6C-1 continued

39. Title: *Soft Tools '84.*

    Company: Psychological Software Services.

    Level: See individual program listings below.

    Description: This disk contains *City Map, Rapid Number Comparison,* and *Time Sense.*

    Compatibility: Apple II+, IIe, IIgs; Atari 800XL, 1200XL, 130XE, 65XE; IBM PC.

    Requirements: Apple, Apple joystick; Atari, Atari joystick.

    Price: $45.00.

    - Title: *City Map.*

      Level: Mild (difficulty).

      Description: A map is drawn on the monitor screen. A small orange-yellow block is used to mark the destination of travel and is randomly placed on one of the streets. The client studies the map for a few seconds to plan a route of travel. Once the map clears from the screen, only the immediate neighborhood around the small white block, indicating the client's position, is visible, moving only when the block moves. Once the client moves onto the destination block, the program ends. The program allows viewing of the entire map during the program, reporting the number of times the entire map is viewed at the end.

    - Title: *Rapid Number Comparison.*

      Level: Mild (difficulty).

      Description: Activities for training attention, memory, discrimination, and decision-making skills are provided. In this program, the client rapidly scans four sets of numbers that appear on the screen. Upon the client's determining which two of the four sets match, digits from the matching set are typed in. The computer reports both accuracy and errors. Variables that can be changed include the number of digits in each set, the length of presentation, and the delay between presentation and recall.

    - Title: *Time Sense.*

      Level: Mild (difficulty).

      Description: A drawing of a clock is presented on the screen. Upon initiation, the clock ticks off at a randomly determined period of time. The client is then asked to reproduce the time period. Five correct responses advance the client from one level to the next. There are a total of nine levels.

Exhibit 6C-1 continued

40. Title: *Soft Tools '85.*

    Company: Psychological Software Services.

    Level: See individual program listings below.

    Description: This disk contains *Digit/Symbol Transfer, Dot-to-Dot, Sequenced Memory,* and *Visispan.*

    Compatibility: Apple II+, IIe, IIgs; Atari 800XL, 1200XL, 130XE, 65XE; IBM PC.

    Requirements: Apple, Apple joystick; Atari, Atari joystick.

    Price: $45.00.

    - Title: *Digit/Symbol Transfer.*

      Level: Mild (difficulty).

      Description: Focuses on attention, concentration, perceptual motor skills, and immediate memory. A key is displayed across the top of the screen showing the numbers 1 to 9 paired with nine symbols. The client must rapidly supply missing numbers on the remaining display to pair correct numbers and symbols. Scoring is automatic after the last number is transferred. The display will remain on screen until another key is pressed, after which the score and time are displayed.

    - Title: *Dot-to-Dot.*

      Level: Mild (difficulty).

      Description: A spatial configuration is displayed, and the program requires the client to reproduce it sequentially from memory. The figure is displayed on a five by five grid of large dots consisting of horizontal, vertical, and diagonal lines interconnecting the dots. As the client encounters success, the computer increases the complexity of the drawing by adding one line to the next display.

    - Title: *Sequenced Memory.*

      Level: Mild (difficulty).

      Description: Provides a structured recall task in which the client recalls the items in the order presented.

    - Title: *Visispan.*

      Level: Mild (difficulty).

      Description: Can be used to assess visual-sequential memory. The client is asked to reproduce the correct sequence of lights using the keyboard. The on-screen display time of the stimulus can be controlled and varied by the client.

Exhibit 6C-1 continued

41. Title: *Soft Tools '86.*

    Company: Psychological Software Services.

    Level: See individual program listings below.

    Description: This disk contains *Delayed Memory, Flash Card,* and *Spots.*

    Compatibility: Apple II+, IIe, IIgs; Atari 800XL, 1200XL, 130XE, 65XE; IBM PC.

    Requirements: Apple, Apple joystick; Atari, Atari joystick.

    Price: $50.00.

    - Title: *Delayed Memory.*

      Level: Mild (difficulty).

      Description: A two by two grid is displayed containing four randomly chosen numbers. The amount of time the display remains on the screen as well as the amount of time that a blank screen is displayed afterward are specified by the therapist and client. The client is asked to supply the numbers on an empty grid when the blank period ends. The computer specifies with a "?" which block of the grid should be filled.

    - Title: *Flash Card.*

      Level: Mild (difficulty).

      Description: Designed as a study aid for clients who are in academic settings as well as those planning to return. It enables the client to enter any question or answer combination by changing the data statements within the program.

    - Title: *Spots.*

      Level: Mild (difficulty).

      Description: Focuses on spatial memory. The client studies the screen for the appearance of one to four small blinking blocks. The positions on the screen where each of the blocks is displayed must be remembered for recall at a later time. After a few minutes the screen clears, and a checkerboard pattern consisting of numbered blocks is displayed. The client must recall the locations where the initial blocks were displayed and enter the numbers of the checkerboard positions that include the small blocks. Immediate feedback is provided.

42. Title: *Soft Tools '87*

    Company: Psychological Software Services.

    Level: Mild (difficulty).

    Description: This disk contains the program *Sound Off,* which addresses auditory attention, discrimination, and recall. The computer presents both a

Exhibit 6C-1 continued

learning and a test mode. In the learning mode, the client can review all possible sound presentations. In the test mode, the program begins with one sound. Upon correct duplication, the program advances by increasing the number of sounds in the sequence by one. Each newly generated sequence is randomly determined. Termination of the program occurs after five errors, at which point the computer produces scores (number of correct responses and highest level obtained).

Compatibility: Apple II+, IIe, IIgs; Atari 800XL, 1200XL, 130XE, 65XE; IBM PC.

Requirements: Apple, Apple joystick; Atari, Atari joystick.

Price: $50.00

43. Title: *Soft Tools '88.*

Company: Psychological Software Services.

Level: Mild (difficulty).

Description: This disk contains the program *Attention,* which focuses on attentional, visual perceptual, and discrimination skills. A randomly chosen number is displayed on the screen. Afterward, the client is asked to recall the number and to type it on the keyboard. Immediate feedback is provided.

Compatibility: Apple II+, IIe, IIgs; Atari 800XL, 1200XL, 130XE, 65XE; IBM PC.

Requirements: Apple, Apple joystick; Atari, Atari joystick.

Price: $50.00.

44. Title: *Soft Tools '89.*

Company: Psychological Software Services.

Level: See individual program listings below.

Description: This disk contains *Easy Street* and *Now Where Did I Leave Those *&%@ Keys.*

Compatibility: Apple II+, IIe, IIgs; Atari 800XL, 1200XL, 130XE, 65XE; IBM PC.

Requirements: Apple, Apple joystick; Atari, Atari joystick.

Price: $50.00.

- Title: *Easy Street.*

  Level: Mild (difficulty).

  Description: Focuses on immediate and delayed recall in remembering directions. The client reads a direction to a certain location. After an optional delay, the client then inputs the remembered direction by

Exhibit 6C-1 continued

choosing from a list of answers determined by a selected level. At level 1 there are two possible answers, at level 2 there are three choices, and so forth. Locations and directions are randomly rearranged between trials.

- Title: *Now Where Did I Leave Those *&%@ Keys.*

  Level: Mild (difficulty).

  Description: Focuses on incidental and spatial memory. From a floor plan view presented on the screen, the client uses the numbered keys 1 to 7 to indicate the correct location of various objects distributed in rooms. Objects are randomly repositioned between turns. Various scores are provided at the end as well as a printed map to aid in the flexibility of the program.

45. Title: *Soft Tools '90.*

    Company: Psychological Software Services.

    Level: Not listed.

    Description: New release; includes letter matching exercises and copy or recall exercises.

    Compatibility: Apple, Atari, IBM PC.

    Requirements: None listed.

    Price: $50.00.

46. Title: *SEQREC.*

    Company: Life Science Associates.

    Level: Not listed.

    Description: A list of nonsense words, shapes, pictures, or short words is shown in sequence on the screen. The client then is shown a list of items and asked to identify the list in sequence. Twenty-one trials are offered.

    Compatibility: Apple, IBM PC and compatibles.

    Requirements: None listed.

    Price: $40.00.

47. Title: *SPAN.*

    Company: Life Science Associates.

    Level: Not listed.

    Description: Addresses short-term memory storage capacity. Consists of 30 lists presented in sets of 5 lists each. In the first set, the client is instructed to recall the last two words. With each set, recall is increased by one word to a maximum of seven.

Exhibit 6C-1 continued

    Compatibility: Apple IIc, IIe, IIgs; IBM PC and compatibles.

    Requirements: None listed.

    Price: $40.00.

48. Title: *Super Challenger.*

    Company: Electronic Courseware Systems, Inc.

    Level: Not listed.

    Description: A musical game that increases the user's ability to remember a series of pitches played by the computer. Pitches are matched to colors on the computer screen.

    Compatibility: IBM PC.

    Requirements: None listed.

    Price: Not listed.

49. Title: *Symbolic Memory.*

    Company: KLS Cognitive Educational System.

    Level: Not listed.

    Description: Consists of six programs addressing memory for symbolic units, classes, relations, systems, transformations, and implications. Varying levels of difficulty for each program. Also includes immediate data feedback for client.

    Compatibility: IBM PC and compatibles.

    Requirements: None listed.

    Price: $100.00 (or $225.00 for a set of three: *Figural Memory, Symbolic Memory,* and *Semantic Memory*).

50. Title: *Task Master.*

    Company: Life Science Associates.

    Level: Not listed.

    Description: User designs own tasks in several cognitive areas, including memory. Tasks can be individualized (e.g., shopping lists) and variables such as timing and sequencing are selected by the user.

    Compatibility: IBM PC.

    Requirements: None listed.

    Price: Not listed.

51. Title: *THINKable.*

    Company: IBM.

    Level: Adolescents and adults (age).

Exhibit 6C-1 continued

Description: A new system that provides practice exercises with four levels of difficulty that focus on visual attention, visual discrimination, visual memory, and visual-sequential memory. Also provides the user with a case management area, enabling the clinician to develop and customize session plans. It also allows the collection and reporting of performance data in tabular or graphic form as well as review of ongoing assessment.

Compatibility: IBM PS/2.

Requirements: OS/2 and color monitor.

Price: $4,800.00. This prices includes all disks, tutorials, manuals, two sets of headphones, and an adaptor board.

52. Title: *Touch and See.*

Company: Exceptional Children's Software.

Level: Not listed.

Description: Organized to teach matching of similar objects while focusing on attention and short-term memory skills. Twelve boxes with pictures or words underneath are displayed. When a box is touched, it reveals a shape, picture, letter, or word. The matching box must be located. Time to complete the task can be varied.

Compatibility: Apple family.

Requirements: None listed.

Price: Not listed.

53. Title: *TRIPREC.*

Company: Life Science Associates.

Level: Not listed.

Description: Can be used as a measure of progress in short- and long-term retention. Also provides practice in various mnemonics. Three words to be recalled are presented sequentially on the screen followed by either zero, three, or nine words to be read but not recalled.

Compatibility: Apple, IBM PC and compatibles.

Requirements: None listed.

Price: $40.00.

54. Title: *VISMEM.*

Company: Life Science Associates.

Level: Not listed.

Description: Exercises focus on visual nonverbal memory. The computer shows patterns on a checkerboard that the client must remember. Variables include complexity of the screens and length of series.

Exhibit 6C-1 continued

> *Compatibility:* Apple IIc, IIe, IIgs; IBM PC and compatibles.
> *Requirements:* None listed.
> *Price:* $50.00.

55. Title: *WORDMEM*.

> *Company:* Life Science Associates
>
> *Level:* Not listed.
>
> *Description:* Exercises to improve rote memory skills through work on immediate span of verbal memory. A random list of words is sequentially displayed on the screen, and the client must respond in the order presented. The number of trials, words per trial, display time, and word list can all be input.
>
> *Compatibility:* Apple IIc, IIe, IIgs; IBM PC, XT, AT and compatibles.
>
> *Requirements:* None listed.
>
> *Price:* $50.00.

56. Title: *Word Radar*.

> *Company:* DLM
>
> *Level:* Not listed.
>
> *Description:* Word matching and memory.
>
> *Compatibility:* Apple II, IBM PC, Tandy, Commodore 64/128.
>
> *Requirements:* IBM PC requires DOS 2.0 or higher 128K, CGA card; IBM PCjr requires DOS 2.1 or higher, 128K.
>
> *Price:* $46.00.

Exhibit 6C-2

Listing of Manufacturers

Advantage Computing
1803 Mission Street
Suite 416
Santa Cruz, CA 95060

American Guidance Services
Publisher's Building
P.O. Box 99
Circle Pines, MN 55014-1796

BrainTrain
1915 Huguenot Road
Richmond, VA 23235

Brain-Link Software
317 Montgomery
Ann Arbor, MI 48103

Computer Advantage Ideas
Berkeley, CA

CREATE
P.O. Box 93541
Milwaukee, WI 53203-0541

DLM
P.O. Box 4000
One DLM Park
Allen, TX 75002
(800) 527-4747

The Einstein Corporation
3111 West Burbank Boulevard
Suite 202
Burbank, CA 91505
(818) 563-1025
Fax (818) 563-1026

Electronic Courseware Systems, Inc.
1210 Lancaster Drive
Champaign, IL 61812
(217) 359-7099

Exceptional Children's Software
P.O. Box 4758
Overland Park, KS 66204
(816) 363-4606

Greentree Group
P.O. Box 28
Mohnton, PA 19540

Hartley Courseware, Inc.
123 Bridge Road
Box 419
Dimondale, MI 48821
(800) 247-1380

KLS Cognitive Educational System
P.O. Box 1257
Ramona, CA 92065
(619) 492-9721

Exhibit 6C-2 continued

Life Science Associates
1 Fenimore Road
Bayport, NY 11705
(516) 472-2111

Merit Software
13635 Gamma Road
Dallas, TX 75244
(800) 238-4277

Microsoft Consumer Products
400 108th Avenue N.E.
Suite 200
Bellevue, WA 98004

Parrot Software
190 Sandy Ridge Road
State College, PA 16803
(814) 237-7284

The Psychological Corporation
555 Academic Court
San Antonio, TX 78204-2498
(512) 299-1061

Psychological Software Services
6555 Carrolton Avenue
Indianapolis, IN 46220
(317) 257-9672

Rehabilitation Psychology Associates
P.O. Box 1510
Beaverton, OR 97075-1510
(503) 228-9117

Slosson Educational Publishers Inc.
P.O. Box 280
East Aurora, NY 14052
(800) 828-4800

Stoelting Company
Oakwood Center
620 Wheat Lane
Wood Dale, IL 60191
(708) 860-9700

Sunburst Communications
101 Castleton Street
Pleasantville, NY 10570-3498
(800) 628-8897

Exhibit 6C-2 continued

Additional Resources

Apple Computer Resources in Special Education and Rehabilitation
DLM Teaching Resources
One DLM Park
Allen, TX 75002
(800) 527-4747
   Provides listings of software, adaptive equipment, and other resources for use with Apple computers.

Brain Injury
Taylor & Francis Ltd.
4 John Street
London WC1N 2ET
United Kingdom
   Brain Injury is the official journal of the International Association for the Study of Traumatic Brain Injury. It will be initiating a computer technology column on a quarterly basis.

Closing the Gap
P.O. Box 68
Henderson, MN 56044
(612) 258-3294
   Provides information on technology, sponsors conferences, publishes a newsletter on computers in CRT. Yearly subscription includes the annual *Resource Directory,* a listing of adaptive software and hardware.

Cognitive Bulletin Board (CBB)
T. Daniel Ridley, MA, PA
The Del Oro Institute for Rehabilitation
HCA Medical Center Hospital
8081 Greenbriar
Houston, TX 77054
(713) 790-8383
   Provides a variety of information about head injury via a telecommunications system. Can be accessed by anyone having a personal computer and a modem. Free of charge to the public.

Exhibit 6C-2 continued

IBM National Support Center for Persons with Disabilities
P.O. Box 2150
Atlanta, GA 30301-2150
(800) 426-2133
   Provides listings of organizations, publications, journals, and other resources available for use with IBM computers.

The Journal of Cognitive Rehabilitation
NeuroScience Publishers
6555 Carrollton Avenue
Indianapolis, IN 46220
   Provides computer programs in each issue. Older issues include reviews of software and articles on cognitive rehabilitation.

7
Compensatory Strategies

OVERVIEW

Compensation, as used in rehabilitation, is based upon the theory of functional adaptation. Functional adaptation assumes that clients need to develop alternative ways to manage deficits rather than work on completely obliterating or restoring a particular deficit area.[1] In rehabilitation, clients will ideally work simultaneously on directly retraining skills (Chapter 6), using compensatory aids (Chapter 8), and learning strategies to assist in compensating for areas that may be permanently impaired. The use of compensatory strategies is extremely important in the rehabilitation of persons with traumatic brain injury (TBI) and is taught in conjunction with opportunities to generalize strategies learned in sessions to the real world into which the client will be returning after rehabilitation.

Most rehabilitation facilities provide direct retraining to TBI survivors via computerized, pen-and-paper, and three-dimensional tasks. These tools are generally task oriented in that clients are given a task, practice it to criterion level, and then move on to another task. Direct retraining is valuable, but this type of rehabilitation in isolation can be seductive. Therapists and rehabilitation facilities may be lured into focusing too much on direct retraining, especially since computer programs are readily available and easily administered and because clients and therapists like them. However, the exclusive use of such tools in rehabilitation is a disservice to TBI survivors.

Effective rehabilitation from TBI involves both the direct retraining of deficits using computerized, pen-and-paper, and three-dimensional tasks, as well as strategies and aids to assist in compensating for cognitive deficits. Indeed, for some clients, the use of strategies and aids may be the only focus of treatment.

The ultimate goal of cognitive rehabilitation is the client's ability to use and generalize skills learned in sessions to the real world to maximize success. Clients may perform admirably on tasks in sessions with the assistance and external structure provided by the therapist; one of the true tests of success, however, is whether the client can transfer these skills to situations in the real world, where the therapist will not be available to assist (e.g., in the workplace, in school, at home, and in relationships). To return to independence, clients need to resume control over their lives, internalizing skills and providing their own structure after rehabilitation.

It should be noted that in teaching compensatory strategies to clients it is not the task of the therapist to tell the client which strategies to use and where to use them. Rather, the therapist acts as a guide who assists the client in identifying particular problem areas and working together to develop strategies for use. Therapists may teach clients a menu of such strategies from which they may pick and choose ones appropriate to situations in which they may find themselves.

To begin the process of teaching strategies, the therapist needs to assist the client in identifying any strategies already being used independently, such as note taking in team meetings to remember information. If the client is already using note taking, the therapist can facilitate the generalization of this strategy to other situations, such as remembering other therapy sessions, using a calendar to remember appointments, making to-do lists to remember daily activities, and so forth. Therapists must also consider personality styles and personal wishes in assisting clients to compensate for memory deficits. For example, the client who independently takes notes in a treatment team meeting may have used this strategy before the accident as compensation. Consider the situation, however, of a client who had an excellent memory before injury and never wrote anything down because this was unnecessary. After injury, this client may have difficulty with the concept of taking notes and may refuse to do so (particularly if the client has not accepted the losses resulting from injury). Therapists must work *with* clients to assist in their empowerment, not force them into situations because the therapist may think it to be effective.

After identification of types of strategies clients are using (or prefer to use), the therapist can then begin the task of maximizing those already in use and teaching others that may fit the client's particular preferences and lifestyle. The therapist can also assist in developing alternative situations in which the client can practice to facilitate generalization.

Compensatory strategies can be used to assist in tasks performed in sessions, such as those on the computer (e.g., the strategy of chunking to remember lists of words). They can also be used in more functional activities of daily living. Depending upon the particular therapy task, strategies can be designed and/or altered as necessary.

In teaching strategies, therapists are encouraged to use a model for treatment such as the Eight-Step Model presented in Chapter 5. Measurements need to be taken both for baseline data and for assessment of change over time as the client learns, practices, and generalizes strategies to real-world settings.

MENU OF COMPENSATORY STRATEGIES

In the sections that follow, a menu of compensatory strategies is presented from which the therapist and client may choose ones applicable to their particular situations. Therapists are encouraged to be creative in developing and expanding upon these strategies and in providing generalization opportunities for their clients. As with other cognitive rehabilitation tasks, it is recommended that therapists structure learning in terms of the Eight-Step Model discussed in Chapter 5.

Active Listening

Remembering is an active process, one that requires the ability to direct attention and sustain concentration. In social situations, the ability to actively attend and listen becomes even more crucial and is the basic building block of communication. The concept of active listening is taken from the psychotherapy literature and adapted for use with clients involved in memory training as well as other cognitive areas.

Active listening involves several components: maintaining eye contact with the speaker, attention to body posture, elimination of distractors, and clarification of understanding (restatement of what the other person said, asking questions, and so forth).

Maintenance of Eye Contact with the Speaker

Maintaining eye contact with another person who is speaking provides both visual and auditory encoding opportunities (multisensory encoding). Maintaining eye contact maximizes the potential for associative learning (which is another strategy) in pairing visual and auditory information. For example, there may be memory of how the person's face looked during a particular comment or of a particular item of clothing the person was wearing as the comment was made.

An example of such associative learning (visual and verbal pairing by maintaining eye contact) occurs with special songs. Most persons have had the experience of remembering where they were when hearing a certain song and can, years later, recall this information. For example, a 16-year-old girl who is out on her first date with a boy named Bob hears the song "I Want To Be Bobby's Girl" playing on the radio as they drive down the road, and she maintains eye contact with him while singing along with the music. Each time that song is heard in the future, the memory of his face, the date, and its details are remembered (this association strategy is discussed later in this chapter).

Maintenance of eye contact also enhances communication skills with other persons, which becomes important in getting needs and wants across to others (and in understanding theirs). It facilitates the respect and acceptance components necessary for empowerment. When a person is looking at another person, it indicates interest in the person and motivation to remember. In rehabilitation settings, eye contact is important in one-to-one situations, such as the therapist-client one. As recovery from head injury occurs, it becomes important for clients and treatment providers to look at the persons with whom they work. This maintenance of eye contact indicates interest and respect for the other person. If the client and therapist are constantly looking at a computer screen and never at each other, the relationship may suffer as well as the client's motivation to remember. In addition, much sensory information that can enhance storage of memories may be lost.

In rehabilitation, clients will often present with multiple physical deformities (e.g., burns, scars, missing or mutilated limbs, and so forth). In these situations, it becomes even more crucial for treatment providers to maintain eye contact. If the therapist is unwilling to look at the client, there may be a feeling of disrespect and a resultant lowered self-concept. On the other hand, the client may feel uncomfortable looking at the therapist (or others), and the ability to encode information and remember it may be impaired. If clients cannot look comfortably at the person with whom they are speaking, they will not be able to concentrate fully and make use of multisensory encoding. Therapists who find themselves not looking at clients with physical deformities (or for other reasons) may benefit from introspection, consultation, and/or training in this area.

Maintaining eye contact is different from staring. There is a balance to achieve between looking at someone or something with interest to facilitate memory and rudely staring. Either too little focus or too much focus can be detrimental to the memory process. Therapists will need to be sensitive to their own level of comfort with eye contact.

In the process of maintaining eye contact, attention must also be paid to facial expressions. Many emotions are expressed through such expressions, including approval, disapproval, sadness, anger, frustration, and confusion. Clients need to increase their awareness of their own emotions and nonverbal expressions of feelings. They also need to monitor the facial expressions of others. Therapists will need to monitor their reactions to clients, particularly since TBI survivors are often hypervigilant about the reactions of others around them. Expressions also communicate respect (or disrespect) and will affect the client's motivation to learn.

While eye contact is important in a one-to-one situation with another person, it is also important in other types of situations involving more persons, such as groups, family gatherings, classes in school, work-related activities, and social situations. For instance, at a family reunion, it may be extremely difficult for a client to concentrate on the amount and intensity of activity occurring, resulting in sensory overload and minimal memory of the content of the gathering. If this client can maintain eye contact with one person who is speaking and then shift eye contact as the next person speaks, the likelihood of remembering is increased (this also lets family members know the client is interested).

Another example involves the student returning to classroom activities. While the instructor is lecturing, the likelihood of learning will be increased if the student looks at the instructor rather than looking around the room or sitting with eyes closed. This again provides for both visual and auditory learning, and the student may remember where the teacher was standing when a certain comment was made or the movement of writing a phrase on the blackboard (association strategy).

The concept of maintaining eye contact is generally related to situations involving people, but the concept can also apply to focusing on inanimate information as well; in such situations it is termed "active attending." For instance, in a therapy situation, the client may need to focus on a paper or the computer screen in addition to periodically maintaining eye contact with the therapist. Focusing and maintaining visual contact is important in the memory process, whether the focus is a person or not.

A valuable way to train clients in maintaining eye contact is through the use of videotaping. As with other tasks discussed in this text, the therapist first takes a baseline measurement, e.g., a five-minute videotape measuring the client's eye contact. Training is then provided with the use of videotapes as part of this process. Clients can critique their own performances along with the therapists, and goals can be set accordingly.

Attention to Body Posture

Most persons do not pay much attention to their body posture as they listen or speak to another person or as they attend to tasks. This is an important element in the process of memory and in communication with others, however, particularly since much of what is communicated among people is done nonverbally. Active listening and active attending mean maintaining a body posture that indicates interest and attention. Erect (but relaxed) body posture and seating that is not overly plush or overly harsh facilitate concentration. While it is possible to concentrate in a prone position, it is not ideal since this may become too relaxed and precipitate drifting into inattentiveness or even sleep. In some rehabilitation settings, clients are sometimes seen while in bed (for testing, therapy, etc.). While this is necessary in some situations, it is not the optimum arrangement to facilitate concentration. It is also not a good situation since it puts the client in a one-down position with the therapist.

Classrooms have long been set up to facilitate active body posturing, which in effect facilitates concentration and learning. We do not feel that seating must be quite so harsh as the wooden seats found in elementary school classrooms, but the principle is a sound one.

Active body posturing forces the listener to attend better; for example, consider the difference between the client who sits comfortably upright in a chair and the one who slouches down in a reclined position or over the arm of the chair. The client who is seated upright will be better able to focus on information and will indicate interest, intent, and motivation to learn.

In communication between two persons, body posturing becomes even more important. If a client or therapist indicates disinterest through body posture, the other person's motivation to attend and remember may be diminished. For example, if a therapist is presenting material to be learned while propped on one arm in the chair, the client may get the message that the material is not interesting or not important or that the therapist is bored, any of which may hinder the client's motivation to attend (i.e., if it is not important to the therapist, why should it be important to the client?).

Therapists will need to be conscious of the messages they convey to clients with their own body posture (e.g., slouching, crossed arms, men with their legs wide open, and so forth). Attention to the client's body posture and skills training in any noticeable deficit areas can facilitate attention and thus facilitate storage of information into memory. Some postures may also send confusing messages to the client by communicating a comfort level used only with very close friends or with spouses. Neither of these communications to clients are appropriate and both violate the boundaries of the therapist-client relationship.

Elimination of Distractors

A distractor is anything that takes away the focus of attention. Distractors can come from the environment (external) around the person, or they can come from internal needs, thoughts, and feelings. Distractors cause the client to have difficulty in attending, concentrating, encoding, storing, and retrieving information. Distractors cause interruption in the process of memory, which may be expressed behaviorally as impulsivity. For example, a client who hears an announcement for lunch over the loudspeaker will not only be interrupted in the task at hand but may also immediately begin moving toward the cafeteria. Similarly, the client who is hungry may suddenly lose concentration on a task and ask when lunch will be ready.

External distractors. Clients recovering from brain injury are often unable to screen stimuli in their environment. For example, the client in an inpatient rehabilitation facility may be required to attend to the physician who is speaking in the hallway while simultaneously being assaulted by people walking back and forth, noises over an intercom, the talking of others, smells, and so forth. In community settings, clients may feel overloaded in shopping malls or large gatherings such as sporting events or family gatherings. Before brain injury, most persons can filter these distractors such that they can focus on the task at hand; brain injury often affects this filtering ability as each stimulus vies for equal attention.

Therapists working with TBI survivors need to attend to the amount of external distraction present in the environment. Clients may initially need to be in rooms that are relatively bare to assist in decreasing sensory overload and facilitating concentration and memory. When clients are participating in retraining of memory skills, the environment first needs to be controlled to eliminate as many external distractors as possible. For clients who are easily distracted, sessions need to be conducted in quiet, private areas. These persons may not do well in group settings either, where they are bombarded with external stimulation.

Even clients who are less distractible should be provided with maximally environmentally sound therapy situations. As a basic requirement, therapists should meet with clients one-to-one and in a private room. Additionally, attention should be paid to objects in the room (i.e., whether there is clutter or too much material on the walls) and the location of the room (i.e., whether it is in a quiet area or a high-traffic one).

Therapists should also attend to their personal ability to distract clients; for example, therapists should be wary of wearing excessive perfume. Therapists must also be aware of distracting personal mannerisms (e.g., excessive use of hands when talking, clearing the throat frequently, constant body movement, and so forth). These behaviors can be extremely distracting for a TBI survivor. Therapists can also distract with their appearance, such as the color and style of clothing (e.g., short skirts on female therapists), hairstyles, or noisy jewelry.

As clients are better able to attend, therapists can begin to reintroduce distractors as a way to measure improvement in concentration. However, it is important to maintain optimum environmental conditions as the learning processes occur. Once the client has succeeded in memory tasks, distractions may gradually be reintroduced to determine the optimum ability of the client to deal with distractors.

For some people, being easily distracted may remain a problem over the long-term. In such situations, external controls and strategies may be necessary to cope effectively. For example, if the client is returning to work, a more structured office situation may be needed, such as one with 2 or 3 persons versus one with 50. If a student is returning to a classroom, tests may need to be taken in an area separate from the rest of the class to minimize distraction and facilitate retrieval from memory (note that distractors not only affect the encoding of information but can also affect its later retrieval).

Internal Distractors. Internal distractors are those generated inside the client that contribute to diminished ability to concentrate. Often, these are more distracting than external distractors. Internal distractors can occur in physical, cognitive, or emotional realms.

Clients who are in some physical discomfort such as being sleepy, hungry, cold or hot, tired, sexually aroused, or in pain may be unable to concentrate and listen actively to information being presented. Likewise, persons who have uncontrolled seizure disorders and those who are on various medications may be distracted by their condition so that the ability to attend and remember information is diminished. Therapists will need to be sensitive to physical distractors and assist the client in getting needs met. If a client is cold in the therapist's office, active listening in the session may be affected as the client is distracted by physical discomfort. Therapists can easily adjust room temperature and provide rest periods and food to assist clients to minimize such distractors. Additionally, they can assess other areas and make appropriate referrals (e.g., the client who is in pain may need skills building in pain management strategies before participating in memory rehabilitation).

The client's internal thoughts may also be distracting. For example, if the client thinks the therapy task is unimportant or stupid, or if its purpose is not understood, motivation to listen actively will decline. Therapists can address this distractor easily by clearly explaining the reasons for tasks or strategies and providing successful experiences for the client. Information is crucial for persons recovering from brain injury. Therapists can both give and obtain feedback from clients regarding the importance of tasks, and work with them to decide which tasks are appropriate. Clients may become bored or unmotivated and have great difficulty actively listening to material that does not feel useful.

Similarly, if the client experiences difficulty with a task, internal messages such as "I am stupid" are often registered. This self-talk diminishes self-concept, motivation, and ultimately the ability to concentrate and actively listen to information to be remembered. Therapists can assist by reframing such thoughts away from the client. Participation in individual psychotherapy sessions can assist clients in improving self-concept and esteem after trauma. TBI survivors may already feel they are in a one-down position, and the added insult of having difficulty with a task will greatly affect the ability to maintain concentration and motivation.

Finally, emotional reactions can greatly distract clients from listening. Much of what a speaker actually says may become distorted by the time it is interpreted by a listener. Listening is often done through a previous template of experiences, knowledge, biases, beliefs, likes, dislikes, and so forth. New information becomes attached to and associated with this previous information and stored alongside it in ways the speaker may not have intended. Neutral comments may become heavily emotionally laden.

For example, in a parent-child relationship, the mother may say to her adult son "What do you think of the way Dad has his hair cut?" This may be an entirely neutral comment, but the son may interpret it differently because of previous experiences when the mother repeatedly criticized him for wearing his hair too long. The message he may be hearing in the present is "I have never approved of the way *you* wear *your* hair. Why don't you do yours like Dad's? I approve of Dad's." In this situation, the adult son may not hear anything else his mother has to say after this comment. His ability to concentrate has been hampered by the emotional listening. This situation can be further complicated when this same client is in a therapy session and the therapist innocently asks, "Have you ever thought of wearing your hair differently?" The client may immediately associate this with a parent message and react with anger. This process (transference) is often unconscious yet is a powerful internal distractor. Therapists who become aware of such reactions can work with clients to separate present situations from past experiences. In some cases this will need to occur in psychotherapy sessions, not CRT sessions.

In rehabilitation, both clients and therapists bring their previous experiences to the therapy situation. A particular therapist may remind the client of someone in the past or present, and comments may be misinterpreted. Therapists may also fall victim to emotional listening as clients "push buttons" from the past or present.

Listening emotionally causes the listener to form judgments about what the other person is saying, which may interfere with memory. It also may cause the listener to feel uncomfortable enough to turn off what is being said. Some material is so uncomfortable that it may be avoided. The listener may become overwhelmed with the complexity of the information and decide it is too difficult; nothing may be heard past that point.

Other emotional reactions may also interfere with active listening and impede the ability to remember information. For example, if a client becomes angry with the nurse as he or she wakes up in the morning, this anger may carry over throughout the rest of the day and interfere with therapy sessions. If a client (or therapist) is angry, tearful, sad, frustrated, or worried, the ability to concentrate on another task may be impaired. Since many clients in rehabilitation have some difficulty maintaining concentration in any case, the addition of emotionally laden information may be devastating.

Therapists can teach clients the strategy of *shelving* emotional, internal distractors. There are many therapeutic ways to *contain* emotional information and avoid spillover into areas where full concentration is needed. Clients can use either concrete or abstract containers to assist in this process. For example, the client may want to visualize all the emotional material being placed in either a real or imaginary container. This container can be left in the client's room so that it can be attended to later but does not have to interfere with present activities. Clients may picture the material in a jar on a shelf, or they may actually purchase a jar in which the material can be visually imagined. The possibilities for containment are endless, but the general principle is the same. It is a way for clients to leave emotional material behind so that they can concentrate on tasks at hand. It does not necessarily mean they forget about the problems; rather, it gives them permission to think about them later and to shelve them temporarily away from present issues.

When clients shelve emotional material temporarily to focus on memory, it is important for them to be able to return to this information if necessary. They should have access to someone who can assist them in dealing with emotional reactions (a psychotherapist or family member) so that the emotions do not continue to build to the point of explosion.

Some clients are not able to shelve emotional distractors, and if this continues to be problematic they may not be ready for work on memory (or other cognitive rehabilitation). They may need to focus on emotional resolution before focusing on cognitive deficits.

Rehabilitation settings are similar to real-life settings where persons are required daily to shelve emotional material. People cannot function adequately on the job or in school if they are worried or angry about something going on in their home situations. They are not able to concentrate on tasks at hand, and their performance may decline, including their ability to remember to complete assignments and so forth. Clients who learn to shelve distractors while in rehabilitation can use these skills when returning to their real-world settings as well, be they school, work, home, or avocational pursuits.

Clarification of Understanding

The final component of active listening involves the listener's clarification of understanding. Understanding can be communicated to the speaker and reinforced for the listener through both nonverbal means (e.g., nodding the head) and verbal means. Acknowledgment facilitates the listener's active participation in the interaction and enhances memory.

Another method of clarifying understanding is through restatement of the information. The listener can restate information back to the speaker (either verbatim or paraphrased) to acknowledge understanding and to provide repetition (to facilitate storage). Therapists should encourage and provide situations in which clients can practice this aspect of active listening. Videotaped feedback is helpful in teaching and practicing this skill. Tasks can be structured such that time limits are established between presentations of material (e.g., the therapist may talk for 2 minutes and then ask the client to restate). Time periods and complexity of information can be gradually increased. Therapists can also alter tasks to accommodate the type of information to be remembered. For instance, is it important for the client to remember the gist of the material, or is it important to remember all the details?

Clients can also ask questions to ensure their understanding of information. TBI survivors are frequently hesitant to do this, particularly as the rehabilitation setting may recreate feelings experienced as a child (e.g., fear of asking questions, so as not to appear "dumb"). Clients may need assistance in being able to ask questions comfortably by learning assertiveness techniques and working on the self-acceptance process (both of which occur in psychotherapy sessions). Therapists must also be careful in this area since many times comfort in the relationship will facilitate the client's willingness to ask. Therapists must endeavor to demonstrate respect for the client and provide an environment that encourages asking questions rather than placing the client in a position of feeling one down.

The clarification of the client's understanding of material is crucial. The therapist must assist in the process in whatever manner is necessary. If the material is inadequately or inaccurately understood, it will be stored as such in memory (or it may not even achieve the status of storage). It is not enough to assume that the client understands what is being said; the therapist must ensure that this process is occurring by periodically checking with the client and monitoring behavioral and verbal demonstrations of understanding.

The ability to listen actively to information is a basic requirement for memory. If the client can attend, concentrate, maintain eye contact, attend to body posture, eliminate distractors, and clarify understanding, the basic building blocks of remembering information are in place.

Note Taking

The concept of writing information down to facilitate memory is not a new one. Most of us have used this strategy since childhood as we learned how to spell words, remember material in classrooms, and so forth. As we grow older, many of us abandon this method of memory, relying more heavily on internal ability. After brain injury, however, it may become important to reinstitute such a strategy to complement and/or substitute for memory limitations. In some cases, note taking skills were never adequately learned prior to injury. Here, the therapist may be in the position of training an entirely new skill rather than retraining an old one.

Advantages and Disadvantages

Note taking has several distinct advantages. The act of writing information down makes the client a more active listener and demonstrates intent to remember. It also facilitates the encoding process via multisensory modalities (i.e., hearing the information, seeing it written down, and using motor functions to write). Writing also provides repetition of information and helps decrease boredom and the potential for distraction.

The disadvantages of taking notes include distraction from interpersonal relationships and the danger of its substituting for good listening skills. When note taking is used, it is a complement to listening, not a substitute. Otherwise, if the client is writing down words but not understanding what is being said, the information will be useless.

Basics of Note Taking

The basics of note taking include helping clients take notes in their own words and balance listening and writing abilities. Note taking also involves knowing when to take detailed notes and when to listen more for main ideas. Elimination of unnecessary words (e.g., *the* and *and*) and the use of abbreviations (e.g., & for *and* and v for *versus*) shortens writing time and makes note taking more effective. Clients may also make up their own abbreviations.

There is a skills component to taking notes. For example, the client may need to take more detailed notes when trying to remember actions agreed upon by team members in a treatment meeting than when trying to remember the plot of a 30-minute television program. The therapist can assist the client in understanding the difference in these types of situations to facilitate effective and efficient note taking. Note taking can be extensive or simply a few key words jotted down to prod memory.

There are situations in which note taking may not feel appropriate. For example, in social situations with friends, taking copious notes while trying to listen to the conversation may feel awkward. While note taking does facilitate the listener's active concentration, it can also detract from some situations, such as those in which the client would need to demonstrate interest (e.g., with intimate friends). Other situations may feel too exposed to some clients (e.g., in church), and they may be hesitant to use this strategy in these situations.

Therapists, in addition to assisting clients in understanding the different types of notes to take in different situations, can assist in the identification of situations that feel appropriate to the client. It is always the client's decision whether or not to use any strategy. Some persons may experience great difficulty with the concept of taking any notes in any situation (e.g., the client who before injury never wrote anything down), and the therapist may encounter resistance if this strategy is forced on the client.

In situations that require extensive note taking (e.g., a classroom), the therapist can either work with the client on the previous method of note taking (if this is the client's preference) or teach alternate note taking skills such as the Cornell method.[2] Cornell is especially useful for students returning to classroom settings as it provides a simple way to organize material to be learned.

In the Cornell method, the client is instructed to use $8\frac{1}{2} \times 11$ paper and draw a vertical line down the center. There are five steps involved in the Cornell method (see Table 7-1).

1. *Record.* The client is instructed to record what is said on the right side of the paper.
2. *Reduce.* Immediately after class (or as soon as possible after the information is presented), the client reduces the information into fewer words (a summary but not an oversimplification) on the left side of the paper.
3. *Recite.* The client covers the right column with a piece of paper, reads the comments in the left column, and then attempts to recite an explanation of the material.
4. *Reflect.* This is the process of thinking about the material and incorporating it into previous knowledge.
5. *Review.* The client then periodically reviews the information to facilitate its permanent storage into memory (repetition).

Basically, the Cornell method is one of actively listening to information presented and taking relevant notes on it. To organize the material and expand the

Table 7-1 Sample Cornell method of note taking.

Life Science
12-16-89

Transport systems	Three systems of body called transport are: circulatory system, respiratory system, excretory system.
Circulatory system does? (3)	Circulatory carries food and oxygen to cells and carries away waste products. Also protects from disease.
Circulatory system composed of? (3)	Circulatory system consists of blood, heart, and blood vessels.
Describe blood	Blood is made up of liquid (plasma) and solids (red and white cells, platelets). Red: carry oxygen to cells' hemoglobin (hemoglobin contains iron and makes blood look red). White: fight infection. Platelets: clotting.
Blood vessels (3)	Veins, arteries, capillaries.
Functions of each	*Arteries: Thick*-walled blood vessels; carry blood *away* from heart. *Veins: Thin*-walled blood vessels; carry blood *back* to the heart (usually carry only waste products). *Capillaries:* Connect veins and arteries; allow food, oxygen, waste to pass directly between blood and cells.
Diseases of circulatory (2)	*Heart attack:* Clogged artery prevents blood from reaching the heart. *High blood pressure:* Pressure against the wall of the artery is too high, causes heart to work harder.
Ways to keep the circulatory system healthy (3)	Eat foods low in fat. Keep weight under control. Exercise regularly.

capacity to remember it, it is then reduced (or chunked) into smaller units. The third step of reciting simply expands the material back again. The memory storage process is similar to the way a song is stored in memory (i.e., a lengthy song may be recalled by simply hearing one or two notes versus the entire song). The material becomes condensed (chunked) and stored via association with a smaller unit of information (chunking and association strategies are discussed later in this chapter).

It should be noted that clients seem either to embrace the Cornell method fully or to reject it fully. Therapists can teach the strategy as a possible method of taking notes but should not force the client to use the method. It is an alien idea for many persons, and there may be resistance to the seemingly complicated set of steps involved. Therapists can assist clients in learning the steps ("the five R's") by using various mnemonic strategies such as rhyming (to be discussed later in this chapter).

Regardless of what method of note taking the client chooses, the therapist can ensure that it is effective. Practice can be given so that both the quality and the quantity of the information obtained can be improved. Notes need to be organized in a manner that facilitates learning, and the writing must be legible. The therapist can work with the client in establishing a comfortable mode of note taking.

Specific Situations

There are numerous situations that lend themselves to using the strategy of note taking. Therapists can encourage clients to purchase a notebook or pad, which becomes one of the items needed in daily activities. The client should always have access to paper, whether this is a small pad carried in a purse or pocket or a larger notebook with sections that can be used in multiple situations. To teach the strategy of note taking, the therapist can use the Eight-Step Model (see Chapter 5) as a structure. Baseline measures are then taken, goals set, practice given, and generalizations developed and practiced. Practice and generalization opportunities can occur in sessions, treatment team meetings, physician appointments, and so forth. The use of pen and paper, for many clients, becomes almost second nature.

New information. New information includes that which the client is required to learn. This may be data from therapy sessions or daily activities of life. In therapy, clients may need to remember names, assignments, and procedures to follow (e.g., operation of computer hardware and software, steps in performing strategies, or programming an aid such as a pill timer). Clients can place a pad of paper by the telephone and take notes on conversations to facilitate memory. In fact, many clients maintain phone logs by the telephone in which they routinely take notes on conversations and record any follow-up steps.

As previously discussed, clients who are entering academic or vocational settings can learn effective and efficient note taking to facilitate memory for course material. Notes can be taken on material presented in the classroom (from the instructor) as well as from textbook material (this area is discussed in more detail later in this chapter). Persons returning to employment may also need to take notes as they learn new job duties, names of persons with whom they will work, company organization, office procedures, and so forth. Notes can also be taken in meetings (e.g., conferences, committees, and church meetings).

Lists. Another situation in which note taking is useful is in the development of lists. Lists of to-do items can be for a specific length of time (day, month, or year) and can include many types of activities (chores, appointments, home practice assignments, or errands). Clients who develop the habit of making a daily to-do list find that they accomplish much more than when they try to remember every-thing without writing it down. As lists are written down, individual items can be prioritized and organized on calendars to ensure that they are done. After the task is completed, it can be marked off and the list reorganized. Most persons find it helpful to do such a list on a daily basis. Not only does this task assist in remembering to complete items, but it also facilitates motivation by the client's seeing items completed and gaining a sense of accomplishment. It also is a way for clients to regain a sense of control over their lives (lists are discussed further in Chapter 8).

Other types of lists include assignments (e.g., from sessions or in the classroom), questions to ask (e.g., in a physician's appointment), shopping items (groceries, clothing, and toiletries), and so forth.

Instructions. Much of daily life consists of receiving instructions in various forms, and this information is well suited to the strategy of note taking to facilitate memory. In rehabilitation, clients are instructed in how to perform tasks (walking, dressing, and remembering). Note taking can be used in academic and vocational areas (discussed above) and activities of daily living, where clients encounter a myriad of instructions, such as:

- cooking (ingredients needed for recipes, proper use of Teflon pans, use of a microwave)
- cleaning (use of vacuum cleaner, how to use oven cleaner or furniture polish)
- laundry (use of detergents, fabric softeners, bleach, washer and dryer)
- safety (electrical appliances or chemicals, first-aid procedures, emergency procedures)
- assembly (bookcases, storage boxes)
- installation (hanging pictures, installing an answering machine)
- repair (patching clothing, replacing fuses)
- personal care (patch-testing products that may cause allergic reactions, weight management and exercise programs)
- driving (car maintenance schedules, using a car wash)
- money management (balancing monthly bank statements, preparation of income tax returns, maintenance of financial records)
- personal health (taking medications)

The above list is only a small sampling of the possible range of instructions that can bombard a client in daily life. It is easy to see how effective note taking can be in these situations. Clients can easily become overwhelmed with so many tasks, and writing down instructions (steps, sequences, and time frames) can assist in this area.

Directions. Clients will also need to learn directions to new locations and may need to relearn directions to old locations. In rehabilitation settings, they may need to learn directions to therapist offices, the cafeteria, and so forth. As the client recovers and moves back into the real world, the need to learn directions increases even more. If the client returns to the hospital for outpatient therapy, the route between home and the hospital may need to be learned. The client who has forgotten how to get to a friend's home will need to relearn this. The client who is pursuing vocational options may need to participate in job interviews at various new locations. Writing down directions (and even drawing a map) can facilitate arriving in a timely and more relaxed manner.

Since learning directions depends on both the ability to remember and the ability to discriminate between spatial elements and directionality, it is often a difficult task for TBI survivors. There are a number of methods for writing down directions. Therapists will first need to assess the client's independent ability to write directions (baseline). Assistance may be required in the sequencing of directions because many clients may write the information down in a jumbled manner. Therapists will need to ensure that the client understands the directions that have been written; otherwise, he or she may still be unable to learn and follow them. For locations that are used frequently, clients can keep a directions log or record information on index cards, which can be filed in a systematic manner (alphabetically, by area, or by category). It is often helpful for clients to obtain an aid such as a message holder, which can be installed in the car to hold the directions that have been written down.

Schedules. The use of calendars is particularly important for TBI survivors, especially for remembering their appointments. Appointments may be made with five or more therapists per day in acute care settings. Clients will attend meetings with physicians, therapists, treatment team members, groups, rehabilitation providers, employers, academic advisors, and so forth. As clients typically experience a decrease in energy after injury, the effective management of time becomes even more critical. Recording information on a calendar will facilitate both memory for the event and a sense of control.

Clients who use to-do lists can record this information on the calendar as well. If the calendar is checked daily, the client will have the day's activities at a glance and can "gear up" for what needs to be done during the day.

Calendars are personal items; clients have definite preferences in the types of calendars they like to use. Some persons prefer small calendars that will fit into a purse or pocket, while others prefer large Day Timers in which many pieces of information can be organized. Therapists can assist clients in discovering the particular style that best fits their individual needs. Regardless of the type of calendar used to record schedules, it should be large enough to allow ample room to write information (clients can be encouraged to use pencil rather than ink since, undoubtedly, schedules change). Clients should also be encouraged to use only one calendar. All information can be recorded on one to minimize confusion and avoid the unnecessary additional steps of recording information more than once (calendars are also discussed in Chapter 8).

Personal information. To remember personal information, clients can keep journals (either for emotional reactions or simply as a listing of activities performed during a day). Names, addresses, and phone numbers of important people in the client's life can be recorded in a central location. The client can also maintain a central record of names, addresses, and phone numbers of physicians who are caring for them. Medication dosages and times can be listed and checked as the medication is taken. Other personal information such as insurance data, financial investments, emergency phone numbers (police and fire department), and safety procedures can all be written down and placed in central locations for easy access. See Chapter 8 for devices that can be used to store personal information.

A particularly useful way to remember personal information is through the use of a memory notebook. This notebook may be organized by the client and may contain sections for appointments, medications, birthdays, emergency numbers, and so forth. Memory notebooks can also contain a section where clients can record daily information such as notes from therapy sessions, phone calls, and conversations.

Audiotaping

For many clients, audiotaping may be the most effective manner of remembering information. Clients who may benefit from audiotaping include those who have motor limitations (which affect writing or typing information), slowed information processing (which affects the speed with which information can be heard, processed, and applied to paper), or visual impairments (limited ability to see what is being written). In addition, there are several types of situations where audiotaping may be appropriate, such as in a classroom where large amounts of information are presented or in other meetings (where note taking may cause the client to feel too exposed). Clients can also use audiotaping as a reminder of items to do. Directions and instructions can also be taped, as can information given over the telephone. Various recording aids are further discussed in Chapter 8.

Advantages

There are several obvious advantages to audiotaping information. The client will be able to go back over the material in a leisurely manner later and fill in any information missed. It also provides the client with repetition and review of information to enhance learning. Finally (and perhaps most important), it alleviates some of the stress the client may feel at having to catch every single word said, which frees him or her to listen more effectively.

Disadvantages

On the opposite side, many clients find listening to an audiotape of information already heard a boring experience. It may actually decrease motivation to remember, particularly if the information is not inherently interesting. Listening to an audiotape is also time consuming; for example, a 2-hour class lecture ultimately becomes 4 hours of listening time (many clients find it useful to listen to information in the car rather than at home). When audiotaping information, clients may find their attention wandering and depend too much on the tape to listen for them. Taping does not require much active participation from clients. A particularly helpful way to deal with this situation is for the client both to take notes and to audiotape information; later the client can listen to the tape and fill in any missed portions of the notes. Finally, in audiotaping, the client may become dependent upon the mechanical ability of the tape recorder (particularly if he or she does not simultaneously take notes). Tape recorders can malfunction, batteries can die, and clients can forget to turn on the recorder or inadvertently erase information.

Repetition and Rehearsal

These two terms are often used synonymously to denote the practice of rehearsing information repeatedly to ensure encoding and memory. Repetition is the skill most persons learn to use early in school when learning dates for a history examination (that is, by saying the material over and over until it is encoded). Repetition can occur in any sensory modality, e.g., verbal (repeating information over and over either aloud or silently), motor (drawing or writing information repeatedly or performing a sequence of actions repeatedly), or visual (looking at information over and over). Repetition of information facilitates overlearning.

The strategy of repetition can be used to remember information that is presented through a single sensory modality or through any combination of these. Repeating information several times can be done either silently or aloud. The more sensory modalities utilized in the repetition of information, the more likely that the information will be remembered. For example, to learn a new telephone number, the client may wish to see the number, repeat it aloud, and write it several times to assist in its encoding. In this manner, the senses of vision, hearing, and touch are used.

Therapists will need to be sensitive to the client's best mode of encoding information. For example, some persons remember information better when hearing it; others need to see information to encode visually; yet others need both to hear and to see information. A TBI survivor will generally have a stronger sensory modality (and in some cases this may be motor), and the therapist can utilize this strength to assist in the learning process.

Using several sensory modalities facilitates the input of information; repetition and rehearsal of sensory data facilitate its storage. Some information only needs to be remembered for short periods of time, such as what has been chosen from a luncheon menu. This may not be critical information for a TBI survivor (or anyone), and the client may not remember it past several minutes or several days and rarely will remember it several months or years later. On the other hand, other types of information may need to be stored for longer periods of time. For example, consider the client who has recently married and needs to remember an anniversary date. This information may need to be reviewed periodically and may even require repetition to ensure its permanent storage in memory.

As with any type of learning, it is usually best to space the material such that the client is not overwhelmed with too much all at once, but is provided with ample opportunity to learn. Therapists will also need to be sensitive to the amount of information provided at any time as well. Clients may only be able to work with one or two pieces initially but may be able to add more pieces later. In addition to the amount of information to be rehearsed, therapists can assist clients in determining the appropriate number of times information needs repeating. Some clients may only need 2 or 3 repetitions, while others may need 50 repetitions to encode the information.

Repetition is the typical strategy used in direct retraining of memory functions (see Chapter 6). It is commonly used in school settings and it is the way most of us learned dates in history, spelling of words, and rules in mathematics. It is undoubtedly a valuable and necessary strategy for use in training memory, and is almost always used to some extent in everything we do. When recovering from a brain injury, however, the amount of repetitions required to learn is usually increased. As a result, therapists who use only this strategy with clients are doing them a disservice. Repetition is only one part of an overall menu of strategies. It must be used judiciously and in combination with other strategies and aids. In isolation, it is inefficient, ineffective, and ultimately frustrating for both the client and the therapist.

Specific Situations

Some of the specific situations in which repetition and rehearsal may be helpful are discussed below.

Lists. In rehabilitation, clients are often exposed to lists of various types such as words, numbers, and so forth. In the assessment process, lists such as the Digit Span Subtest of the Wechsler Adult Intelligence Test or the Rey Auditory Verbal Learning Test are used to measure span of attention and capacity for learning (see Chapter

3). These tests are designed to obtain baseline measures and are not designed as therapeutic tasks. No assistance is given by the examiner, and the client must independently determine how to memorize the information.

In therapy sessions, clients may also be exposed to computerized or pen-and-paper lists of words, numbers, or pictures. Ideally, the therapist would take a baseline measure on the task, teach the strategy of repetition and rehearsal, allow the client to practice, and then measure performance. This technique is useful when clients are required to learn small amounts of information for small amounts of time and gradually increase their learning capacity. The training must, however, go beyond this point. The therapist must assist the client in applying this strategy to real-life situations and provide practice such that generalization occurs (see Chapters 5 and 6).

Using repetition to learn lists can be helpful if the lists are useful to the client. For example, learning lists of items to purchase in the grocery store or a list of to-do items for the day will mean more to the client than learning a list of unrelated words or numbers. Other useful lists may include sequences of events (e.g., personal historical data or history of the accident), lists of medications to take, lists of emergency phone numbers, and so forth.

Instructions and directions. Repetition, like note taking, can be a valuable strategy in learning instructions and directions. Instructions and directions can first be written down and then rehearsed a sufficient number of times to encode into memory. Repetition of directions can be particularly important, especially if these are learned before getting into the car to drive. It is distracting to drive and read directions at the same time; previous learning of directions (through repetition) can decrease both the likelihood of getting lost and the potential for distraction (and accidents) caused by the client looking away from the road to read written directions.

Schedules. From the moment a client enters an acute care facility, he or she encounters schedules. The daily schedule will include established times to rise, sleep, attend therapies, and so forth. One of the typical ways therapists measure memory in such settings is whether or not the client can remember the schedule. Repetition proves especially helpful in this regard, and as the client is able to remember the daily schedule, control and empowerment are facilitated.

As the client moves out of acute care into other settings, schedules may continue to be important and may continue to be complicated. For instance, many clients continue to see various medical personnel and may simultaneously return to work or school. Some clients may also use a calendar for scheduling (discussed above) and then use repetition to remember as much as possible.

Personal information. Other information especially amenable to repetition and rehearsal is personal information such as birthdates, anniversaries, date of accident, date of hospitalization, and so forth. For clients who are disoriented, repetition may be used to assist them in remembering the present date, time, and location. Since most clients do not remember their accidents, family members can assist in the reconstruction of events so that the client can build a personal history; repetition can assist in encoding this history.

Medical information can also be learned with repetition of the names, purposes, and dosages of medications and what time of day to take them. Other medical information may include the names and addresses of physicians, dates of appointments, and findings of medical procedures.

Clients may also need to remember names of persons from the past or new persons, and repetition can be useful in these situations as well. In rehabilitation, the names of therapists, physicians, and other clients are important. In employment and academic situations, clients may need to remember names, titles, and other pieces of information about persons with whom they come in contact.

Association

Association involves joining two items together to form a connection. Association can be used to link various types of information (e.g., auditory, visual, and motor) to form a chain of memory. Associations can be formed between new pieces of information, or new information can be associated with what the client already knows. The forming of associations is the basis for all memory.

Most people are familiar with this strategy, even if they are not familiar with its name. For example, when the television sitcom husband ties a string around his finger to remember to bring home the milk for dinner, he is using a strategy of association (the string and milk become linked so that when he sees the string he will remember the milk). In addition, when hearing the word *milk,* most of us can form a visual image we associate with this word, and we can form the visual image regardless of whether the word is spoken to us or we read it.

The use of association assists in the process of encoding information (i.e., reducing it to a form that can easily be stored). It also assists in the retrieval process. Associations can be made within cognitive, physical, and emotional realms and can consist of combinations of information gained from all sensory modalities. We can associate a particular feeling with a particular picture or song heard on the radio; a person may associate fear with an object or person from childhood; we may associate nausea with a food that caused this sensation at an earlier point in life.

In rehabilitation, therapists must be sensitive to clients' internal, preexisting positive and negative associations, many of which can be used to strengthen desired associations or may cause distraction in therapy sessions. For example, if the therapist wears a particular perfume that the client associates with a negative past experience, it may be difficult for the client to participate in sessions. Similarly, the therapist's office may evoke pleasant associations for the client, as it reminds him or her of a parent's office. It should be noted that while some associations are known to individuals many may remain subconscious while continuing to affect the person in the present (e.g., the client may not consciously know why that particular perfume causes an adverse reaction).

Therapists can assist clients in forming associations to aid in remembering information. For example, clients can remember the placement of items (keys, purse, wallet, or checkbook) using this strategy. Associations can be formed by placing the items in the same location each time (forming an association of place) or by placing a colored sticker on the item and in another visible place (such as the front door). In this technique, the client would see the colored dot on the door and associate it with the colored dot on the object to be remembered. Other associations can be used in addition to dots (i.e., any cue that has significance for the client will work). Associations can be formed by representational images (i.e., pictures and words) and in various other ways.

Sample tasks can be designed in therapy sessions, such as practicing associating words with objects. For example, suppose the client needs to remember the following list of words: pencil, paper, and red. The therapist can assist the client in associating these words with various objects in the room. The pencil could be imagined under the sofa, the paper could be imagined in the closet, and the word *red* could be imagined written on the wall. After the images are strongly formed, the therapist could test memory by saying the associated words (i.e., *sofa, closet,* and *wall*) and asking the client to recall the original words to be remembered.

Clients may need practice in forming these visual associations and in repetition to ensure encoding into memory. The stronger the visual imagery available to the client, the stronger associations will become. The important aspect of lasting associations is links of significance to the client. If the client can draw upon personal information to form the associations, the storage process may be more permanent.

The possibilities of forming associations are endless. Several examples follow, but therapists are encouraged to work with clients in developing links appropriate for these individuals.

1. A client has difficulty monitoring the passage of time and forgets to check his watch periodically to structure this. He writes the word *time* on a piece of paper and places this in a visible location to remind him to check the time. Each time he sees the word, he is reminded to check his watch.

2. A client has difficulty remembering to record automatic teller card withdrawals in her checkbook. She places a small star on both her checkbook cover and her automatic teller card to associate these two items.

3. A client has trouble remembering to fasten her seatbelt when getting into her car. She attaches a small piece of yellow paper to her steering wheel as a visual reminder.

4. A client who has difficulty with circumlocutous speech is working on monitoring this but needs external cuing as he forgets to do this internally. The therapist assists by touching her earlobe when the client is going off track. Each time the client sees this, he remembers he is digressing and returns to track (eventually, this strategy becomes internalized).

5. A client cannot remember his therapist's name (Eileen), so he pictures an "island" in her hair. Each time he looks at the therapist's hair, he sees the island, which then reminds him of the therapist's name.

6. A client who repeatedly forgets whether the dishes in the dishwasher are clean or dirty develops a system of placing magnets on the door. Red is associated with clean dishes, while black is associated with dirty ones.

7. A client who must remember to call a friend back the next day moves the telephone to a location where she will be sure to see it. Seeing the phone reminds her to call the friend.

The important aspect of association strategies is to form strong links of meaning to the client.

Pegging

Pegging is a strategy that assists in remembering names. It involves a three-step process: creating a peg name for a person's real name (such as the word *barrel* for the name *Darryl*), identifying some salient visual characteristic of the person (such as height or an unusual facial characteristic), and then associating the peg name to the visual characteristic. The goal of this strategy is to enable the client to identify a person by the use of this visualization.

Suppose a client meets a man named Darryl. The client should ask himself or herself "What feature really stands out about this person?" The client notices that Darryl's nose is unusually large. The client develops a peg for the name *Darryl;* in this case, the client chooses the word *barrel*. Another person may choose a different peg, such as "plaid shirt" (associating Larry, Darryl, and Darryl on television wearing their plaid shirts). In the final step, the client visualizes Darryl with a barrel (or some other image, such as a plaid shirt) on his nose. If a strong visual image is formed, the name should be stored into memory (repetition will enhance the process). Suppose the client then meets Darryl again 2 weeks later and tries to remember his name. As the client looks at Darryl, he or she notices the nose again, immediately pictures a barrel sitting there, and associates *barrel* (the peg) with the name *Darryl*.

Pegging is a personal process. It works best when clients are encouraged to develop their own pegs and visualizations. Pegs work best when they are concrete objects or nouns that can be easily visualized. For example, the client may wish to use the peg *Ferrell* (the name of a business where the client used to work); however, this peg will be difficult to use since it is not easily visualized (or, if it can be visualized, it may involve several additional and unnecessary steps for the client to do so). Pegs work best when they are simple and developed by the client rather than the therapist.

In the visualization process, it is helpful to have the client focus on the feature of the person that is most outstanding. This may or may not be the same feature the therapist notices. For example, a client may look at a person and notice blue eyes; the therapist may notice high cheekbones. The feature chosen should be relatively stable (i.e., each time the person is seen, the same feature is likely to be noticed). Features such as weight or hair color can be tricky associations since they are subject to change. If an association is formed with blonde hair, it may be difficult to recall the name if the person changes hair color to black. Also, the more vivid and absurd the associations formed, the more strong the memory is likely to be. We tend to remember things that stand out more than those that are commonplace.

The strategy of pegging can be taught via pen and paper, three-dimensional tasks, or computer. Therapists can use pictures from magazines or photographs from real life. The therapist can also produce a simple videotape of several persons introducing themselves. In producing such a videotape, it is suggested that the therapist use an identical background for all subjects; otherwise, clients may identify the person with his or her environment rather than remember a feature. Situation-specific learning is common with TBI survivors, and therapists can easily avoid it in this situation. After practice in therapy sessions, the therapist should provide practice in the real world to facilitate generalization. The therapist should also assist the client in rapidly performing the sequence of steps necessary in this process so that it becomes a smooth process when the client is rapidly introduced to a new person.

Pegging is also taught via computerized instruction. *The Einstein Memory Trainer*[3] is a computer software program that offers extensive practice in this technique. Initially, the client is exposed to peg names for 40 common male and female names. Some examples are *Joe-Toe, Bruce-Noose, Harry-Hairy, Alice-Palace,* and *Joyce-Juice.* The client is given the option of substituting his or her own peg names and should be encouraged to do so during this phase of learning. For example, the peg name for *Mike* is *Microphone.* If a client's auto mechanic is named Mike, he may wish to substitute the word *mechanic* for the word *microphone* as it will be easier for him or her to recall.

Once the client has exhibited proficiency in remembering all 40 peg names, he or she is given the opportunity to match peg names with real names. The computer presents a face on the screen and indicates the name of the person below it. Depending on the client's memory skills level, he or she may choose to use a program option that allows him or her to have the peg name exhibited on the screen with the real name. The length of exposure can be controlled as well as the number of faces to be shown on the screen in one test trial. The client's goal at this time is to create a visual picture associating the peg name with the salient characteristic of the face shown on the screen. This is frequently the step with which the client will require some assistance initially.

Once the client has been exposed to all the names, recall is tested. The faces will appear on the screen in random order, and the client will be asked to type in the correct name. After each trial, the client's performance is shown on the screen. This can be graphed or charted separately so that the client has some sense of progress.

One caution that should be employed with this program initially is to limit practice to perhaps only two trials per session since the computer will occasionally generate the same face in two consecutive trials but ascribe different names to it. This can be a source of confusion to the client in the early stages of learning. Once confidence and expertise in this technique are developed, this will be less of a factor.

If therapists use such computerized programs with clients, it should be considered a first step. A viable hierarchy for the skill attainment of pegging would be to use *The Einstein Memory Trainer,* practice using magazine pictures, practice using real photographs, practice with videotaped persons, and finally practice with real-life persons.

Pegging is a process that requires much practice, and many clients are unwilling or unable to expend this much energy to remember names. Therapists will need to be sensitive to the client's wishes in learning this or any other strategy. However, clients who feel defeated before they try this technique may be selling themselves short and losing an opportunity to learn an effective strategy for remembering names (see Appendix 6C for more information on *The Einstein Memory Trainer*).

Loci

The concept of loci (location) is centuries old. It was used by ancient Greeks and Romans to help them remember long speeches and sermons. The technique involves memorizing a set of locations that are extremely familiar to the client, for example his or her room, a favorite movie theater, a classroom, or an office. It is essential, however, that the locations fulfill these three requirements: They must be easily memorable to the client so that they can be easily recalled, they must lend themselves to easy visualization (door, window, etc.), and they must be in an order that is easy to remember (to facilitate remembering items in the correct sequence). Once the various locations in the familiar room or area have been memorized, they can be used repeatedly to assist in remembering lists of words, key elements of a speech, and the like. Associations are formed between the information to be remembered and the locations.

This technique is particularly effective with those clients who enjoy a better visual than auditory memory. Loci can be taught using pen-and-paper tasks as well as computer programs. There are two basic steps involved in learning information through the strategy of loci: determining a familiar location and series of items within it, and visualizing the items to be remembered along with the loci (association).

Suppose the client wishes to remember several items on a shopping list (e.g., bread, butter, and jelly). The first step is to decide upon a familiar area (which can be used over and over with different sets of information to be remembered). The client may choose his or her living room. As the client imagines the living room, he or she may want to take an imaginary walk around it and notice items that become pegs. For example, the client passes by the following items on the imaginary walk: the television, door, fireplace, table, lamp, sofa, and chair (note that the client can develop as many pegs as necessary). The next step is to picture the words to be remembered connected with the pegs in the living room. Thus the client may visualize

- a loaf of *bread* sitting on top of the *television,*
- a stick of *butter* spread on the *door,* and
- a jar of *jelly* burning in the *fireplace.*

After these visualizations are formed, the client should be able to recall the list of words by simply taking an imaginary walk around the living room and remembering the pegs of television, door, and fireplace (all of which should evoke visual images).

One effective way to present and practice this technique is with *The Einstein Memory Trainer.*[4] This computer software program introduces the client to a set of loci (ten locations in a movie theater: entrance, cashier, ticket-taker, lobby, popcorn stand, theater doors, aisle, seat, screen, and exit). Once these locations have been memorized, the computer generates a list of ten words to be memorized. Each word is associated with one of the ten locations described above. The client is asked to visualize each word to be remembered and associate it with a theater location. For example, the word *frog* is paired with the first location, the entrance to the theater. A large frog is shown on the screen sitting on the theater marquee. The client is also assisted with visualizing one or two additional words and locations but is then required to generate personal, unique, visual pairings. After exposure to the list of ten words, the client is asked to type in the ten words in order. Results are shown on the screen. If the ten locations have been learned, the majority of the words should be recalled. To emphasize further the efficacy of this technique, the therapist may wish to have the client attempt to memorize the ten words in order before using the loci technique.

Initially, the word list to be remembered involves association of concrete words (*frog, boot, egg,* and *elephant*) to the various loci. As some expertise in this technique is acquired, more abstract items can be introduced (e.g., visualizing a picture for the abstract word and then associating it with the appropriate location).

For example, the word *freedom* may be visualized as the Statue of Liberty or the American flag (these visualizations will vary from person to person). The visualized word is then associated with the appropriate location (the Statue of Liberty on the theater marquee) to assist in recall of the abstract word.

After training in this technique (which takes much practice), the client should be given ample opportunity to transfer the strategy to real-life situations, and the therapist can assist in any problem areas that may arise (most frequently, problems occur because of faulty visualization).

An appropriate use of this technique in the real world may involve helping the client remember to bring materials to a therapy session, prepare for an oral presentation in class, recall to-do lists, and so forth.

One definite drawback to this strategy is the length of time required for most clients to learn it. Also, much practice is needed for some clients to remember the initial set of pegs and/or the sequence of steps required to perform the strategy.

Chunking and Grouping

Chunking and grouping are terms generally used synonymously to describe a strategy involving grouping large pieces of information into smaller chunks to remember them. The principle of chunking is to break down information so that it can be stored effectively. It is based on the premise that the immediate store available for encoding information is 7 ± 2 pieces of information at a time. These pieces can either be individual items or larger chunks. For example, the telephone number 229-7338 can be learned one number at a time (2 2 9 7 3 3 8), in which case all seven "slots" in memory would be filled. Alternatively, it can be chunked into smaller pieces, which would fill fewer slots (229 and 7338 for two slots, or 229 73 38 for three slots). Chunking is an efficient way to manage and encode information to enhance learning.

Chunking is a way to organize information. It is similar to a filing system or the way information is stored on a computer disk. It involves grouping information in some organized fashion and storing it that way to facilitate retrieval. Information can be chunked in many ways.

Ways to Chunk

Categories. Development of categories is a useful way of grouping information. For example, a grocery list can be remembered by grouping dairy products and vegetables. Categories are general and include specific items; they can be concrete (fruits and vegetables) or abstract (freedom).

Properties. The client and therapist can review information to be learned and decide upon any identifying properties that can assist in chunking items together.

Properties are diverse and can be used to group like (or unlike) items; some examples of properties are

- color (same colors, shades of color),
- shape (round, square, diamond, triangle, solid, empty, transparent),
- size (large, small, fat, skinny),
- texture (smooth, bumpy, silky, made from wood, plastic, etc.),
- temperature (hot, cold, cool, warm), and
- parts.

Functions. Items can also be grouped according to functions they perform (what they do) or uses that can be found for them. Examples include grouping items that can be used in the kitchen or items that can cut.

Origins. Identifying where items originate can also be a means of grouping (e.g., items grown in warm climates or items derived from plants).

Definitions. Information can be grouped by what it means (e.g., words that are synonyms or antonyms can be grouped together).

Specific Situations

Material can be chunked in any manner that the client finds personally meaningful. The therapist can again assist in developing grouping strategies that will apply to the individual client's life. Often, clients will group material in a way that the therapist may find difficult to follow but that has meaning for the client.

In therapy sessions, several pictured items can be presented that the client must group independently (the therapist takes a baseline measurement, sets goals, monitors practice, and so forth). Any number of items can be used, but 20 seems to work particularly well with most clients since it provides enough material to group effectively into several chunks. The broader the chunks, the easier the memory process in this task will be. For example, if the client discovers 10 categories, there will only be 2 items in each one, and it may be difficult to chunk this much information. To facilitate learning, chunks should be kept to 7 ± 2 categories (or fewer if the individual client's available store is diminished after injury).

Many activities lend themselves to chunking. In therapy sessions, clients can use pen-and-paper, three-dimensional, or computerized tasks and can group both auditory and visual information. Chunking can be used to remember numbers such as phone numbers, social security numbers, license tags, credit card numbers, addresses, and so forth. Dates can also be remembered using chunking, such as birthdates, anniversaries, holidays, and historical events. Items on lists can also be chunked, including grocery store and personal items, to-do lists, appointments, and so forth.

Clients can also be taught to chunk together sequential information, such as steps involved in performing a task or the parts of a speech. Outlining written information is another way of chunking large pieces of information into smaller ones.

Rhythm and Rhyming

Rhythm

Many persons use rhythm to remember information without realizing that they do so. Rhythm is most apparent in songs and poems but is also used in daily speech. A popular current use of rhythm (and rhyming) is the musical style of rap. Anyone who has heard this music will immediately be able to identify its possibilities in facilitating memory. When information is spoken (or sung) in a monotone with minimal voice inflection, clients become bored and unmotivated to learn. Varying pitch, tone, and rhythm all facilitate encoding into memory. When words are added to rhythm, the brain is using both sides, and storage can be more effective.

Suppose a client wants to remember a list of items to pick up from the grocery store. He or she could make up a song linking these items together in some way or use the melody and rhythm of a song he or she already knows and simply fill in the words.

Rhyming

Rhyming involves the use of rhythm but adds the factor of similar sounds. Common rhymes are learned throughout our lives, such as "Thirty days hath September, April, June, and November. All the rest have 31, save February." This rhyme helps us remember how many days are in each month of the year.

Most persons are familiar with poems, many of which utilize both rhythm and rhyming. Poetry is, as a general rule, much easier to remember than a paragraph of equal length. For example, using the above example of days in the months of the year, consider the difference in learning the information in the format of a poem versus a format such as: "September has 30 days. So does November, April, and June. All the other months have 31 days, except February."

Clients can be encouraged to make up their own rhymes and apply them to areas of daily living. Rhythm and rhyming can be used to remember lists, classroom material, instructions, and so forth. Therapists are encouraged to be creative with clients in helping them develop these strategies.

Word Finding Strategies

Word finding difficulties are not solely memory deficits but are often experienced and defined that way by clients. When a client is in the middle of a conversation and suddenly cannot think of the word he or she wishes to say, it can be extremely frustrating, and, to some clients, embarrassing.

Most often the words are stored in long-term memory, but the client may have difficulty gaining access to and retrieving them. The client may be able to recognize a word when given several choices but may be unable to recall it independently without cues. The therapist's task is one of teaching strategies to the client so self-cuing and compensation can occur.

Therapists can assist clients in identifying the purpose of the communication. In some cases, it is important for the listener to get the meaning of the speaker's words but not necessarily the details. It may not be essential that the client continue struggling to find the exact word. It may be enough to convey the gist of it instead. If the client can give himself or herself permission to convey meaning in appropriate situations, he or she may feel less stressed and less critical of his or her abilities (which in turn will facilitate improved self-confidence and perhaps the ability to remember more). The use of videotaping is valuable in teaching word finding skills to clients.

Pacing Speech

For clients to "buy time" in which to use any word finding strategy, the therapist can teach a slowing down strategy. Clients can pace speech patterns slowly so there is time to search internally for the appropriate word. In some cases, this strategy will not be adequate, but it can serve as a way to minimize obvious and embarrassing incidents of word loss.

Talking Around the Word

Clients who experience word-finding difficulties can learn strategies to compensate. They can learn to talk around the word they wish to say by describing it (either verbally or by writing it down). Descriptions may be similar to the ways in which information can be chunked (discussed previously in this chapter). For example, the client can describe a category, a property, a function, and so forth. Suppose the word the client is trying to recall is *purple*. He or she may talk around it by saying "It's a color, a deep shade, and it's often used in robes of kings." Often, as a client describes the word, he or she will think of it. This probably occurs because the correct memory file has been tapped. The client can also describe the word by using an antonym ("It's the opposite of large") or by using a sentence with blanks ("It's the _____ that counts.").

Mental Imagery

Another strategy for remembering words is for the client to form a mental picture of the word and then describe it, mimic it, or draw it. Suppose the word to be recalled is *baby*. The client could picture a baby in his or her mind and then try to describe it, (e.g., "It's a small person, it's newborn, and it cries"). The client could also demonstrate or act out the image (as in the game Charades) by pretending to cradle a baby in his or her arms and rocking it back and forth. Finally, the client could attempt to draw a baby. As with talking around the word, this mental imagery often facilitates the client's recall of the word.

Word Substitution

If the client is ineffective in using any of the previous strategies, he or she can substitute a synonym for the word (e.g., the word *yells* for *screams*). Another strategy is to substitute an antonym for the word (e.g., the word *whispers* for *screams*).

Gestures

If the client has great difficulty in finding the appropriate word, gestures can be used as substitutes. For example, clients may draw a circle in the air or on paper instead of saying the word *circle* or make a hammering gesture for the word *hit*. Some clients can draw the word or even write it when saying it is difficult or impossible.

Remembering Written Information

We encounter written information constantly in our lives. Some of this material is short (directions on a frozen dinner), while some is more lengthy (a textbook). Therapists can work with clients to determine their particular needs in remembering written information. For example, the person who only needs to read frozen dinner labels may not need to remember this information, while the person reading a textbook will need to remember what the book contains. The strategies presented in this section can be adapted, depending upon the individual needs of the client.

Regardless of what the client's particular needs are, there are a number of basics that are important in remembering written information.

Maladaptive Habits

Regression. Persons who continually go back over information before the initial reading is completed may have difficulty in remembering the information. If the client reads and rereads sections of the material before the entire material is completed, comprehension may be impaired and concentration interrupted. This is similar to the advice given to writers: Do one task at a time; either write or edit, but don't do both. The same applies to reading: Either read or reread, but don't do both at the same time.

Vocalization. Many persons learn to read by moving their lips to the words. This can be distracting behavior that may take away from concentration on the material at hand. This is different from reading aloud, which provides multisensory encoding.

Subvocalization. Another type of this behavior is subvocalization. When persons subvocalize, they do not say the words or actually move their lips; however, they are exerting effort in muscles as they think each word and almost say it.

Reading with distractors. A final bad habit while trying to remember written information (or any type of information) is reading with distractors. Persons who try to remember information while simultaneously listening to television or radio may have great difficulty in accurately and adequately encoding this information. Some clients may be reluctant to change this behavior, particularly since it is often learned early in life. Therapists may need to creatively demonstrate differences in the client's memory by giving tasks in situations with and without distractors, and testing memory after each. Effective remembering takes concentration, and persons who are recovering from TBI often have little to spare and should be discouraged from reading with distractors (either internal or external; see the previous discussion in this chapter on distractors).

Adaptive Habits

There are a number of strategies that clients can develop to facilitate remembering written information.

Preview information. A preview of the information to be remembered will assist the client in gathering a "big picture" of how the material is organized and how much material there is. If the material has an introduction, it is helpful to read the topic sentence (or abstract) to gain an understanding of what the material is about. Likewise, reading the summary at the end will provide a general overview of the information.

Skim and scan. A preview of material often involves skimming and scanning the information before actually beginning to read it. For example, many people scan a magazine before beginning to read. They will briefly look through the contents or flip through the articles to assess what material is covered and then move through in a more leisurely fashion, reading each article of interest. The preview provides an overall structure within which the client can operate.

Find the main idea. Depending upon the client's reason for reading the material, it may be important to remember main ideas or details. A determination of which ideas are important can save both time and energy. In any case, finding the main idea can be helpful in understanding the material, even if the client is also required to know details.

Repetition and rehearsal. This strategy has been discussed previously in this chapter. As material is read, it is important to repeat and rehearse it to facilitate memory. This is particularly true with lengthy and detailed information, such as that from a textbook used in classroom work.

Note taking, outlining, and highlighting. Note taking has been discussed earlier in this chapter and is an important aspect of remembering written information. Taking notes facilitates understanding and assists the client in organizing the material into manageable chunks. Clients may need guidance and practice in taking notes and attending to types of information, purpose, etc. Some clients prefer to take notes during an initial reading of material while others prefer to read once for content and take notes on the second reading. Therapists can provide practice situations and assist clients in determining the optimal manner and timing of taking notes.

Writing an outline of material is also helpful in organizing and condensing information and is an association strategy as well (the information can be condensed and stored and then expanded when retrieved). Many clients do not do well with outlines, either because this skill was never learned prior to injury, or because other cognitive limitations have interfered. Therapists can teach a variety of outlining techniques, from formal outlines using upper and lower case, roman numerals, etc., to more informal ones with the focus on content of the outline instead of form.

Finally, clients can learn the use of highlighting when reading. This simply means marking important information in some manner, e.g., underlining or marking with a colored highlighting pen. This cues the client to important information and serves as an associative and organizing strategy as well.

Vary reading speed. Depending on the purpose for reading the material, the client can learn to vary the reading speed. For example, if the client is required to remember details, he or she may need to read the information slowly; if the client is reading for the main idea, he or she can read the material quickly; and if the client is reading for pleasure, he or she may want to read at a more leisurely pace.

Read material three times. It is generally a good idea to read information at least three times (some TBI survivors may need to read more than three times). The first reading is to analyze the information (i.e., to find out what it is about). The second reading is to understand the material in depth, and the third reading is to incorporate the material in knowledge already held, such that the information makes sense.

NOTES

1. E. Miller, *Recovery and Management of Neuropsychological Impairments* (Chichester, England: John Wiley & Sons, 1986), 56–61.

2. W.H. Saleebey, *Study Skills for Success* (Elmsford, N.Y.: National Publishers of the Black Hills, 1981), 30-32.

3. M. Samet, *The Einstein Memory Trainer* (Burbank: Preface, 1983).

4. Ibid.

8

Compensatory Aids: Prosthetic and Cognitive Orthotic Devices

In the previous chapters, we discussed the direct retraining of memory and the use of compensatory strategies. This chapter focuses on the use of external compensatory aids. Two types of compensatory aids are discussed: prosthetic devices and cognitive orthotic devices. Several authors have pointed out the usefulness of such devices,[1,2] and Parenté and Anderson[3] have documented the variety and complexity of devices presently available. Most therapists may be aware of some types of external aids but may not be aware of others. We have found the use of such devices to be extremely helpful in assisting survivors of head injury to address memory problems.

This chapter presents practical information for therapists about the various devices that are available as well as information about how to use the aids with clients. At the end of the chapter, two appendixes are provided that include purchasing information (manufacturers, addresses, phone numbers, and prices) for aids discussed in the text, as well as additional vendors.

Clients can use prosthetic and orthotic devices to gain control over their lives and increase their independence (empowerment). Most devices are generally acceptable to clients, and because they are concrete and provide immediate relief from nagging problems, most clients can immediately see the relevance of their use.

These devices are adjuncts to other cognitive rehabilitation therapies and are not used in isolation. When therapists teach clients to use such devices, the approach to doing so is the same one used to teach other skills and strategies, and it is helpful to use a treatment model such as the Eight-Step Model discussed in Chapter 5. Clients must participate in the process of choosing devices applicable to their individual situations. Therapists can introduce a variety of such devices from which the clients can pick and choose.

PROSTHETIC DEVICES

Fowler, Hart, and Sheehan[4] were perhaps the first to use the term *prosthetic memory* in relation to training persons with memory impairment. Prosthetic memory aids are designed to help the client perform some memory function by substituting a device to obviate the problem. These devices are typically electronic or nonelectronic aids and do not usually involve the use of a computer.

Prosthetic devices have the advantage of being inexpensive compared to many of the other interventions discussed in this book. Learning to use a prosthetic device typically takes a short period of time.

These devices also may have disadvantages. Clients may be resistant to using them. Some clients feel that if they just try hard enough these devices will not be needed. Other clients may fear becoming too dependent on the aids or may feel embarrassed to use them around other people.

A variety of different prosthetic devices are outlined in this chapter. The list is ordered in terms of the level of complexity of the devices. In most cases, the rule of thumb when using these devices is keep it simple.

Aids for Timeliness, Completeness, and Accuracy

These devices ensure completeness and accuracy of performance. Many simply cue the person to perform a task at a certain time or organize a task so that it can be performed rapidly and with a minimum of frustration. Most can be created from paper-and-pencil materials or are available at local department stores or from specialty catalogs.

Alarm Clocks and Watches

Alarm clocks are, of course, common devices in use by most of the population, typically as a way to awaken on time in the morning to get to work or school. In addition to this use, however, clocks can be helpful to clients with traumatic brain injury (TBI). For example, clients may set alarms to remind themselves to keep an appointment or turn off the stove. In fact, some stoves have this as a built-in feature. Clocks can be used to remind clients to take medication, turn the television on to watch a certain program, call a friend, and so forth.

This type of device is readily available. It must have certain features to be useful to the TBI survivor, however. First, it must be easy to operate. Many alarm clocks are quite complex because of the number of built-in functions. These types are less useful for a TBI client because of the memory necessary to operate the various features. Moreover, the person must read a technical manual to understand the clock's operation. Therefore, although alarm clocks can provide a vast array of different useful features, the rule again is keep it simple.

The alarm should also have a large, readable array to accommodate those persons with visual impairments. The display must be readable without having to press a button to illuminate the dial. Ideally, the person should be able to read the dial from a distance of 12 feet in a darkened room. The clock should also have a multialarm feature such that it can be set to go off at different times during the day. Moreover, the alarms should go off at the same times each day unless otherwise programmed. This will facilitate reminding the client to take medications.

There are a variety of clocks that have these features. They are commonly available in department stores and vary in price from $5 to $20.

Several wrist watches have alarm features that can be programmed to beep at half-hour and hour intervals. The Seiko Corporation has recently marketed a talking wrist watch that will speak to the client to remind him or her of an appointment. A similar watch is sold by Hammacher Schlemmer.

Signs

Signs are any visual display that can be used as a reminder either to do something or not to do something. Signs can be made with instructions, one or two words to serve as a reminder to the client, or visual images (icons) to represent an idea. The general rule when using signs is that they must be visible to the client but unobtrusive. While signs are helpful prosthetic devices, they are not in common use in most homes, probably because they are embarrassing to the client. They are often highly noticeable to an observer. The use of signs is particularly effective when used with strategies such as association (see Chapter 7).

Signs are relatively simple to construct from household materials such as colored pencils and white typing paper. Even the simplest signs have a cuing and association function and warning capability. For example, signs placed in different locations can be used to remind clients to do something or direct their attention to some location. This is especially important in a large rehabilitation facility or house. It can be useful to post lists of things to do before leaving the house at strategic locations or anywhere the person frequently exits. This ensures that the client is continually reminded of this important sequence of safety checks. Signs that describe how to operate kitchen appliances should be placed in plain view and near the area where the client would operate the appliance. This type of sign also warns the client of things to avoid when operating the appliance.

Signs obviously vary in their level of complexity. However, for most TBI survivors, more than three short statements is difficult to process and recall, especially if the sign is designed to cue a rapid reaction. The most important elements of the sign should be printed in the largest type and placed at the top of the list, since that is where most people will begin reading. Warning signs should be printed in red ink or on red paper, so that the color will suggest importance.

Visual images (icons) can also be used in making signs and are helpful particularly for those clients who process better visually (e.g., artists). Catalogs of these are available from Media Materials (see Figure 8-1).

The client and therapist can make simple lists of common signs and warning labels from household materials (e.g., backs of cans, electronic devices, and appliances). Once the list is constructed, the client can memorize the appropriate response by using repetition, rehearsal, chunking, or other strategies (see Chapter 7).

Figure 8-1 Sample Media Materials signs.

Cuing Cards

Cuing cards are a type of sign that reminds the client of something he or she is supposed to do in a certain situation. Cuing cards may also specify a sequential action or an appropriate response in a variety of situations. For example, most of us are familiar with the various icons and simple cues on copiers. These are generally embossed in various places, typically nearest the point where the action would take place. To change the paper, there is an explanation next to the paper tray. To sort the document, there are buttons and brief explanations or icons next to the sort tray. The placement of the cues illustrates the principle of *point of access*. This means that the cues are not effective unless they are placed near the object or area where the action takes place. Therefore, if the client uses the object frequently, association, repetition, and rehearsal will ensure permanent memory storage.

It is also necessary to *cluster* cues to describe multiple or complex behaviors. This is especially necessary in situations where some behavior must follow another to complete the task. For example, placing paper in a copier requires taking out the tray, opening the magazine, placing the paper into the magazine in a certain manner, and inserting the loaded tray back into the copier. Sometimes, levers or latches must be set or locked. Operating a microwave oven typically requires pressing two or three buttons in a certain sequence. In these types of situations, it is necessary to position the cuing cards directly adjacent to the devices that the client operates. The sequence of instructions should read from left to right. The description of any one step should not involve more than seven words. Critical steps should appear in red or other forms of highlight (see Exhibit 8-1).

Colored Key Jackets

Simple and inexpensive, colored plastic key jackets allow the client to organize his or her key chain and to associate certain keys with certain colors. Color coding keys eliminates confusion and search time. The plastic key covers are available at most locksmith shops and cost about 25¢ each. An entire key chain can usually be coded for less than $3. Newer varieties glow in the dark for easy nighttime searching.

Exhibit 8-1 Cuing card for microwave.

HOW TO WORK THE MICROWAVE

STEP 1: Put Your Food Inside
STEP 2: Press Time Start Button
STEP 3: Press Numbers For Correct Cooking Time
STEP 4: Wait For 3 Beeps
STEP 5: Take Out Food and Press Clear Button

Checklists

A checklist is a paper-and-pencil device that allows the person to complete a task consistently. They have proven effective for ensuring that TBI clients perform work-related tasks correctly, for training accurate completion of sequential steps, and for creating convenient lists of routine behaviors around the home. For example, if a client who returns to work must perform routine daily tasks, it will be easy to construct checklists that will ensure that the tasks are done consistently. The same technique works around the home. For example, checklists can be placed on doors or next to exits to list the things that the client must do before leaving home.

Checklists can also increase the client's feelings of control and decrease obsessive worrying or compulsive behaviors. For example, if the client has a routine to complete every day, the checklist can be used to avoid rechecking steps.

Appointment Calendars

Appointment calendars are a mainstay of any cognitive rehabilitation training program. Calendars provide structure as well as serve as reminders later for the client who needs to recall what happened on a certain day. As with some other types of devices, however, some clients will be hesitant to use calendars, especially if they have never needed to use one before. Therapists will have to be sensitive to this issue when introducing the aid.

Clients can learn to use appointment calendars easily, and the devices are relatively inexpensive. There are, however, many different types of appointment calendars, and the utility of any one type depends greatly on its features. There are certain features that any appointment calendar must have to provide a useful prosthetic service to the client.

First, the calendar must be large enough to accept messages, directions, and instructions. Calendars smaller then 7 by 10 inches may be too small, but calendars larger then 8½ by 11 inches are usually too large and bulky to carry. Second, the calendar should have 30-minute markings for the client to write in important messages at the appropriate time of day. Third, it is useful for the calendar to include sheets of plain lined paper along with each time-marked page. Clients can then write down instructions, directions, phone messages, and so forth on these pages. The pages are also useful for making diary entries at the end of each day. In these ways, the calendar can be used not only as a way to add structure and to remember appointments but also for taking notes, which is an extremely useful strategy (see Chapter 7).

We have evaluated many appointment calendars to determine which work best with TBI survivors. Few commercially available calendars have all the features outlined above. One calendar, available from EZ Record company, has parts that the client can purchase separately. The calendars come in a variety of sizes and colors and are reasonably priced. This calendar is especially compatible with another device, the SONICA appointment minder, which is described below.

Although this calendar has worked quite effectively for most clients, it is important to remember that the client must ultimately choose a calendar that he or she feels is useful. The therapist must not impose his or her particular preference.

Appointment Minder

This is a useful device for many TBI survivors. It is a multipurpose beeping reminder that is inexpensive and extremely easy to use. It is produced by SONICA Corporation and consists of a plastic bar approximately 1 by 6 inches in size. The bar supports various white levers that mark off the day in 30-minute increments, starting at 8 A.M. and ending at 5 P.M. There is also a clock at the bottom of the bar and a calendar function that will display the day and date. The client simply slides the bar for a given time to the side, and at that time of day the appointment minder will begin to beep. The device will continue beeping until the client presses the stop button at the bottom. The client can set any or all of the alarms each day or simply leave them set for daily reminding.

The appointment minder is especially useful in conjunction with the EZ Record appointment calendar because the time markings are identical (see Figure 8-2). The appointment minder affixes to the cover of the appointment calendar and functions to remind the person to look at a particular time on a certain page. The device costs only $12.

Pillbox Reminders

These devices are special types of timers that are designed to hold the client's medications and to remind the client when it is time to take certain ones. They are generally available at department stores or from specialty catalogs. The devices are easy to operate and can be conveniently carried in a purse or pocket. Many are battery operated with lights above each compartment in the pillbox. The lights are set to blink at a certain time of day and to continue blinking until the client lifts the lid on that compartment. Therefore, the device signals the client to take the correct medication at the right time, eliminating the need to remember which medication is appropriate at a particular time of day. These devices are available from local suppliers such as department stores, pharmacies, etc. or may be ordered from the West Bend Company.

Other versions of the pillbox reminder are simply plastic boxes that are subdivided for various medications. With this type of device, compartments can be labeled and a beeping wrist watch used to keep the medication regimen on track. If the client takes only one medication, the device can be set to beep at that time every day.

Information Storage Devices

Business executives have used this type of device for years to keep convenient records of phone numbers, addresses, and other forms of personal information. The simpler versions are also useful for TBI survivors to consolidate their personal information in one easily accessible place. However, many of these devices are actually miniature computers that are difficult to operate. Some clients may

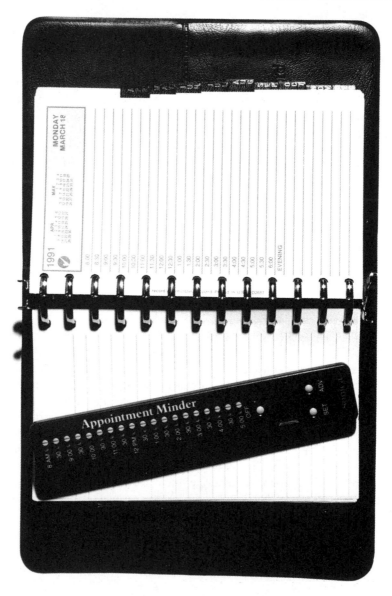

Figure 8-2 EZ Record appointment calendar and appointment minder.

therefore have a difficult time using them or accepting them. The therapist may need to help the client enter personal information and demonstrate how to use the device to gain access to that information. Only after the client can use the device is it feasible to expect that he or she will be able to enter or update the information.

Digital Diaries

Casio corporation makes a variety of high-capacity information storage devices called digital diaries (see Figure 8-3). These are relatively complex devices and are often useful with relatively high-functioning clients. There are several varieties, ranging in price from $70 to $200. See local suppliers of Casio products (e.g., department or jewelry stores). The level of sophistication has increased markedly over the years, and now the devices can transmit information to and from most IBM-compatible computers. The device has a calendar, telephone number storage directory, and address directory, and it can also store reminders and appointments. It will also mark a day on the calendar to remind the client that he or she has an appointment that morning or afternoon.

The device is compact (about 3 by 5 inches) and is easy for most clients to use. It is relatively easy for most clients to learn to recall needed information from the

Figure 8-3 Casio digital diary.

digital diary. It is more difficult to learn how to input personal information; therefore, the therapist may initially need to enter the client's personal information and then help the client learn how to use the device. With practice (repetition), the client can learn how to update the information already entered and then input new information.

Phone Banks

This device is a limited version of the Casio digital diary. Many companies market phone banks. In our experience, however, the Texas Instruments phone bank is the most reliable and least expensive. The phone bank holds a limited number of phone numbers and names, has a calculator feature, and is considerably smaller than other models. It is easy to use and highly reliable. It costs about $19 and is available at most department stores (Figure 8-4).

Telememo Scheduling Watches

Casio corporation also makes a variety of different wristwatches that not only keep the time, date, and day but also store information such as phone numbers and memos. These are called Telememo watches (Figure 8-5). One version also dials

Figure 8-4 Texas Instruments phone bank.

the phone numbers for the client. The DB (short for data bank) series comes in a variety of capacities that differ in terms of the number of phone numbers or messages that can be stored. For example, the DB-50 can store as many as 50 names and phone numbers and/or memos. The DB-30 model stores only 30 names and numbers and/or memos.

We have found that the DB-30 is perhaps the most useful of the watches for TBI survivors. First, it is waterproof, which eliminates the need to remove it when showering or bathing. Clients therefore seldom misplace it. It holds 30 phone num-

Figure 8-5 Casio Telememo watch.

bers and names, which is more than adequate for most clients. It is also easy to operate.

The DB-50 phone-dialer model is unique because it actually dials the phone numbers. The client simply holds the watch up to the mouthpiece of the phone and presses one button on the side of the watch. The watch then sounds the number into the phone, which completes the connection. This dialing feature is quite accurate and easy for most clients to learn to do. The phone-dialer model has one drawback, however. It is not waterproof and must be removed when bathing. Consequently, this model may be lost or ruined, and if it must be replaced, all the phone numbers must be input again.

The Telememo watches come with a 5-year lithium battery and seldom need servicing. They range in price from $25 to $50. It takes approximately 1 hour to train the client to use the watch and an additional 1 hour to input all the phone numbers he or she would commonly use.

Information Pendant

Mediscope Corporation makes a necklace that can store large amounts of information on microfilm in a convenient gold pendant costing about $50. The client compiles a list of useful information, including phone numbers, bank card numbers, blood type, medication, birthdates, and so forth. The list is sent to the company, which reduces it to a piece of microfilm and inlays the film into the Mediscope pendant. The device was originally used to store medical information, but any information can be inserted. Moreover, large amounts of personal information can be input into the device. The pendant is an attractive amulet that is suspended on a gold chain and worn as a piece of jewelry. The client simply looks through one end of the pendant through a lens that magnifies the film, making the information easy to read (Figure 8-6).

Memory Card

We have found that another version of the Mediscope system is also quite useful and easy to construct. Simply typing the information in large bold letters will make it readable when it is reduced several times. Therefore, it is easy to record large amounts of personal information on plain paper and then reduce it several times on a photocopier to approximately the size of a credit card. This paper is then laminated to ensure that it is not destroyed by water or effaced over time. The client can then carry this information in a wallet or purse for ready access. It is easy to make many copies for multiple placement or in case of loss. Although the Mediscope pendant is more convenient, this system is about as effective and certainly less costly.

Figure 8-6 Mediscope pendant.

Dictation Tape Recorders

Microcassette recorders are perhaps the most useful device discussed in this section. They are inexpensive, typically less than $50, and are available in office supply stores, electronics stores, etc. They are compact and can fit easily into a shirt pocket, purse, or glove compartment of a car. The device allows the client to take messages much faster and more accurately than is possible by writing down the information. For example, the client can record phone messages without the embarrassment of asking for repetition of directions and instructions. Students can use the recorder to tape lectures and instruction and then write their notes later when reviewing the tape. Clients can record directions and instructions from conversations or lists of things to buy at the store. Clients can read into the tape recorder, rewind the tape, and listen to it while rereading the material to improve memory for the text. See Chapter 7 for additional discussion on tape recorders.

It takes less than 1 hour for most clients to learn how to use the tape recorder. The low cost, limited learning time, and multiple applications of this device make it generally useful with most clients (See Figure 8-7).

COGNITIVE ORTHOTIC DEVICES

Cognitive orthotics are devices and computer software programs that perform an artificial thinking skill for the client. Therefore, the therapist teaches the client to use an external device in a real-world setting to obviate a memory or intellectual impairment.

The term *cognitive orthotic* has also been used to describe a variety of training procedures. Several authors[5-7] have described how cognitive orthotic devices can be effective for training a person with TBI to operate a word processor. There is also software that supports activities of daily living.[8] Parenté and Anderson[9] have shown how a laptop computer with an expert system shell program can be used to do the job that a person with TBI previously performed, thereby allowing the person to return to work and to function successfully. COGORTH (short for COGnitive ORTHoses) is a computer programming language specifically designed to create computerized training simulations for persons with head injury. This language is described below.

Clearly, there are a variety of applications of cognitive orthoses. It is perhaps the most exciting area of prosthetic research and one that will have an obvious payoff in the future.

Simple Retrieval Devices

This class of device stores information and retrieves it easily. In some ways, the devices are similar to the information storage devices outlined above. The difference is that these devices process the information and make a decision about how best to recall.

Automated Telephones

Telephone answering machines ensure that phone calls are answered, and there is an audio record of who called and what messages were left. The special features available in these machines vary greatly; certain features are quite useful for certain

Figure 8-7 Microcassette recorder.

types of TBI survivors. The voice-digitizing feature is useful for those clients with physical disorders such as spasticity, missing limbs, or an inability to use their hands to hold the receiver or to dial. The device records not only incoming messages but also stores phone numbers and names by digitizing the client's voice. The client need only say the person's name out loud and the phone will dial the correct number. The client can also talk to the person without using the receiver simply by speaking at the phone.

Dialing telephones store as many as 200 phone numbers and dial them with the push of a single button. These are especially useful for those clients who may eventually return to work in a clerical capacity. The often-used phone numbers are entered into the device along with relevant information, such as the person's name and address. The client can then use this information to cue recall of the person's number. The phone then dials the number without error, which eliminates the additional time and frustration of misdialing. These telephones are generally available wherever phones are sold.

Spelling Checkers

Spelling checkers are devices for checking spelling, which is often a problem for persons after TBI. Several companies make spelling checkers that sell for less than $100. Most can fit easily into a purse, wallet, or briefcase. The devices are easy to use and store more than 100,000 commonly used and misspelled words. Each works in a similar fashion. The client spells the word the way it sounds, and the device returns the word the way it is actually spelled. For this reason, electronic spelling checkers are frequently referred to as phonetic spellers.

Several companies make devices for checking spelling. For example, Franklin Corporation, Seiko, and Selectronics Corporation all make spelling checkers for less than $100 (see local suppliers of these materials).

The advantages of electronic spellers are obvious. First, a book that would hold 100,000 or more words would be bulky and difficult to carry. Second, the spelling machine is also a training device. Each time the client spells a word phonetically and then sees the correct spelling, there is a paired association between the phonetic and the correct spelling. Third, some electronic spellers come with additional features, such as a thesaurus and dictionary definition capability. Therefore, these spellers are actually three machines in one. Also, a talking speller, which reads the words aloud to the client, is available through the Franklin Corporation.

The one machine with the most features and the lowest cost is produced by Selectronics Corporation. It sells for $50 to $100 and has a spell-checking function and thesaurus capability, and it will also return the dictionary definition for all its words. It stores 100,000 commonly used words with 220,000 synonyms. It measures approximately 3 by 5 inches and is easy to operate.

Spelling checkers are especially useful for those clients who will eventually return to school or to a job that requires a good vocabulary and grammar. The devices are also useful for training word meaning. Other electronic spellers have different word games, such as hangman, that the client can play. In that way, it serves as a simple multifunction therapy tool.

Grammar, Punctuation, and Style Checkers

Rightwriter 4.0 and *Grammatik IV* are designed to work with most popular word processors. These programs check the document for literally thousands of grammatical errors. Each flags the various errors and makes suggestions for how to fix them. Although each program differs in the way it parses the text, each provides a summary of weaknesses, general suggestions for improving writing style, and an analysis of critical writing features such as adjective/adverb use and readability.

Grammar, punctuation, and style checkers require that the person know how to operate a computer and use a word processor. This type of software is therefore best suited for students or working people who have to generate reports and memos on a regular basis. Each costs about $100. *Rightwriter 4.0* is probably a little better for checking the overall style of the document, whereas the *Grammatik IV* package is better for individual statements and sentences. The packages also differ in terms of how each processes the document.

In either case, the end result is a document that is free of grammatical errors. When these are used in conjunction with the spelling checkers discussed above, the client can be assured of a paper that is free of spelling and grammatical errors. These packages also serve to train the person's grammar and punctuation by constantly alerting the person to problems and providing suggestions for correcting them. As a result, the client's writing style generally improves with time, and he or she is less likely to make these kinds of errors in the future.

Expert Systems

Expert systems are computer programs that are used by business and industry in lieu of high-priced experts. The program is written to mimic the decision-making process of an expert and to make this expertise available to anyone who needs it. In the last 5 years, a variety of shell programs have become available that allow the user to develop expert system programs without any knowledge of computer programming. An expert system is most applicable in situations where the job can be reduced to a set of rules or steps. Those skilled in defining and implementing the programs are called knowledge engineers.

Expert systems may be quite useful for those TBI survivors who were previously employed in a job where the task demands were easily specified or could be reduced to a rule-based system. A computer program can be produced that would make the same decisions for the client. He or she could learn how to operate the program and return to work.

This concept is quite feasible now that laptop computers are generally available. The client and employer provide information concerning decision-making rules, which is loaded into the expert system shell. The system is then field tested to eliminate the flaws in logic and programming. The client could then take the expert system to work and begin using it to make many of the decisions he or she previously made independently. The system therefore serves two purposes. First, it allows the person to return to work rapidly and to perform at the same level of speed and accuracy. Second, the expert system actually retrains the person to recall the rules of the job. Over time, the client becomes progressively less dependent on the expert system and eventually may not need it at all.

Several case studies using the expert system are presented below. Although the approach has generally proven successful, it is not without drawbacks. First, the client must have a laptop computer or access to one at work. A set of rules that are sufficient to perform the job must be developed, and the client must be willing and able to learn to operate the computer. The system must be refined to work effectively with a variety of potential choice situations. This may take considerable time and may result in constant updating. It may take months before the program works perfectly.

In the future, continued expansion in this field will require therapists to have different skills to implement this type of treatment. Technical as well as people skills will be needed, along with the patience to break down the training into simple tasks and stages. The therapist must be able to work with computer software, to explain hardware operations, and to work patiently so that the client eventually learns how to operate the various devices independently. The therapist must also keep abreast of the vast array of electronic devices and computer applications to determine which innovations are most appropriate for use with TBI survivors.

Case study 1: Alice. Alice had worked as a legal secretary before her head injury. She was unable to return to her job at the law firm for about a year after leaving the hospital. During that period, she was involved in a program of stimulation therapy that produced modest improvement in attention and concentration. Alice was still unable to manipulate information effectively in working memory. For example, she had difficulty doing arithmetic problems in her head and keeping up in complex conversations.

She eventually returned to the law firm, where she worked as a typing pool manager and was responsible for distributing case reports and briefings to several word processors. At any one time, she was responsible for tracking 50 documents at various stages of completion. Even though she kept lists of the various documents, it was clear that her system would have to be improved before her performance would be considered adequate.

We created a computer program to teach domain-specific skills. The program required Alice to give out various case reports to the secretaries and mentally keep track of the status of each document. The program used the names of the secretaries and lawyers with whom Alice worked, and it simulated the task she normally performed. Like her job, the program required high levels of complex mental control. We developed a new checklist for Alice so that she could determine the status of any report. She practiced for an hour after work each day, and her job performance improved immediately.

Alice also began using a single-digit dialing telephone that stored 200 names and numbers that she could gain access to by entering a short code. She purchased a dictation recorder so that she could take accurate telephone messages without having to ask for repetition. Alice is still working full time and does not report any difficulty with her job.

Case study 2: Lois. Lois had worked as a dispatch advisor for a trucking firm before her stroke. Potential clients would call the company, and she would provide advice about the least expensive way to ship freight. Following the stroke, she could no longer perform her job functions and was eventually placed on medical leave. Fortunately, her job was easily reduced to a set of rules, which made it a good candidate for expert system modeling. After intensive interviewing, her rules for advising clients were entered into an expert system, and she was trained to use a laptop computer that operated the system. She took the laptop computer to work each day and set it up on her desk next to the telephone. When a client called, she would simply ask the sequence of questions that appeared on the screen, and the system would provide the least expensive way for the client to ship freight. Eventually, Lois received so much applied training using the expert system that she no longer needed it to perform the job.

Case study 3: Ted. Ted was a college-educated man who experienced memory loss after an automobile accident. He lost his job as a teacher but was eventually hired by a sheltered workshop. Part of his job responsibilities involved keeping track of various workers' productivity. This portion of the job called for exactness and accuracy. He made many mistakes and spent long hours checking his work.

The problem was solved by creating a simple computer program that would accept his tallies and tabulate the results in the form of a report that he could turn in at the end of each day. Ted had only to enter the data correctly, which was a considerably simpler and shorter process than hand-tallying. The computer program did the rest.

COGORTH

COGORTH is a computer language designed to develop instructional programs for cognitively impaired clients who still require cuing, reminding, or guidance to complete daily activities. Complex activities are broken down into simpler tasks that are further subdivided into stages. Each stage presents several options. Responses at each stage yield different corrective feedback. In this way, COGORTH is similar to a computerized self-paced instructional system that can greatly facilitate a client's training. Kirsch and colleagues[10] have demonstrated the use of COGORTH for improving a client's ability to bake cookies. Presumably, the language can be used to train practically any activity.

The application of computer software technology to facilitate training and to mimic clients' job functions is an exciting field that is currently in its infancy. The COGORTH language is already developed, and there has been one successful test of its training capability. The successful use of an expert system shell to expedite return to work has also been demonstrated.[11] This line of research has only scratched the surface of its potential.

NOTES

1. G. Jones and J. Adam, "Toward a Prosthetic Memory," *Bulletin of the British Psychological Society* 32 (1979): 165–167.

2. J. Harris, "Methods of Improving Memory," in *Clinical Management of Memory Problems,* eds. B. Wilson and N. Moffit (Rockville, Md.: Aspen Publishers, 1984), 46–52.

3. R. Parenté and J. Anderson, *Retraining Memory: Techniques and Applications* (Houston: CSY Publishers, 1991), Chap. 12.

4. R. Fowler, J. Hart, and M. Sheehan, "A Prosthetic Memory: An Application of the Prosthetic Environment Concept," *Rehabilitation Counseling Bulletin* 15 (1972): 80–85.

5. E. Cole, "Interface Design as a Prosthesis for an Individual with Brain Injury," *SIGCHI Bulletin* 22 (1990): 28–32.

6. N. Abbot, M. Foschi, and E. Cole, "Word Processing as a Compensatory Device in the Traumatic Head-Injury Survivor," *Cognitive Rehabilitation* 9 (January/February 1989): 36–38.

7. W. Lynch, "Cognitive Retraining using Microcomputer Games and Commercially Available Software," *Cognitive Rehabilitation* 1 (1983): 19–22.

8. D. Chute, G. Conn, M. DiPasquale, and M. Hoag, "Prosthesware: A New Class of Software Supporting Activities of Daily Living," *Neuropsychologia* 2 (1988): 41–57.

9. Parenté and Anderson, *Retraining Memory,* Chap. 12.

10. N. Kirsch, P. Simon, M. Fallon-Krueger, and L. Jaros, "The Microcomputer as an Orthotic Device for Clients with Cognitive Deficits," *Journal of Head Trauma Rehabilitation* 2 (1987): 77–86.

11. Parenté and Anderson, *Retraining Memory,* Chap. 12.

Appendix 8A
Manufacturers of Prosthetic and Cognitive Orthotic Devices

This appendix contains the following exhibits:

- **Exhibit 8A-1** Vendors of Prosthetic Devices
- **Exhibit 8A-2** Additional Vendors of Prosthetic Devices

Exhibit 8A-1

Vendors of Prosthetic Devices

Vendor	Address	Telephone
Casio Computer Co.	PO Box 7000 Dover, NJ 07801	201-361-5400
DAK Industries, Inc.	8200 Remmet Avenue PO Box 7120 Canoga Park, CA 91304	800-352-0800
Damark International, Inc.	7101 Winnetka Ave, N. P.O. Box 2990 Minneapolis, MN 55429	800-729-9000
E–Z Record	PO Box 829 Westminster, MD 21157	301-876-2511
Hammacher Schlemmer	147 East 57th Street New York, NY 10022	800-543-3366
Media Materials	1821 Portal Street Baltimore, MD 21224	301-633-0730
Reliable Home Office	PO Box 804117 Chicago, IL 60680	800-869-6000
Seiko Corporation	540 Fifth Avenue New York, NY 10019	212-977-2800
Texas Instruments	PO Box 655474 Dallas, TX 75265	214-995-2011

Exhibit 8A-2

Additional Vendors of Prosthetic Devices

Vendor	Address	Telephone
Attitudes	1213 Elko Drive Sunnyvale, CA 94089	800-525-2468
Markline	PO Box 8 Elmira, NY 14902	800-225-8390
Sharper Image	660 Davis Street San Francisco, CA 94111	800-344-4444
Solutions	PO Box 6878 Portland, OR 97228	503-643-4876
Syntronics	Building 42 Unique Merchandise Mart Hanover, PA 17333	800-621-5800

Appendix A
Additional Readings

For those readers who wish to learn more about the topics and issues addressed in this book, the authors have provided this listing of additional readings. The list is not exhaustive, but will provide the reader with an overview of available materials. The readings are arranged in alphabetical order.

Adamovich, Brenda, Jennifer Henderson, and Sanford Auerbach. *Cognitive Rehabilitation of Closed Head Injured Patients: A Dynamic Approach.* San Diego: College Hill Press, 1985.

Albrecht, Karl. *Brain Power, Learn To Improve Your Thinking Skills.* Englewood Cliffs, N.J.: Prentice-Hall, 1980.

Barrett, Susan L. *It's All in Your Head.* Minneapolis: Free Spirit, 1985.

Batchelor, J., E. Shores, J. Marosszeky, J. Sandanam, and M. Lovarini. "Cognitive Rehabilitation of Severely Closed-Head-Injured Patients Using Computer-Assisted and Noncomputerized Treatment Techniques." *Journal of Head Trauma Rehabilitation* 3 (1988): 78–85.

Ben-Yishay, Y., J. Rattok, B. Ross, P. Lakin, O. Ezzrachi, S. Silver, and L. Diller. "Rehabilitation of Cognitive and Perceptual Defects in People with Traumatic Brain Damage: A Five Year Clinical Research Study." *Working Approaches to Remediation of Cognitive Deficits in Brain Damaged Persons.* Rehabilitation Monograph no. 64. New York: New York University Medical Center, Institute of Rehabilitation Medicine, 1982.

Bernard, Larry C. "Prospects for Faking Believable Memory Deficits on Neuropsychological Tests and the Use of Incentives in Simulation Research." *Journal of Clinical and Experimental Neuropsychology* 12 (October 1990): 715–728.

Berrol, Sheldon. "Issues in Cognitive Rehabilitation." *Archives of Neurology* 47 (February 1990): 219–220.

Berrol, Sheldon, and Mitchell Rosenthal, eds. Cognitive Rehabilitation issue. *The Journal of Head Trauma Rehabilitation* 4 (1989).

Binder, Laurence M., and Loren Pankratz. "Neuropsychological Evidence of a Factitious Memory Complaint." *Journal of Clinical and Experimental Neuropsychology* 9 (April 1987): 167–171.

Boake, C., R. Parenté, P. Mazmanian, and J. Kreutzer. "Progress Toward an Independent Society for Cognitive Rehabilitation." *Cognitive Rehabilitation* 6 (May–June 1988): 8.

Bornstein, Robert A. "Report of the Division 40 Task Force on Education, Accreditation and Credentialing: Recommendations for Education and Training of Nondoctoral Personnel in Clinical Neuropsychology." *Journal of Clinical and Experimental Neuropsychology* 5 (January 1991): 20–23.

Bornstein, Robert A. and Gordon J. Chelune. "Factor Structure of the Wechsler Memory Scale—Revised." *The Clinical Neuropsychologist* 2 (March 1988): 107–115.

Bracy, Odie L. "Computer Based Cognitive Rehabilitation." *Cognitive Rehabilitation* 1 (January-February 1983): 7–8, 18.

Bracy, O., W. Lynch, R. Sbordone, and S. Berrol. "Cognitive Retraining through Computers: Fact or Fad." *Cognitive Rehabilitation* 3 (March-April 1985): 10–23.

Buzan, Tony. *Use Both Sides of Your Brain*. New York: E.P. Dutton, 1983.

Buzan, Tony. *Use Your Perfect Memory*. New York: E.P. Dutton, 1984.

Caplan, Bruce, ed. *Rehabilitation Psychology Desk Reference*. Rockville, Md.: Aspen Publishers, 1987.

Chelune, Gordon J., and Robert A. Bornstein. "WMS–R Patterns among Patients with Unilateral Brain Lesions." *The Clinical Neuropsychologist* 2 (March 1988): 121–132.

Chute, Douglas, Gretchen Conn, Madeline DiPasquale, and Melanie Hoag. "Prosthesis Ware: A New Class of Software Supporting the Activities of Daily Living." *Neuropsychology* 2 (1988): 41–57.

Cooper, Patricia V., Bobbie K. Numan, Bruce Crosson, and Craig A. Velozo. "Story and List Recall Tests as Measures of Verbal Memory in a Head-Injured Sample." *Neuropsychology* 3 (1989): 1–8.

Crainer, James F., and Howard E. Gudeman. *The Rehabilitation of Brain Functions: Principles, Procedures, and Techniques of Neurotraining*. Springfield, Ill.: Charles C. Thomas, 1981.

Crook, Thomas H., and Glenn J. Larrabee. "Interrelationships among Everyday Memory Tests: Stability of Factor Structure with Age." *Neuropsychology* 2 (1988): 1–12.

Crook, Thomas H., James R. Youngjohn, and Glenn J. Larrabee. "The Misplaced Objects Test: A Measure of Everyday Visual Memory." *Journal of Clinical and Experimental Neuropsychology* 12 (December 1990): 819–833.

Crook, Thomas H., James R. Youngjohn, and Glenn J. Larrabee. "TV News Test: A New Measure of Everyday Memory for Prose." *Neuropsychology* 2 (1990): 135–146.

Crossen, John R., and Arthur N. Wiens. "Wechsler Memory Scale—Revised: Residual Neuropsychological Deficits Following Head Injury." *Journal of Clinical and Experimental Neuropsychology* 2 (November 1988): 393–399.

Crosson, Bruce, Thomas A. Novack, Max R. Trenerry, and Paul L. Craig. "California Verbal Learning Test (CVLT) Performance in Severely Head-Injured and Neurologically Normal Adult Males." *Journal of Clinical and Experimental Neuropsychology* 10 (December 1988): 754–768.

D'Elia, Lou F., Paul Satz, and David Schretlen. "Wechsler Memory Scale: A Critical Appraisal of the Normative Studies." *Journal of Clinical and Experimental Neuropsychology* 11 (August 1989): 551–568.

Edelstein, Barry A., and Eugene T. Couture. *Behavioral Assessment and Rehabilitation of the Traumatically Brain-Damaged*. New York: Plenum Press, 1984.

Ellis, David W., and Anne-Lise Christensen. *Neuropsychological Treatment after Brain Injury*. Boston: Kluwer Academic Publishers, 1989.

Engum, Eric, Robert Sbordone, and Tamara Story. "Hard Talk about Software." *Cognitive Rehabilitation* 5 (July-August 1987): 8–16.

Filskov, Susan, and Thomas Ball. *Handbook of Clinical Neuropsychology*. Vol. II. New York: John Wiley & Sons, 1986.

Franzen, Michael D., Amy Tishelman, Stan Smith, Brian Sharp, and Alice Friedman. "Preliminary Data Concerning the Test-Retest and Parallel Forms Reliability of the Randt Memory Test." *Journal of Clinical and Experimental Neuropsychology* 3 (January 1989): 25–28.

Fussey, Ian, and Gordon Muir Giles, eds. *Rehabilitation of the Severely Brain-Injured Adult: A Practical Approach*. London: Croom Helm, 1988.

Glisky, Elizabeth L. and Daniel Schacter. "Remediation of Organic Memory Disorders: Current Status and Future Prospects." *Journal of Head Trauma Rehabilitation* 1 (September 1986): 54–63.

Glisky, E.L., D.L. Schacter, and E. Tulving. "Computer Learning by Memory Impaired Patients: Acquisition and Retention of Complex Knowledge." *Neuropsychologia* 24 (1986): 313–328.

Golden, Charles, "Using the Luria-Nebraska Neuropsychological Examination in Cognitive Rehabilitation." *Cognitive Rehabilitation* 6 (May-June 1988): 26–30.

Goldstein, Gerald, and Elaine A. Malec. "Memory Training for Severely Amnesic Patients." *Neuropsychology* 3 (1989): 9–16.

Goldstein, Gerald, Michael McCue, Samuel M. Turner, Cynthia Spanier, Elaine Malec, and Carolyn Shelly. "An Efficacy Study of Memory Training for Patients with Closed-Head Injury." *The Clinical Neuropsychologist* 2 (July 1988): 251–259.

Grant, Igor, and Kennth M. Adams, eds. *Neuropsychological Assessment of Neuropsychiatric Disorders.* New York: Oxford University Press, 1986.

Haut, Marc W., Thomas V. Petros, Robert G. Frank, and Greg Lamberty. "Short-Term Memory Processes following Closed Head Injury." *Archives of Clinical Neuropsychology* 5 (1990): 299–309.

Heilman, Kenneth M., and Edward Valenstein. *Clinical Neuropsychology.* 2nd ed. New York: Oxford University Press, 1985.

Herman, David O. "Development of the Wechsler Memory Scale—Revised." *The Clinical Neuropsychologist* 2 (March 1988): 102–106.

Hodges, John R., and Susan Oxbury. "Persistent Memory Impairment following Transient Global Amnesia." *Journal of Clinical and Experimental Neuropsychology* 12 (December 1990): 904–920.

Imes, Cheryl. "Cognitive Rehabilitation of Brain Damaged Patients: An Annotated Bibliography." *Cognitive Rehabilitation* 3 (May-June 1983): 8–19.

Jarvis, P. "The Importance of Patient Friendliness in CACR Software and Tips for Improving It." *Cognitive Rehabilitation* 8 (July-August 1990): 24–33.

Kerner, Michael, and Mary Acker. "Computer Delivery of Memory Retraining with Head Injured Patients." *Cognitive Rehabilitation* 3 (November-December 1985): 26–31.

Kreutzer, J.S., and C. Boake. "Addressing Disciplinary Issues in Cognitive Rehabilitation: Training, Credentialing, and Organization." *Brain Injury* 1 (1987): 199–202.

Kreutzer, Jeffrey, Mark R. Hill, and Catherine Morrison. *Cognitive Rehabilitation Resources for the Apple II Computer.* Indianapolis: NeuroScience Publishers, 1987.

Laatsch, L. "Development of a Memory Training Program." *Cognitive Rehabilitation* 1 (July-August 1983): 15–18.

Lawson, Michael J., and Donald Rice. "Effects of Training in Use of Executive Strategies on a Verbal Memory Problem Resulting from Closed Head Injury." *Journal of Clinical and Experimental Neuropsychology* 11 (December 1989): 842–854.

Leonberger, F. Timothy, Sandra Nicks, Peggy R. Goldfader, and David C. Munz. "Factor Analysis of the Wechsler Memory Scale–Revised and the Halstead-Reitan Neuropsychological Battery." *Journal of Clinical and Experimental Neuropsychology* 5 (January 1991): 83–88.

Levin, Harvey S. "Cognitive Rehabilitation: Unproved but Promising." *Archives of Neurology* 47 (February 1990): 223–24.

Levin, Harvey, Arthur Benton, and Robert Grossman. "Memory Function." In: *Neurobehavioral Consequences of Closed Head Injury,* 99–122. New York: Oxford University Press, 1982.

Levin, Harvey S., Jordan Grafman, and Howard Eisenberg, eds. "Memory Disturbance after Head Injury: Recent Strategies for Research." In: *Neurobehavioral Recovery from Head Injury,* 293–352. New York: Oxford University Press, 1987.

Lezak, Muriel Deutsch. *Neuropsychological Assessment.* 2nd ed. New York: Oxford University Press, 1983.

Loring, David J. "The Wechsler Memory Scale–Revised, or The Wechsler Memory Scale–Revisited?" *Journal of Clinical and Experimental Neuropsychology* 3 (January 1989): 59–69.

Loring, David W., and Andrew C. Papanicolaou. "Memory Assessment in Neuropsychology: Theoretical Considerations and Practical Utility." *Journal of Clinical and Experimental Neuropsychology* 9 (August 1987): 340–358.

Luria, Alexander R. *Higher Cortical Functions in Man.* New York: Basic Books, 1980.

Luria, Alexander R. *The Working Brain.* New York: Basic Books, 1973.

Lynch, Bill. "A Review of the 'The Einstein Memory Trainer.' " *Cognitive Rehabilitation* 2 (March-April 1984): 16–18.

Lynch, William J. "Cognitive Retraining using Microcomputer Games and Commercially Available Software." *Cognitive Rehabilitation* 1 (January-February 1983): 19–22.

Lynch, William J. "Microcomputers in Cognitive Rehabilitation: New Directions." *Journal of Head Trauma Rehabilitation* 4 (September 1989): 92–94.

Lynch, William J. "The Ten Commandments of Rehabilitation Software." *Neuropsychology* 2 (1988): 111–115.

Mack, James L. "Clinical Assessment of Disorders of Attention and Memory." *Journal of Head Trauma Rehabilitation* 1 (September 1986): 22–33.

Mateer, Catherine A., McKay Moore Sohlberg, and Jeff Crinean. "Focus on Clinical Research: Perceptions of Memory Function in Individuals with Closed-Head Injury." *Journal of Head Trauma Rehabilitation* 2 (September 1987): 74–84.

Matthews, Charles G., J. Preston Harley, and James F. Malec. "Guidelines for Computer-Assisted Neuropsychological Rehabilitation and Cognitive Remediation (Division 40, American Psychological Association)." *Journal of Clinical and Experimental Neuropsychology* 5 (January 1991): 3–19.

Meier, Manfred J., Arthur L. Benton, and Leonard Diller. *Neuropsychological Rehabilitation.* New York: Guilford Press, 1987.

Miller, Edgar. *Recovery and Management of Neuropsychological Impairments.* New York: John Wiley & Sons, 1984.

Milton, Sandra. "Compensatory Memory Strategy Training: A Practical Approach for Managing Persisting Memory Problems." *Cognitive Rehabilitation* 3 (November-December 1985): 8–16.

Naugle, R., M. Prevey, C. Naugle, and R. Delaney. "New Digital Watch as a Compensatory Device for Memory Dysfunction." *Cognitive Rehabilitation* 6 (July-August 1988): 22–23.

Nissen, Mary Jo. "Neuropsychology of Attention and Memory." *Journal of Head Trauma Rehabilitation* 1 (September 1986): 13–21.

Norman, Donald A. *Memory and Attention: An Introduction to Human Information Processing.* New York: John Wiley & Sons, 1969.

O'Hara, C., and M. Harrell. *Rehabilitation With Brain Injury Survivors: An Empowerment Approach.* Gaithersburg, Md.: Aspen Publishers, 1991.

Parenté, Frederick J., and Janet K. Anderson. "Use of the Wechsler Memory Scale for Predicting Success in Cognitive Rehabilitation." *Cognitive Rehabilitation* 2 (March-April 1984): 12–15.

Parenté, R., and T. Bennett. "Training of Cognitive Rehabilitation Specialists: Reflections by Two Psychologists." *Cognitive Rehabilitation* 7 (November-December 1989): 18–20.

Parenté, Rick, and Janet K. Anderson-Parenté. "Retraining Memory: Theory and Application." *Journal of Head Trauma Rehabilitation* 4 (1989): 55–65.

Parenté, R., and J.K. Anderson-Parenté. *Retraining Memory: Techniques and Applications.* Houston: CSY Publishers, 1991.

Prigatano, George P. *Neuropsychological Rehabilitation after Brain Injury.* Baltimore: Johns Hopkins University Press, 1986.

Reitan, Ralph M., and Deborah Wolfson. *The Halstead-Reitan Neuropsychological Test Battery: Theory and Clinical Interpretation.* Tucson: Neuropsychology Press, 1985.

Rosenthal, M., E. Griffith, M. Bond, and J.D. Miller, eds. *Rehabilitation of the Head Injured Adult.* Philadelphia: F.A. Davis, 1983.

Roth, David L., Thomas J. Conboy, Kenneth P. Reeder, and Thomas J. Boll. "Confirmatory Factor Analysis of the Wechsler Memory Scale–Revised in a Sample of Head-Injured Patients." *Journal of Clinical and Experimental Neuropsychology* 12 (December 1990): 834–842.

Ruff, Ronald M., Rudolph H. Light, and Margaret Quayhagen. "Selective Reminding Test: A Normative Study of Verbal Learning in Adults." *Journal of Clinical and Experimental Neuropsychology* 11 (August 1989): 539–550.

Ryan, Joseph J., Michael E. Geisser, David M. Randall, and Randy J. Georgemiller. "Alternate Form Reliability and Equivalency of the Rey Auditory-Verbal Learning Test." *Journal of Clinical and Experimental Neuropsychology* 8 (October 1986): 611–616.

Schacter, Daniel L., Susan A. Rich, and Michele S. Stampp. "Remediation of Memory Disorders: Experimental Evaluation of the Spaced-Retrieval Technique." *Journal of Clinical and Experimental Neuropsychology* 7 (February 1985): 79–96.

Sohlberg, McKay Moore, and Catherine Mateer. *Introduction to Cognitive Rehabilitation: Theory and Practice.* New York: Guilford Press, 1989.

Sohlberg, McKay Moore, and Catherine Mateer. "Training Use of Compensatory Memory Books: A Three-Stage Behavioral Approach." *Journal of Clinical and Experimental Neuropsychology* 11 (December 1989): 871–891.

Uzzell, Barbara P., and Yigal Gross, eds. *Clinical Neuropsychology of Intervention.* Boston: Martinus Nijoff, 1986.

Volpe, Bruce T., and Fletcher H. McDowell. "The Efficacy of Cognitive Rehabilitation in Patients with Traumatic Brain Injury." *Archives of Neurology* 47 (February 1990): 220–222.

Whyte, John. "Outcome Evaluation in the Remediation of Attention and Memory Deficits." *Journal of Head Trauma Rehabilitation* 1 (September 1986): 64–71.

Wiens, Arthur, Mark R. McMinn, and John R. Crossen. "Rey Auditory-Verbal Learning Test: Development of Norms for Healthy Young Adults." *The Clinical Neuropsychologist* 2 (January 1988): 67–87.

Wilson, Barbara. *Rehabilitation of Memory.* New York: Guilford Press, 1987.

Wilson, Barbara and Nick Moffat, eds. *Clinical Management of Memory Problems.* Rockville, Md.: Aspen Publishers, 1984.

Wilson, Barbara, Janet Cockburn, Alan Baddeley, and Robert Hiorns. "Development and Validation of a Test Battery for Detecting and Monitoring Everyday Memory Problems." *Journal of Clinical and Experimental Neuropsychology* 11 (December 1989): 855–870.

Wonder, Jacquelyn, and Priscilla Donovan. *Whole-Brain Thinking, Working from Both Sides of the Brain to Achieve Peak Job Performance.* New York: Ballantine Books, 1984.

Index

About the Authors

Minnie Harrell

Minnie Harrell, M.S. is a Licensed Professional Counselor who provides psycho-therapy to individuals, couples, families, and groups at the Center for Psychological and Rehabilitation Services in Decatur, Georgia, where she is also Supervisor of Cognitive Rehabilitation Services and provides case management.

Ms. Harrell received a Bachelor's degree in psychology from Drexel University in Philadelphia and her Master's degree in counseling from Georgia State University in Atlanta. Over the last 10 years, she has provided direct clinical services to survivors of neurological trauma (e.g., head injury, cerebrovascular accidents, aneurysm, cancer, and tumors). She has worked in both inpatient and outpatient facilities in Pennsylvania and Georgia with clients at various impairment levels (severe to mild).

Ms. Harrell is a member of various professional organizations, including the American Congress of Rehabilitation Medicine, International Society for Traumatic Stress Studies, National Rehabilitation Association, American Trauma Association, and American Mental Health Counselors Association.

Ms. Harrell is an ad hoc reviewer for the *Journal of Mental Health Counseling* and is an editorial advisor to the *Journal of Traumatic Stress*. She is also on the board of reviewers of *Cognitive Rehabilitation*. She is president of the national Society for Cognitive Rehabilitation, Inc., which is in the process of developing guidelines for the training and certification of cognitive rehabilitation therapists. She is coauthor of the text, *Rehabilitation with Brain Injury Survivors: An Empowerment Approach;* and has presented many papers at national and international conferences on the topic of brain injury rehabilitation. She has also provided consultation and training to individuals and facilities in the provision of cognitive rehabilitation services.

Frederick Parenté

Frederick Parenté, Ph.D. is Professor of Psychology at Towson State University in Towson, Maryland and Associate Professor of Physiology at the University of Maryland Dental School in Baltimore. He graduated from the University of New Mexico in Albuquerque in 1975 with a doctoral degree in psychology with emphasis

in cognition, memory, biostatistics, and computer simulation of memory processes. He completed postdoctoral training at the University of Maryland Dental
School, Department of Physiology, where he created computer models of muscle
electricity and perception of pain. He is currently the Neuropsychology Consultant
at the Maryland Rehabilitation Center, where he has worked with traumatically
brain-injured persons for the past 5 years. His work with traumatic brain injury
extends back to 1982 and includes individual therapy for cognitive and memory
remediation. He is the author of multiple books, chapters, and articles on head injury
rehabilitation and has presented many papers on head injury and workshops on
memory at local, national, and international conferences.

Eileen G. Bellingrath

Eileen G. Bellingrath, M.S. is a Cognitive Rehabilitation Therapist at the Center
for Psychological and Rehabilitation Services in Decatur, Georgia, providing
direct individual and group cognitive rehabilitation therapy. She also serves as
psychometrist, administering neuropsychological test batteries.

Ms. Bellingrath received the Bachelor of Arts from Newton College of the
Sacred Heart in Newton, Massachusetts and the Master of Science in Psychology
from New Mexico Highlands University in Las Vegas, New Mexico. Over the past
5 years, she has worked in the Center for Psychological and Rehabilitation
Services in Decatur, Georgia providing cognitive rehabilitation services to
survivors of brain injury. She has also provided training in computer-based
cognitive rehabilitation therapy to the staff of a local rehabilitation facility and
consultation services in study skills to the Counseling Department of a local
medical college.

Ms. Bellingrath is a member of the National Head Injury Foundation, Georgia
chapter, and is a charter member of the Society for Cognitive Rehabilitation.

Katherine A. Lisicia

Katherine A. Lisicia, M.Ed., CCC-SLP is a licensed speech/language pathologist
who provides cognitive rehabilitation and speech therapy services to individuals at
the Center for Psychological and Rehabilitation Services in Decatur, Georgia. She
also provides speech and language therapy to survivors of traumatic neurologic
insults in other facilities in the Atlanta area.

She received her Bachelor's degree from Armstrong State College in Savannah,
Georgia and her Master's degree in education at the University of Georgia in
Athens, Georgia.

Ms. Lisicia is a member of many professional societies, including the American Speech-Language-Hearing Association and the Georgia Speech-Language-Hearing Association. She is a charter member of the Society for Cognitive Rehabilitation, Inc. In addition, she participates in an in-state interest group in the area of cognitive rehabilitation.